"What do you get when a top-notch bik join forces to write on the gospel and the church's mission? A book that not only is sensitive to the finer elements of the biblical storyline but also guides you through its theological implications for our present cultural moment. *The Gospel of Our King* is highly accessible and academically informed as well as biblically grounded and culturally insightful. Highly recommended."

—**Joshua Chatraw**, director, New City Fellows; theologian-in-residence, Holy Trinity Church, Raleigh, North Carolina

"This book is a glorious reminder of the fact that, as believers—no matter where, when, or under what conditions we live—we serve the King of all. Bruce Ashford and Heath Thomas remind us that God is King over creation, culture, politics, education, and our individual lives. Their robust theology seasoned with wise understanding makes me want to bow down before this King again and again and serve him better in all ways, in all my days."

—**Karen Swallow Prior**, author of *On Reading Well: Finding the Good Life through Great Books* and *Fierce Convictions: The Extraordinary Life of Hannah More—Poet, Reformer, Abolitionist*

"Some expositions of the biblical narrative as the foundation for our Christian worldview lack contemporary application. And some cultural analyses of the idolatries of Western culture lack solid biblical foundations. This book lacks neither. Ashford and Thomas have combined their respective areas of expertise most effectively, giving us a book that is biblically rich, theologically thorough, spiritually insightful, holistically missional, and practically relevant. Western Christians today need to become much more rooted in the whole Bible story as active participants in its great drama. And we need to open our eyes to recognize and renounce the false gods and idols that masquerade within our culture—even in Christianized costumes. This book helps us do both."

—**Christopher J. H. Wright**, Langham Partnership; author of *The Mission of God*

"In *The Gospel of Our King*, Ashford and Thomas introduce the Christian worldview while also attending to Christian action. In the first half of the book they take a story approach to review the grand narrative of Scripture in order to define and describe the Christian worldview. The second half of the book explicates the real-life difference that the good news of the gospel and a Christian worldview make in the day-to-day life of a believer. Fitting for those unfamiliar with the jargon of biblical and theological studies, this book will enjoy a wide readership. If you are looking for an effective survey of the whole biblical narrative that connects directly to the gospel message and spills forth naturally into Christian living in the twenty-first century, this book is for you."

—**Douglas S. Huffman**, Talbot School of Theology, Biola University

"*The Gospel of Our King* is a sheer delight. This is what happens when you bring together close attention to the Bible as a whole, worldview, and mission, just as they should be, with the overarching focus on the glory of God. Ashford and Thomas wear their considerable academic abilities in Bible, theology, and mission lightly in this creative, accessible, and eminently practical work. This is a book that we urgently need today, and my hope is that it will receive the wide reception it deserves. Take and read . . . and buy extra copies for friends!"

—**Craig G. Bartholomew**, director, Kirby Laing Institute for Christian Ethics, Cambridge

"This is a wonderful book. Ashford and Thomas take us to the heart of the Christian faith: the biblical story centered in Jesus and the kingdom as the true story of the whole world, the mission of God's people to embody that good news in all of life, and a missionary encounter with the idolatrous story of our Western culture. Their writing is engaging and the idols they challenge are timely, making this a book full of insight for faithful Christian living today. May this book find a wide readership for the sake of God's kingdom."

—**Michael W. Goheen**, Missional Training Center, Surge Network of Churches–Phoenix, and Covenant Theological Seminary

THE GOSPEL of OUR KING

BIBLE, WORLDVIEW, AND THE MISSION OF EVERY CHRISTIAN

BRUCE RILEY ASHFORD & HEATH A. THOMAS

Baker Academic

a division of Baker Publishing Group
Grand Rapids, Michigan

Published by Baker Academic
a division of Baker Publishing Group
PO Box 6287, Grand Rapids, MI 49516-6287
www.bakeracademic.com

Printed in the United States of America

Library of Congress Cataloging-in-Publication Data
Names: Ashford, Bruce Riley, author. | Thomas, Heath, author.
Title: The Gospel of our king : Bible, worldview, and the mission of every Christian / Bruce Riley Ashford and Heath A. Thomas.
Description: Grand Rapids : Baker Publishing Group, 2019. | Includes bibliographical references and index.
Identifiers: LCCN 2018036389 | ISBN 9780801049033 (pbk. : alk. paper)
Subjects: LCSH: Bible—Theology. | Mission of the church.
Classification: LCC BS543 .A84 2019 | DDC 230—dc23
LC record available at https://lccn.loc.gov/2018036389

ISBN 978-1-5874-3432-7 (casebound)

19 20 21 22 23 24 25   7 6 5 4 3 2 1

For Craig G. Bartholomew,
friend, scholar, encourager, co-conspirator
who lives *for the King*

CONTENTS

ACKNOWLEDGMENTS

Writing a book is dicey business. All the more so if you are *co*writing a book. The process can draw friends together or drive them apart. So, what is the verdict on our friendship at the close of this book? Well, we still talk with each other, laugh together, share meals, and dream about how the Lord might work in and through our labors together. We suppose we made it through the gauntlet! But a wonderful team helped bring us through.

We wish to thank Jim Kinney, Melisa Blok, and the editorial team at Baker Academic for their commitment to this project. We are also grateful for those persons who, through critical feedback, research, editing, and proofreading, made this manuscript better than it would have been: Dennis Greeson and Grant Taylor for research assistance, and Jackie Sanderlin and Cindy Hotchkiss, who assisted in preparing the manuscript for submission. We are also thankful for good friends and colleagues who have sharpened our thinking, including but not limited to Craig Bartholomew and Michael Goheen. I (Heath) would also like to express my deepest heartfelt gratitude to my mentor and friend, Dr. Jay Strack, who introduced me to worldview in Student Leadership University. He challenged me to aim high and not settle. His life for the King is exemplary. Jay taught me that I will be the same person today in five years' time except for the books I read, the people I meet, and the places I go. Well, that is dangerous—and sage—advice! I pray that I have dreamed big, thought deeply, served others, read extensively, and traveled widely for our King. Thank you for your leadership, friendship, and ability to see the best in all of us.

And finally, we wish to express love and appreciation to our families and friends who made this book possible. I (Heath) would like to offer gratitude to my wife, Jill, and to my children for giving me extraordinary delight and the privilege of living our lives together. I (Bruce) express my love and appreciation for my wife, Lauren, who has been my partner in thinking and writing since 2007, and for my young children—Riley, Anna, and Kuyper—whose ceaseless conversation and constant encouragement have made life such a joy and writing nearly impossible.

ABBREVIATIONS

Old Testament

Gen.	Genesis	Song	Song of Songs
Exod.	Exodus	Isa.	Isaiah
Lev.	Leviticus	Jer.	Jeremiah
Num.	Numbers	Lam.	Lamentations
Deut.	Deuteronomy	Ezek.	Ezekiel
Josh.	Joshua	Dan.	Daniel
Judg.	Judges	Hosea	Hosea
Ruth	Ruth	Joel	Joel
1–2 Sam.	1–2 Samuel	Amos	Amos
1–2 Kings	1–2 Kings	Obad.	Obadiah
1–2 Chron.	1–2 Chronicles	Jon.	Jonah
Ezra	Ezra	Mic.	Micah
Neh.	Nehemiah	Nah.	Nahum
Esther	Esther	Hab.	Habakkuk
Job	Job	Zeph.	Zephaniah
Ps./Pss.	Psalm/Psalms	Hag.	Haggai
Prov.	Proverbs	Zech.	Zechariah
Eccles.	Ecclesiastes	Mal.	Malachi

New Testament

Matt.	Matthew	1–2 Cor.	1–2 Corinthians
Mark	Mark	Gal.	Galatians
Luke	Luke	Eph.	Ephesians
John	John	Phil.	Philippians
Acts	Acts	Col.	Colossians
Rom.	Romans	1–2 Thess.	1–2 Thessalonians

1–2 Tim.	1–2 Timothy	1–2 Pet.	1–2 Peter
Titus	Titus	1–3 John	1–3 John
Philem.	Philemon	Jude	Jude
Heb.	Hebrews	Rev.	Revelation
James	James		

Secondary Sources

AnBib	Analecta Biblica
ANF	*Ante-Nicene Fathers*
AYBC	Anchor Yale Bible Commentaries
AYBRL	Anchor Yale Bible Reference Library
BTCL	Biblical and Theological Classics Library
CTJ	*Calvin Theological Journal*
IBMR	*International Bulletin of Missionary Research*
JETS	*Journal of the Evangelical Theological Society*
NCBC	New Century Bible Commentary
NICOT	New International Commentary on the Old Testament
NIGTC	New International Greek Testament Commentary
NSBT	New Studies in Biblical Theology
NTS	*New Testament Studies*
PNTC	Pillar New Testament Commentary
SAHS	Scripture and Hermeneutics Series
TWOT	*Theological Wordbook of the Old Testament*
VT	*Vetus Testamentum*
WBC	Word Biblical Commentary
WCC	World Council of Churches

INTRODUCTION

The renowned poet Wendell Berry asks a very good question: What are people for?[1] His response is stimulating, but let's focus on his question for a moment. For what purpose do you and I live on this earth? His is not really a question of action first and foremost, as if he is trying to answer the question, "What do people *do*?" Rather, Berry's question is first one of purpose. Only after we understand the *purpose* of people can we begin to explore responsible human *action* in our world.

Have you ever considered Berry's question? If not, you should. It has occupied theologians and philosophers since the dawn of time, and our guess is that it has crossed your mind as well. The way the question formed in your thoughts may not have been, "Why are *we* here?" but more pointed, "Why am *I* here?" Both "I" and "we" questions are vital, and this book will help you, the reader, explore each of them.

We do provide a robust answer to Berry's question in this book. Our answer—to be concise to the extreme—is that the world exists, you and I exist, *for the King*. This answer draws us to identify both the purpose of humanity and what counts as responsible action in the world.

No doubt "for the King" is a strange idea. After all, living for a king sounds, well, *old*. People in Western society do not live under the authority of kings or queens today—at least not as they once did. Royal figureheads might occupy ceremonial positions in a country, but they are not thought to hold real power. Real power is invested in other political offices: president, prime minister, minister of parliament, or congressperson.

1. Wendell Berry, *What Are People For? Essays* (New York: North Point, 1990), see esp. 123–25.

1

But the King we speak of is no figurehead. The King we speak of is more than a symbol. The King we discuss in this book *does* hold real power. More to the point, this King holds the entirety of the universe together, imbuing it with wonder and significance. And knowing and loving this King enables us to discover the wonder and purpose of life and how to live well in the world. So if we want to come to grips with life, its purpose, and meaningful action in our world, we must get to know this King.

Biblical Story

The Bible tells the story of the King. It reveals that the King is God and tells the story of his actions in regard to the world. It is a true story. From it, we can come to know and love the King and find purpose for our lives. We can discover how to live responsibly in our world, all *for the King*.

The first four chapters of this book trace the Bible's main storyline. While the Bible is not composed exactly like the stories one might find in world literature, it does, in fact, tell the mysterious and powerful story of God's intentions for the world and his interactions with it.[2]

In our modern world, many overlook the overarching story the Bible tells. We have seen this especially in the churches, universities, and seminaries we have served. Because of the Bible's inherent complexity and how it has been used (and abused) throughout history, readers associate the Bible with many things other than a comprehensive narrative. A few of the categories that some (and maybe you!) use to understand the Bible are the following:

- Literature: a collection of random literary genres, tales, and songs
- Ethics: a collection of moral lessons from which we can learn
- Doctrine: a compilation of truths or principles that we can apply
- History: a collection of facts about people who lived a long time ago

Each of these touches on truth. Of course, the Bible contains a multifaceted set of literary genres, each drawing its readers to experience the awesomeness of God and his dealings with the world. And it is certainly true that the Bible provides ethical norms that reveal God's virtues and values and how humanity

---

2. For a recent discussion on how the Bible has been understood as a story, or *narrative*, with strengths and weaknesses, see Craig G. Bartholomew and Michael W. Goheen, "Story and Biblical Theology," in *Out of Egypt: Biblical Theology and Biblical Interpretation*, ed. Craig G. Bartholomew, Mary Healy, Karl Möller, and Robin Parry, SAHS 5 (Grand Rapids: Zondervan, 2004), 144–71.

should relate to him. It is surely accurate to insist that the Bible teaches truths about God and the world in the form of doctrine. And we affirm that the Bible gives an accurate historical presentation of the patriarchs and matriarchs, the people called Israel, the life and ministry of Jesus, and the early church. Still, each of these categories finds its fit within the big story of the Bible.

We will see this reality in the chapters ahead. But for now, consider how the Bible presents God and Jesus within a universal story. And consider how early Christian interpreters understood Jesus in light of Scripture's story rather than some other idea.

God in the Biblical Story

When Scripture describes God, it does so on the basis of what God has said and done. In other words, the one true and living God is a personal being rather than an impersonal force. He *speaks and acts* within the world rather than existing as an abstraction. God is an actor, the *primary* actor, in a world-encompassing and true story.

Note God's self-description in Exodus 3:14–15. After God calls Moses to lead the people of Israel, Moses is confused about how to describe God to the people, so Moses asks God how to describe God to them. God's response to Moses is enlightening:

> God replies to Moses, "I AM WHO I AM. This is what you are to say to the Israelites: I AM has sent me to you." God also says to Moses, "Say this to the Israelites: The LORD, the God of your fathers, the God of Abraham, the God of Isaac, and the God of Jacob, has sent me to you. This is my name forever; this is how I am to be remembered in every generation.

God begins by telling Moses, "I AM WHO I AM." Then he continues to identify himself by recalling his relationship to Abraham, Isaac, and Jacob. Instead of describing himself with abstractions, he does so in a concrete and vivid fashion by placing himself at the center of a story. So we can rightly say the God of Scripture is a "storied" God. Scripture discloses who he is and what he has done.

Jesus in the Biblical Story

In his exceptional work *Ethics*, Dietrich Bonhoeffer identifies Jesus as the "center" of Scripture. Bonhoeffer says, "He [Jesus] is the centre and strength of the Bible, of the Church, and of theology, but also of humanity, of reason, of justice, and of culture. Everything must return to Him; it is only under

His protection that it can live."[3] For Bonhoeffer, Jesus is the central reality revealed in Scripture; he is the one who gives life and meaning to everything else. We will explore this fully in the chapters on redemption in this volume.

Bonhoeffer's concept of Jesus as the "center" of Scripture helps us to see that Jesus fulfills all the major symbols and stories of the Old Testament. Jesus is the prism through which the bright light of the Old Testament is broken into its full color. It is not that the colors of the light were absent prior to Jesus but that they were, in different ways, concealed. But in Jesus the full spectrum of color in Scripture emerges. N. T. Wright summarizes Jesus's centrality in the Bible: "Jesus intended to bring the story of Israel to its god-ordained climax, in and through his own work. His prophetic praxis was designed to challenge his contemporaries to abandon their agendas, including those agendas which appeared to be sanctioned in, or even demanded by, the Torah and the Prophets. He summoned them to follow him in a way of being the people of [God] which was, according to him, the true though surprising fulfilment of the whole scriptural story."[4]

In other words, Jesus sits at the center of the biblical narrative that discloses God and his world, and he invites us to participate with him by following him. Jesus's life and ministry culminate in his crucifixion, resurrection, ascension, and promise to return one day to set the world aright. In his own words, he describes his relationship to Scripture by saying, "Don't think that I came to abolish the Law or the Prophets. I did not come to abolish but to fulfill" (Matt. 5:17). But if it is true that Jesus fulfills the totality of the symbols and stories that went before him, then it follows that we must understand the biblical narrative in order to understand Jesus.

Christian Interpretation of the Biblical Story

It is no wonder that early Christian interpreters understood the Savior in light of the biblical storyline. Two of the best examples of this form of reading come from the works of Irenaeus and Augustine. In *Against Heresies*, one of Christianity's most significant early writings, Irenaeus (ca. AD 202) refutes those who are misreading Scripture by demonstrating that they don't interpret the Bible's story correctly, namely, in light of Jesus. Famously, he chides those with whom he disagrees by saying that they take little bits of the Bible and read them how they want, without any reference to the Bible's overarching story, which reveals Jesus. Similarly, in *City of God*, one of the greatest Christian writings of all time, Augustine (ca. AD 354–430) refutes

3. Dietrich Bonhoeffer, *Ethics*, trans. N. H. Smith (New York: Macmillan, 1965), 56.
4. N. T. Wright, *Jesus and the Victory of God* (London: SPCK, 1996), 473.

the Roman despisers of Christianity, and he does so primarily by showing that the Bible's narrative trumps Rome's founding narrative and any other narrative that claims to be the true story of the whole world.

Considering Israel's God, Jesus's presentation of himself in light of Israel's Scriptures, and early Christian interpretation, we argue that it is vital to read the Bible with an eye toward discerning its overarching story. But how does this story proceed?

A Brief Overview of the Story

The story begins at the beginning, with God's creation of the world. We will explore this first plot movement in close detail in chapter 1. God created the world and declared it good. He created humanity and called us to be religious, social, and cultural beings. If we would live according to his good design, we would flourish under his good rule. At the time of creation, the first couple—Adam and Eve—flourished as they lived in right relationship with God, with each other, and with the rest of creation.

In a dark twist of the narrative, however, the first couple rebel against their Maker, a rebellion we will explore in chapter 2. Adam and Eve commit treason against the King. As a result, every dimension of human life becomes corrupted and misdirected. We experience a broken relationship with God, with our fellow humans, and with God's good creation. That is why we often feel listless and directionless in life; we have been disconnected from our source of life—God—because of our sin. Theologians call this development "the fall."

Fortunately, the story does not end there. In response to humanity's rebellion, God could have destroyed the world. But instead of scrapping what he has made, God promises to redeem and restore, a promise we will explore in chapters 3 and 4. He promises to heal what has been corrupted, redirect what has been misdirected, fix what has been broken. So he sets his redemptive and restorative plan into motion. He calls forth a people for himself—Israel—so that people could be a light to the other nations, illumining the path of righteousness so the nations could walk in that path and flourish under God's cosmic reign. Through Israel, God provides the world a messiah who will set the world aright. This messiah is his Son, Jesus:

> For God loved the world in this way: He gave his one and only Son, so that everyone who believes in him will not perish but have eternal life. For God did not send his Son into the world to condemn the world, but to save the world through him. (John 3:16–17)

Because God loved our broken and sinful world, he sent Jesus, his very own Son, "to save the world through him."

What does it mean that the "world" might be saved through Jesus? Scripture teaches that one day Christ will return to renew and restore his good creation. He will save sinners *and* he will save the created order so that one day worshipers from every tribe, tongue, people, and nation (Rev. 5:9–10) will live with him eternally in a restored heavens and earth, the same heavens and earth he created in Scripture's first plot movement (21:1–4).

Worldview and the Biblical Story

The first four chapters of this book are devoted to articulating the Bible's overarching story, or *narrative*, in more depth. From the story of Scripture, basic beliefs about God, the world, and appropriate human action in the world coalesce into what can be understood as a *worldview*. For now, we define worldview as follows:

> A set of basic beliefs that are embedded in a shared narrative of the world and rooted in a religious commitment that shapes and directs the lives of individuals and communities.

All human beings navigate the world and operate within it based on some sort of worldview that shapes their lives, even if that worldview is never fully realized or reflected on. As we have lived in Russia, the United Kingdom, and the United States, and because we have worked in dozens of countries around the globe, we have witnessed several worldviews at work. Some worldviews are more dominant and actively compete with the Christian worldview. In our experience, the following worldviews are the most dominant:

- Islamic Theism: in which God is a monochrome uniformity rather than a triunity
- Deism: in which God exists but does not interact personally with the world
- Naturalism: in which there is no God and humans rule their own lives
- Nihilism: a type of naturalism in which life is meaningless; there is no absolute truth, goodness, or beauty
- Existentialism: a type of naturalism that goes beyond nihilism in which humans assert themselves in the world, creating their own truth, goodness, beauty, and meaning

- Monistic Pantheism: in which, instead of God, there is an impersonal, one-world soul[5]

Each of these worldviews exerts a significant shaping influence on the lives of those who fall under their sway. Even when a person is not consciously able to articulate it, one's worldview shapes basic desires and intuitions, impacts how one sees the world, and influences how one speaks and acts.

Gospel and the Biblical Story

Worldview provides a framework to respond to significant questions humans share, like, What has gone wrong in the world? and, What is being done to set things right? Both find robust answer in the good news of Jesus Christ, which is the *gospel*.

Christians often use the term *gospel*, but do we really know what it is and what it means? As we see it, the gospel is the announcement that God's kingdom arrived in the life, death, and resurrection of Jesus, who is King and Savior, in fulfillment of Old Testament prophecy. The gospel calls for belief, trust, and repentance; God promises that those who heed this call will live with him eternally in the new heavens and earth. Another, and briefer, way we summarize it is to say that the gospel is the announcement that Jesus the King died and rose again to save us *from* our sins and *for* renewed life in him.

We will argue that a proper understanding of the gospel of Jesus Christ arises directly from the biblical story. If we try to describe the gospel apart from the biblical story, our description will be deficient at best and misleading at worst. Trying to describe the gospel as a logical syllogism is not wrong. In fact, doing so can be helpful. But if the gospel is reduced to nothing but a logical syllogism, it loses much of its meaning.

From this summary, you will notice that, just as the Christian worldview makes sense only with reference to the biblical narrative, so the gospel is comprehensible only in light of the biblical story. Chapter 5 is devoted to an exposition of the Christian worldview and gospel in light of the biblical story. Having reflected on story, worldview, and gospel, we are then prepared for the last four chapters of this book, which reflect on the *mission* God has given to us, his people.

5. For an introduction to worldviews, see James W. Sire, *The Universe Next Door: A Basic Worldview Catalog*, 5th ed. (Downers Grove, IL: InterVarsity, 2009); Tawa J. Anderson, W. Michael Clark, and David K. Naugle, *An Introduction to Christian Worldview: Pursuing God's Perspective in a Pluralistic Age* (Downers Grove, IL: IVP Academic, 2017).

Mission and the Biblical Story

The final four chapters of this book will help us understand the Christian mission. We can begin to answer the question What are people *for*? in a robust manner through these chapters. In them, we draw on the biblical story in order to grasp the holistic nature of our *mission* as God's people.

If we ignore any one part of the biblical storyline, we will end up with a mission that is incomplete at best and harmful at worst. In fact, we think that people are often tempted to think about mission in ways that ignore or underemphasize the beginning and end of the biblical narrative—creation and new creation. Our exposition of the Christian mission draws on all four plot movements (creation, fall, redemption, new creation).

To help bring order and clarity to the Christian mission, we have divided our discussion of it into four aspects:

Theological
Social
Cultural
Global

As you read the final four chapters, you will notice that these four aspects overlap with one another quite a bit. They are not airtight categories but heuristic devices that help us think about the Christian mission in all its multifaceted glory.

First, we show how the Christian mission is *theological*. By this, we mean that the Christian mission centers on the God of Jesus Christ. The Bible calls us to love God with all our hearts, and in biblical terms, the heart is the central organizer of our lives. But precisely because true religion is personal, it can never be merely private; because it is heartfelt, it radiates outward into everything we do. When we love God with all our heart, that love shapes the way we approach every relationship and activity in life. Our affection for God overflows in our words and deeds. It fuels the mission. In our secular age, the theological nature of our mission is especially challenging.

Then we expose the way in which the Christian mission is thoroughly *social*. By that, we mean that genuine Christian mission involves interaction with other people made in the image of God. Our interaction with them is itself part of the Christian mission. When one person speaks to another person about the good news that Jesus is Lord and Savior, that conversation is social. When the inner life of a local church is marked by Christian love and obedience and that church becomes a window into which the world can peer to see Christ, it is bearing witness to Christ in a social manner. When the members of a church engage in a ministry to help single mothers who are financially destitute, their ministry is social. So the Christian mission is social in diverse ways.

Following a discussion of the social aspect of mission, we argue that the Christian mission is deeply and pervasively cultural. *Culture* is anything that humans produce when they interact with one another and with God's creation. When we cultivate the ground (grain, vegetables, livestock), produce artifacts (clothes, housing, cars), build institutions (governments, businesses, schools), form worldviews (theism, pantheism, atheism), participate in religious communities (Christian, Hindu, Buddhist, Muslim, atheist), and speak languages (English, Mandarin, Arabic), we produce culture. At the same time, our cultural context shapes us and affects who we are, what we think and do, and how we feel. Everything we say and do is cultural, so as Christians, we should work hard to ensure that our cultural doings point to Christ.

We conclude these chapters by talking about the *global* scope of the Christian mission. Immediately after Christ's resurrection, he commanded his followers to take the gospel to the nations. And in fact, the entire biblical storyline is consummated with international worship in a new heavens and earth. So global mission is near to God's heart and is central to the Christian mission. We want to preach the gospel and plant churches among every known people group and every known language on earth. When we do so, those global Christian communities will be able to live out the Christian mission—theologically, socially, and culturally—among their own people and extend it outward— globally—to other peoples.

After our journey through the biblical story, we will gain a deeper understanding of the Christian worldview, the centrality of the gospel, and the scope of the Christian mission. We will also be able to give an answer to Wendell Berry's question about purpose: we exist . . . *for the King.*

1

CREATION

God the King and His Good Creation

> *In the beginning God created the heavens and the earth.*
>
> *Genesis 1:1*

Introduction

"In the beginning God created the heavens and the earth." So begins Genesis 1, the starting point of the biblical narrative. That chapter, like this chapter, is about *creation*. But what is meant by *creation*? At least two things, both of which help us to frame the remainder of our discussion.

First, creation is an activity undertaken by none other than God himself. God's creation of the heavens and earth provides the home environment for humans to live out our calling before God, and it composes the grand stage on which the rest of the Bible's narrative plays out. As we will see, God's creative activity could be compared to the labors of a skilled craftsperson. After a long day, the craftsperson looks at the work of his or her hands and declares, "Very nice. Exactly as I intended!" Similarly, the world in which we live is the work of God's hands, the skillful work of the ultimate craftsperson.

Second, creation is the "stuff" of reality. When we talk about *creation*, we are talking about not only the divine activity of creating but also the finished product itself—all the created world in both its material and immaterial aspects. Of course, the meanings of the word are really two sides of one coin. If we are talking about one, we must always necessarily be talking about the other. The stuff of creation cannot exist without its Creator. Likewise, the Creator cannot be known except through his creation. Even as we observe the life of Christ and read the words of Scripture, we are learning about God in an embodied manner and through human language.

It is not uncommon in our world, however, for people to separate the two aspects of creation. On the one hand, some well-meaning Christians seem to believe that we ought to orient ourselves toward God by escaping from his good creation. They see salvation as something that takes us up and away from the world. But that picture is not right; as we will see, God's salvation will renew the heavens and earth so that we can dwell with him forever in this context.

On the other hand, atheists and other types of naturalists speak about nature without reference to God. Take, for example, Richard Dawkins's *The Greatest Show on Earth: The Evidence for Evolution*. In it Dawkins, a biologist, argues that the world as we know it is a result of impersonal forces that give the illusion that the world was designed by an intelligent mind (God). But in actual fact, he argues, the appearance of design is nothing more than a mirage. The world, as he sees it, created itself via natural processes. But something is deeply and profoundly wrong with this view of the world. As philosopher Alvin Plantinga argues in *Where the Conflict Really Lies: Science, Religion, and Naturalism*, it is impossible to sufficiently understand and explain reality (science) from within a worldview (naturalism) that has no recourse to a Divine Mind. The natural world is best understood and explained with reference to God, that God being none other than the divine craftsperson of Genesis 1.

Beginning at the Beginning

Thus we begin at the beginning. We shouldn't take for granted that the Bible begins at the beginning. Other religious texts, such as the Islamic Qur'an, the Hindu Bhagavad Gita, and the Analects of Confucius, do not begin at the beginning. These other works may speak of the creation of the world in one way or another, but they do not *begin* with the creation of the world.

Genesis was composed from within the context of a postfall world, looking back to the origin of the world. The book of Genesis is contemporary with ancient civilizations such as Egypt, Canaan, Sumer, Assyria, and Babylon, each of which had its own account of the world's origins.[1] Their accounts are in some ways similar to the creation account of Genesis but in many ways quite different. Note some of the general differences in table 1.1.

Table 1.1: Differences between Creation Stories

Pagan Myths	Genesis 1–2
many gods	God
grumpy gods	personal God
gods dependent on humanity for food	God utterly independent; humanity dependent on God
world is God's body	God is distinct from his creation; world is ordered and good
humanity is gods' slave	humanity is created in God's image; humans as priest-kings

As we can see, there are significant and defining ways in which the biblical account goes against the pagan accounts. This is why some commentators think, to our minds rightly, that the Genesis creation account has an apologetic edge to it. The first chapter of Genesis reflects God's view of the world, a view that he reveals to the people of Israel so that they will pass it along to the pagan nations, enlightening them and inviting them to worship the God of Israel rather than the false gods of the nations.

Significantly, the Genesis creation account is presented in a narratival manner, providing the point of departure for an extended story that develops throughout the canon of Christian Scripture. None of the other ancient Near Eastern creation stories function in this way. Leon Kass argues that Genesis's opening is utterly unique in that it "is not an account of human life or even of human beginnings, but rather an account of the whole world and its creation."[2] So the Genesis creation narrative is ambitious—it aims to provide an explanatory framework for the whole of reality. Nothing falls outside the scope of the Genesis account.

As we will see, the story that begins in Genesis culminates in the final book of the Bible, the Revelation of John. In that last book, God reveals to the beloved disciple that Jesus will return one day to institute a new creation, which,

1. J. B. Pritchard, ed., *Ancient Near Eastern Texts Relating to the Old Testament*, 3rd ed. with supplement (1969; repr., Princeton: Princeton University Press, 1992). See also Cyrus H. Gordon and Gary A. Rendsburg, *The Bible and the Ancient Near East*, rev. ed. (New York: Norton, 1997), 33–51.

2. Leon R. Kass, *The Beginning of Wisdom: Reading Genesis* (Chicago: University of Chicago Press, 2006), 25.

as we will see, is this fallen creation renewed and restored. Thus creation and new creation serve as bookends to Scripture, beginning and ending the story and holding together everything in between.

In fact, creation is the stage on which the drama of salvation plays out.[3] God provides salvation through a Savior who takes on created flesh and speaks human language. He inscripturates his word in a Bible that is composed of paper and communicated in human language. He redeems us—we who are created in his image and likeness, we who are part of his creation. He calls us to live out our salvation within the created order rather than trying to escape the physical and material nature of our existence. So if one does not understand creation, one does not understand what God has saved in Jesus Christ. Creation cannot be tossed aside. It cannot be passed over. It cannot be ignored.

God

We mentioned earlier the great German theologian Dietrich Bonhoeffer. He opens his *Creation and Fall* by noting that the phrase "In the beginning God" is a striking way to cause the reader to reflect on God's identity.[4] It forces us to recognize that the God of creation is neither one whom we make for ourselves nor one who fits into our world. Rather, the God on display in Genesis is the uncreated Creator of the universe into whose world we fit. He is the King of it.

The psalmist describes God in this way: "The LORD has established his throne in heaven, / and his kingdom rules over all" (Ps. 103:19). The God of Genesis is none other than the King of the universe, who has created his kingdom, the world in which we live. "Scripture begins by declaring that God, as Creator and triune Lord, is the sovereign ruler and King of the universe. In this important sense, the entire universe is God's kingdom since he is pres-

3. So we fundamentally disagree with the thought of Gerhard von Rad, who suggests that themes such as election and salvation are more important in biblical faith than creation is. He says that a belief in creation is not a central subject in Old Testament faith. Gerhard von Rad, *Genesis*, rev. ed. (Philadelphia: Westminster, 1972), 45. Marginalizing the doctrine of creation often occurs in biblical studies and Christian theology, unfortunately. Even if one follows the old historical-critical line that a teaching on creation is a late development in Israel's history, one must still grapple with the fact that the creation account was intentionally placed at the *forefront* of Israel's Scripture, providing the introductory shape and meaning to the story of the world, a story that will later develop into the stories of Abraham and Israel. Because of this, the stories of Abraham and Israel continue the story that begins at creation.

4. Dietrich Bonhoeffer, *Creation and Fall / Temptation: Two Biblical Studies* (New York: Touchstone, 1997), 13.

ently Lord and King."[5] So the Genesis account makes clear that the world is a kingdom with God as its King.

God the King is distinct, majestic, powerful, good, and personal. He is *distinct* from his creation in that he created the universe. The universe is not part of him and is not on par with him. It cannot exist without him and remains utterly dependent on him. He is *majestic*, and his majesty is reflected in the resplendent, ordered diversity of his magnificent creation. He is *powerful*, and his power is reflected in the fact that all the forces of the natural world find their starting point in his limitless authority—from the inescapable gravity of a black hole to the incomparable heat at the center of a star. He is *good*. When God the King looks at the world he has made in Genesis 1, he says that it is good no fewer than seven times. God creates a good world because he is good. In him, there is no evil. Finally, he is *personal*. In Genesis 3:8 we see him walking in the garden, conversing with the first couple. God the King is not an abstraction, a force of nature, or a one-world soul. He is a God who relates personally to his good creation.

An astute reader will notice that the first two chapters of Genesis provide different but complementary accounts of creation. Genesis 1:1–2:3 offers a grand and cosmic approach to the creation of all things in which everyone and everything finds its place and order before God. But Genesis 2:4–25 offers a specific and focused perspective on creation by zeroing in on the first man and woman and their special relationship with God and with each other. The God who made the heavens and the earth and created Adam and Eve in Genesis 1 gives them names, a home, and a job in Genesis 2. He even convenes their wedding (so to speak)! God's majestic power in Genesis 1 is matched by his relational presence in Genesis 2. From the second creation account, we discover the personal and relational character of the Creator God.

Bonhoeffer rightly says that Genesis's account presents God as utterly free in creating the world.[6] It was his choice. He was not bound to do this work. It was not even necessary! After all, Christian theology reminds us that God is perfect in himself, apart from the world he has made. He does not need the world. He does not need us. But God, in his wonderful love and creative power, freely created everything that is and will be. And he made you and me. This means that all of creation is a free act of great love from a great God.

5. Peter J. Gentry and Stephen J. Wellum, *Kingdom through Covenant: A Biblical-Theological Understanding of the Covenants*, 2nd ed. (Wheaton: Crossway, 2018), 648.
6. Bonhoeffer, *Creation and Fall*, 16.

God's Kingdom (The Created World)

Genesis 1 especially shows us that God made the world as the natural habitat for humanity. He did not design us to float on clouds or walk on water. He designed us to walk, build, plant, till, cultivate, and multiply. In other words, God made us to be at home in this world. We are made for this place. Genesis teaches us that God's good world is our rightful home and we cannot be fully human without it!

It is not uncommon for Bible-believing Christians to think that the point of the Christian life is to bide our time on this old earth until God helps us to escape from it one day so that we can live with him in heaven. There is an element of truth to this, for in heaven we will not be part of the broken world infected as it is with sin. But Jesus taught that the Christian hope is not heaven but heaven on earth: "Your kingdom come. / Your will be done / on earth as it is in heaven" (Matt. 6:10–11). In other words, God will bring heaven to earth one day, cleansing this world of sin and its consequences so that we can dwell here together with God forever.

God designed us to build a relationship with him within the context of the world he has made: his kingdom. Heaven is not our final home. Heaven on earth—the fulfillment of God's kingdom—is our home. Because of this fact, it is understandable that Genesis 2 presents God working in his garden, fashioning it, making Adam and Eve, and placing them there to tend and till (v. 15) that beautiful place. He made humanity to work in his kingdom. God is known as he relates to his world, and humans know God by relating well to him in the world he has made, by living under his reign, and by following his rules.

A helpful way to view Genesis 1 is as the opening act of the story of God's kingdom. Note the structure of Genesis 1:1–2:3. The text begins with God creating the world by means of his word (Gen. 1:3). God speaks the world into shape, but he does so in six days. There was a time before the six days, a time before God had created something from nothing, when everything was shapeless and uninhabitable and darkness covered the face of the deep (v. 2). For practical purposes, we call this day 0. It is a period of formless emptiness. But this shapeless void was not without God, for the "Spirit of God was hovering over the surface of the waters" (v. 2). God's Spirit was present even in the midst of the void, moving, hovering, and waiting to bring shape and purpose. And indeed, God brought shape and purpose. His six days of creative activity resulted in a distinctive order that reveals both the domains of creation (days 1–3) and the filling of those domains (days 4–6). Notice figure 1.1.

Most of us, perhaps, have not read the creation account in this way. Certainly, the Bible does not contain a figure 1.1. But this order is present

Figure 1.1
The Structure of Genesis 1:1–2:3

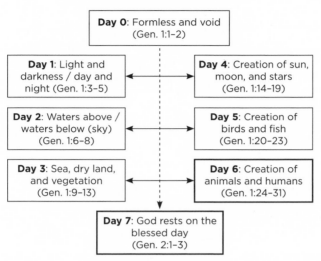

in the Bible, and we can recognize it through the repetition of language that demarcates the days and the way that the days match one another topically and spatially. Light and dark (day 1) are filled with luminaries (day 4). Waters and sky (day 2) are filled with animals that belong in them, like birds and fishes (day 5). Dry land (day 3) is filled with humans and land animals (day 6), with vegetables given for food. So the structure makes sense of information that would otherwise be confusing (such as, How can there be measurable "day" and "night" on days 1–3 without a sun? That makes no sense!). The beauty and symmetry of the creation narrative imply that God provided this account not to give us the precise mechanics of creation so much as to tell us that God created the world from nothing and ordered it according to his purposes. From within this theologically and literarily structured account, we can glean several significant theological insights.

God's world displays the orderliness of its Creator. Note the close correspondence between days: day 1 // day 4; day 2 // day 5; day 3 // day 6. This pattern exposes symmetry and order in the creative act of God. The world that God has created displays regularity, symmetry, and a discernible structure. It sings his praises, speaks of his greatness, and is comprehensible to his creatures (Ps. 19). Old Testament scholar William Brown writes, "All hints of conflict and opposition are effectively banished from this account. The elements of creation are poised to fulfill God's bidding at the drop of a word. Creation is gently yet decisively led to its fulfillment in a process of formfulness, an execution of separation and ful*fill*ment. Nothing lies outside God's creative direction and approbation, not even 'chaos.' . . . First and foremost, God is creator of an order par excellence."[7]

In other words, God designed the world for it to be understood. Nothing is outside God's control or design. When you look at our world, you see the fingerprints of God all over it. The regularity and orderliness of the world is one reason why the writer of Proverbs instructs students about the ways of the world to help them attain wisdom (Prov. 8:1–36). The King's creation is designed in such a way that its orderliness and comprehensibility reflect *God's* orderliness and comprehensibility.

God's world displays the goodness of its Creator. God structured the world in a certain way, according to his good intentions for creation as a whole and for humanity in particular. As God stepped back to observe his creation, he pronounced it "good." In fact, he called it "good" seven times within this one brief narrative, with the number seven signifying both God's completion and its inherent goodness.[8] Within this good creation, God's imagers could flourish in right relationship with him, with each other, and with the rest of the created order.

As we read the Genesis account, we cannot help but be reminded that something went awfully awry. Through our experiences of sin and tragedy, we know that something went wrong, but through them we also intuit that this is not the way the world ought to work. That intuition is a gift from God, reminding us that God is not the cause of the injustice, disorder, disharmony, and confusion we now experience. Rather, as we will discover in the next chapter, God created the world whole and good, but human sin frustrated his purposes.

God's world displays a hierarchical pattern. Each of the days in the creation account is ordained by God, but each of the days is not equal. Day 1 establishes light and darkness, but day 4 ordains how those domains will be ordered: the great lights will "rule over" day and night, times and seasons (Gen. 1:14–16). Birds and fishes fill the sky and seas on day 5, while animals are created to inhabit the land on day 6. Humans and animals alone are "blessed" by God on days 5 and 6 and are given the commands to "be fruitful" and "multiply" (1:22, 28). Kass beautifully exposes the hierarchical and ordered world according to Genesis 1:

7. William P. Brown, *The Ethos of the Cosmos: The Genesis of Moral Imagination in the Bible* (Grand Rapids: Eerdmans, 1999), 46, 47, italics original.

8. A number of elements in the narrative are associated with the number seven. For discussion, see J. McKeown, *Genesis* (Grand Rapids: Eerdmans, 2008), 308–9.

- Humanity is the peak of creation as stewards of God's world (day 6).
- Humanity has the rational capacity to discern and govern and is higher than the remainder of the created order (day 6).
- Humanity alone images God in the world (day 6), as opposed to the animal world (land animals, day 6; fish and fowl, day 5).
- Animals (fish, fowl, and land animals) are higher than heavenly bodies (day 4) by virtue of the fact that they have greater freedom (day 5).
- All animals are blessed and commanded to multiply (days 5 and 6).
- All animals produce according to their kinds (days 5 and 6), and, unlike the heavenly bodies (day 4), animals display the powers of awareness (such as the gift of hearing).[9]

God the King made a kingdom for himself within which, significantly, human beings would lovingly manage the world under his wise and good leadership. While the moon and sun may exert dominion over the sky to govern time and seasons, humanity is given the unique task of representing God in his kingdom, managing the created animals and dry land. Of this hierarchy, Kass summarizes, "Living things are higher than nonliving things; and among living things, some are more alive than others—that is, their powers of awareness, action and desire are more fully developed. Who could disagree? The special powers of human beings make the case most boldly."[10] His comment drives us to think about the place of humanity in creation, to which we will soon turn.

God's world is a unified diversity. God created a multiplicity of animals and plant life "according to their kinds" (1:11–12, 21, 24–25). In recognition of this wonderful diversity, Abraham Kuyper writes, "Where in God's entire creation do you encounter life that does not display the unmistakable hallmark of life precisely in the multiplicity of its colors and dimensions, in the capriciousness of its ever-changing forms?"[11] This infinite diversity extends beyond the non-human aspects of creation to human beings, among whom God distributes diverse appearances, aptitudes, and talents. Additionally, as Paul says to the Colossians, this multisplendored diversity finds its unity in Christ, who holds all things together (Col. 1:17). So God's creation is a cosmos (a richly diversified

9. Kass, *Beginning of Wisdom*, 35–36.
10. Kass, *Beginning of Wisdom*, 36. Kass goes on to suggest that evolutionary theorists would disagree with him. However, he provides a compatibilist view between the biblical vision of Genesis 1 and evolutionary theory, which he supports.
11. James D. Bratt, ed., *Abraham Kuyper: A Centennial Reader* (Grand Rapids: Eerdmans, 1998), 34.

yet coherently unified whole) rather than a chaos, and God's Word helps us see its ordered unity, which undergirds the full range of our lives.

God's People (Humanity)

Genesis 1 is significant for its wide-lens perspective, as it informs its readers that God's world is a habitat for humanity, specially designed for humans to know and love their Maker and live before him. Genesis 2, however, is unique for its focused and up-close perspective on the first couple and their life in the garden of Eden. This garden is depicted as a kind of sanctuary, or temple, in which God dwells and God's people minister. This is important because it reveals the nature of humans as worshipers of God who minister before him in the whole of their lives. How does the text show us this?

God's Word speaks through the text's symbols and its connections with other biblical texts. First, notice the *physical* symbolic relationships. The garden of Eden was on a mountain (Gen. 2:10–14; rivers run downhill from Eden), just as God's sanctuary would later be located on a mountain (Ps. 48:1–2). Eden was entered from the east (Gen. 3:24), as was Israel's sanctuary (Num. 3:38; Ezek. 44:1). A river flowed through Eden (Gen. 2:10), just as a river flowed out of Jerusalem (Ps. 46:4) and out of the new temple (Ezek. 47:1). There were precious stones in Eden (Gen. 2:12), just as there were ornate decorations in the temple (Exod. 25:7; 28:9). Also notice the *temporal* symbolic relationships. God created the world in six days (Gen. 1:1–2:3), just as he gave six commands concerning the temple's construction (Exod. 25–40). God rested on the Sabbath (Gen. 2:1–3), just as he rested by dwelling within the sanctuary (Exod. 40:34–35). Finally, notice the *verbal* symbolic relationships. God walked in the garden (Gen. 3:8), which is the same language used of his presence in the temple ("I will walk among you," Lev. 26:12). Adam worked in the garden (Gen. 2:15) and the same language is used to describe the priests' ministry in the sanctuary (Num. 3:7–8; 8:26; 18:5–6).

Collectively, these clues imply that God created Eden as a natural temple, a pattern that would inform Israel's sanctuary later in the biblical story. Gordon Wenham describes well the relationship between the sanctuary and Eden when he writes, "Like the garden of Eden, the tabernacle was a place where God walked with his people. To be expelled from the camp of Israel or to be rejected by God was to experience a living death. . . . The expulsion from the garden of delight where God himself lived would therefore have been regarded by the godly men of ancient Israel as yet more catastrophic than physical death."[12]

12. Gordon J. Wenham, *Genesis 1–15*, WBC 1 (Waco: Word Books, 1987), 90.

God created the world as his kingdom within which human beings would represent him and rule underneath his wise and good kingship, but he also created the garden as a temple in which man and woman would worship him, giving honor and glory back to God like priests who do their work as unto the Lord. But *what* is their worshipful work, and *how* should they represent God and give glory and honor back to him? To that we now turn.

In a significant moment during the Genesis 1 account, we are told that God created man and woman in God's image and likeness, or, as the Latin rendering puts it, in the *imago Dei*: "So God created man in his own image; he created him in the image of God; he created them male and female" (Gen. 1:27).

A discerning reader will immediately intuit that this moment in the narrative is heightened and set apart from other moments. The animals were created "according to their kinds," but man and woman were created "in the image of God." Their creation in God's image is intuitively significant, but the meaning of the *imago Dei* is not so immediately obvious.

Most patristic and medieval theologians interpreted the image as being seated in the human intellect (largely because of Plato's influence). The Reformers, however, departed from this view, with Martin Luther linking the image with humanity's original righteousness and John Calvin linking it with the whole human being, including humanity's relational and physical dimensions. Karl Barth dismissed all of them by calling their interpretations "inventive genius" and setting forth his own view that the image of God is relational: it is our ability (together as male and female) to be addressed by God and to respond to him.[13] Many contemporary theologians define the *imago Dei* functionally by what human beings are able to do.

Given the historic disagreement about the image of God, how should we think about it? What is the *imago Dei*, and why is it important for understanding humanity? In response, we recognize that although Scripture never provides a dictionary definition of the image of God, the Genesis account does provide significant clues concerning its meaning. The image of God should be understood as structural, functional, and relational.

Imago Dei: *Structural*

As we noted, many interpreters understand the image of God exclusively in functional (what God created humans to do) or relational (our ability to be addressed by God and to respond to him) terms. But this is not quite right.

13. Karl Barth, *Church Dogmatics* III/1 (Edinburgh: T&T Clark, 1958), 192.

Although the image of God is functional and relational, it is not exclusively so. It is also structural, meaning that the whole person, in his or her God-given structure, *is* the image of God. Human beings image God by virtue of being human rather than some other part of God's creation. The whole person is the image of God. For this reason, we prefer to call human beings "imagers" rather than "image bearers" (for "bearing" the image implies that it is located in some limited aspect of our being).[14]

To illustrate the point, consider the following examples. An infant does little but coo, cry, or smile. An infant cannot "rule" or "be fruitful" as described in the language of Genesis 1:26 and 28. Yet we suggest that an infant images God all the same. Another example comes in a body at rest. Consider a person who is taking a nap. Does that napping person image God despite the fact that they are not actively *doing* something? Yes. A body at rest loses nothing of God's imprint on it by virtue of its sleep. A body at rest images God beautifully, as does a helpless infant with their bright, beautiful eyes.

This is to draw out a simple but profound theological point. Although it is appropriate to suggest that bearing God's image is *closely* tied to certain functions, such as being fruitful and multiplying, tilling the soil, or having dominion, it is not *exclusively* tied to this functional terminology. The image of God is not a property of humanity, as if one could take it off like a coat. Instead, it is a given. "We *are* imagers of God," writes theologian Gordon Spykman. "Imaging God represents our very makeup, our constitution, our glory, and at the same time our high and holy calling in God's world."[15]

Imago Dei: *Functional*

Human beings image God, therefore, by the very fact that we exist as human beings. We image God whether we are aware of it or not, whether we like it or not. Yet we also image God by doing certain things in certain ways. Consider, for example, the *kingly* command God gave to humans when he instructed them to have dominion over the world he created (Gen. 1:26, 28). God says, "Let us make humanity in our image, according to our likeness, so that they may rule over the fish of the sea, and over the birds of the sky, and over the beasts, and over all of the earth, and over every creeping thing that creeps upon the earth" (Gen. 1:26, author's translation). Verse 28 reiterates this command, surrounding the poetic center of verse 27. But God's design

14. Gordon Spykman, *Reformational Theology: A New Paradigm for Doing Dogmatics* (Grand Rapids: Eerdmans, 1992), 224.

15. Spykman, *Reformational Theology*, 224, italics original.

for humanity is not governance gone wild! Rather, human governance over God's world *imitates* God's governance over his creation. To the first couple, God was saying something to the effect of, "Just as I exercise my wise and loving kingship over the created order, so you should go and do likewise. Just as I rule with an eye toward order, harmony, peace, and flourishing, so you should rule."

The language "to rule" is followed by another charge given by God, "to subdue" (Gen. 1:28). This latter language is profoundly *cultural*, describing how humans fashion the created world into a state of productivity.[16] William Brown perceptively comments about the meaning of "to subdue": "Human beings must work *in* creation in order for creation to *work* for human beings by providing sustenance and the means of their livelihood. Nevertheless, such a commission does not require exploiting the earth's resources, as the specific language of subduing might suggest."[17] A similar intent is implied in God's wish for humanity to till the soil (Gen. 2:5). Although God was referring to an agricultural task, based on a close reading of the rest of Scripture and on human history, we know that he surely was also referring to other cultural tasks. He was saying something along the lines of, "See the good world I created? Good. Now take what I made and make something of it. Bring out its hidden potential."

So human beings image God socially, regally, and culturally by promoting the flourishing of the whole of creation. God's command to Adam in Genesis 2:15 reminds us of this fact as well. He gives Adam the role of tending and tilling the garden. But as any close reader of the Hebrew text knows, the language, while certainly connoting good farming that leads to productivity, also foreshadows the kind of work priests would do at the temple. The work of humanity is that of ruling and developing God's world so that it produces good fruit, but that work should always be done as an act of love and worship before God. "The creation comes into existence progressively as a coherent whole," Bartholomew writes, "and part of humankind's stewardship will be to continue to ensure that the earth brings forth vegetation in a way that is 'good,' so that birds, fish, and animals are able to flourish in the environments designated for *them*."[18] As God's imagers, therefore, we are called to image God worshipfully and to represent him by the things we *do* in the world.

The psalmist reflects the functional aspect of the *imago Dei*:

16. So Brown, *Ethos of the Cosmos*, 44.
17. Brown, *Ethos of the Cosmos*, 44–45.
18. Craig G. Bartholomew, *Where Mortals Dwell: A Christian View of Place for Today* (Grand Rapids: Baker Academic, 2011), 16.

> What is a human being that you remember him,
> a son of man that you look after him?
> You made him little less than God
> and crowned him with glory and honor.
> You made him ruler over the works of your hands;
> you put everything under his feet:
> all sheep and oxen,
> as well as the animals in the wild,
> the birds of the sky,
> and the fish of the sea
> that pass through the currents of the seas. (Ps. 8:4–8)

Imago Dei: *Relational*

Human beings are made in the image of God as relational beings, and as such, it is *not good* for a human being to be alone. The Triune God (cf. Gen. 1:26: "Let *us* make . . .") , whose persons exist in unbroken communion with one another, created humans to live in relationship with one another. We suggest that humanity's unique nature and calling as God's image bearers involve at least four relationships.

First and foremost, God created us to know and love him. If God created us, then it makes sense that our purpose in life stands in direct relation to our Creator. Indeed, the highest call is to love the Lord God (Deut. 6:5; Matt. 22:37; Mark 12:30; Luke 10:27). To bear God's image in the world whether by structure or function implies a deep and abiding capacity for humans to know and relate to the God who created us.

But the creation account also reveals that God created us to know and love one another. In Genesis 2:18, God says that "it is not good for the man to be alone" and that he will make a helper for Adam, one who is fitting for him and he for her. This is an important development because it implies that the *imago Dei* reveals itself in humanity not only individually but corporately as well: humans relate to one another and thereby image God one to the other. Humans, then, imitate God by enabling one another to flourish in a divinely intended interdependence with one another. And this interdependence is a reflection of God's own Trinitarian being. In the case of Genesis 2, it is man and woman depending on each other as they both depend on God.

The movement from loving God to loving others is not uncommon in the Bible. When Jesus speaks of loving God, he speaks also of the second command like it, to love one's neighbor (Matt. 22:39; Mark 12:31; Luke 10:27). In Romans 12, when Paul exhorts Christians, in view of God's rich mercy, to love God by presenting themselves as living sacrifices, he then proceeds to instruct them to love others by using their gifts to build up the church, to love even enemies, to submit to civil authorities, to avoid being judgmental, and to avoid causing a brother to stumble. All these actions should be understood as expressions of love one to another. Such love for others is definitive of what it means to be Christian (John 13:34–35; 15:12–17; 1 John 3–4). But we would go further and suggest that such love expressed in relationship to others is what it means to be human.

So imaging God means loving God and others, but another aspect is often neglected: loving oneself. Imaging God means loving ourselves by seeing ourselves the way God sees us and by becoming who God wants us to become. The command to love neighbor as self (Matt. 22:39; Mark 12:31; Luke 10:27) calls for a proper response to all humanity, oneself included.

Only Christian theism can properly explain humanity. Other worldviews, philosophies, and religions tend either to denigrate or to enthrone humanity, viewing humans as nothing more than mere matter, on the one hand, or as the pinnacle of all that exists, on the other hand. But the Christian Scriptures make clear that humanity is neither mere matter nor divine being. Instead, our great dignity is that we are *like* God, able to image him, while our great humility is that we are *not* God, as we live under his authority and owe our very existence to him.

Finally, the *imago Dei* is carried out by humans in the way that we relate well to the world. In Genesis 2, there was no one to work the ground (v. 5), and then immediately the narrative tells us that God created such a person (vv. 7–15) to do the work! God thought it good to create Adam, who would work the soil that God had made. The reader should note that God was asking humanity to change, and even enhance, the good creation that God had given. It is good for humans to work; it is good for them to shape, form, and develop God's good creation. Moreover, the narrative tells us that God gave humans stewardship over the whole of the created order (1:26–30) so they could flourish in mutual interdependence.

God's Commands

As we have already noted, God gave humans certain directives. These commands are not optional; they cause us to flourish and help us understand what it means to be human. They reveal how we are distinct from the rest of the created order; God charged us to rule over the terrestrial world. Although Genesis 2:7 tells us that we are formed "out of the dust from the ground," "human beings are, however, not 'landlings'; they are rather 'landlords.'"

Humanity has the "tasks and trappings of royalty and cult, the offices of divine representation and habitation." In the Genesis account, God "imbued humanity with royal blessing and task in the world."[19] Humanity is blessed by God, indeed, but to be a blessing to the rest of the created order, to "rule" and "subdue" it (Gen. 1:28). Humans are given the great privilege and responsibility of being God's vice-regents in the world that he has made. Note the responsibilities God gives his people in Genesis 1–2:

1. Humanity: Be fruitful and multiply (1:28).
2. Humanity: Fill the earth and subdue it (1:28).
3. Humanity: Rule over the animal world (1:28).
4. Adam: Tend and till the earth (2:5, 15).
5. Adam: Eat from any tree (2:16).
6. Adam: Do not eat from the tree of the knowledge of good and evil (2:17).

These responsibilities are not optional; they are commands, or laws, that God gives to humanity to image him in the world. To grasp our purpose as human beings, we must carefully understand these responsibilities.

The first four in the list above remain vitally important, as we will see in the next chapter. Humanity is called to reproduce, to rule and fill the earth, and to rule over the animals. In addition, God commands Adam to work the ground in Genesis 2:15 (but the command is also implied in 2:5). This command to cultivate the earth remains in force even after Genesis 2 . . . for we all have to eat! These responsibilities, or creational laws, appear again and again in different ways throughout the rest of the story of Scripture, and we will make connections back to the creational laws as we move through the story.

Although these are laws that God has built into creation, nonetheless, these responsibilities neither oppress nor depress humanity. The first commands are set in the context of God's blessing. The commands are part of God's good world, not a result of sin or inadequacy. God's laws in creation are designed to bless his people as they relate to him.

We live best when we live within God's laws. God's laws are given to humans as a way for us to live well in God's world. As an illustration, consider the law of gravity. We can rebel against the law of gravity, but it is best not to, especially when climbing Mount Everest or flying an Apache helicopter! Tending, tilling, filling, reproducing, and cultivating the world in a manner that imitates the life-giving power of God is how he designed the world for humanity. We

19. Brown, *Ethos of the Cosmos*, 44.

live best when we live within his responsibilities. If we rebel against God and disobey his laws, then we suffer as a result of our disobedience. Not only is God displeased with our rebellion, but we shall also see in the next chapter the great price of our disobedience to God and the law he has given us.

God's Goal (The Seventh Day)

In the narrative of Genesis 1, the sixth day is the longest in terms of the number of words used to describe the day. And it is also true that the sixth day is climactic in terms of God establishing his image in humanity so we can govern the created world. And it is further apparent that after he completed the sixth day, God pronounced the world "very good" (Gen. 1:31). Yet creation is not complete without the Sabbath day (the seventh day).

The Sabbath day stands as the *culmination* of creation itself. But what does it mean for the Sabbath to be the culmination of creation? It means that the Sabbath day depicts all of creation enjoying God and God enjoying all of his creation. The Sabbath reveals the flourishing of creation.

While the first six days of creation reveal a world that is habitable for God's vice-regents, the creation account as a *whole* shows us that the *aim* of creation is Sabbath rest. God takes "formless and empty" (day 0) and ordains a *world*: "the heavens and the earth . . . in all their vast array" (Gen. 2:1 NIV).

The seventh day is unique for both literary and theological reasons.

Literary
1. The language of "the heavens and the earth" (1:1) appears again (2:1), bracketing day 0 and day 7.
2. The formulaic conclusion that appears with days 1–6 ("evening came and then morning") is notably absent in day 7, leaving the time frame of the day open ended. This day is not bounded by the evening/morning constraints of the other days. For this reason, it is doing something *other* than providing a rationale for the later Sabbath law that would be given to Israel. The Sabbath in the creation account is not bounded in time, even if demarcated by the term *day*.

Theological
1. God blesses (only) the seventh day.
2. God declares (only) the seventh day holy.
3. God rests from his creative activity described in the first six days of creation.

4. What was "formless and empty" (1:2) is now fully established and identi-
fiable as "the heavens and the earth . . . in all their vast array" (2:1 NIV).
This alerts the careful reader to the progression of creation: from empty
to filled, from a formless mass to an ordered world.

Later laws in Israel invoke the Sabbath day to ground their teaching (Exod.
20:8–11; Deut. 5:12–14). Some think that the teaching on the Sabbath day
is given late in Israel's history as a way to explain the reason for the laws.
But we suggest that the seventh day in Genesis 2:1–3 does *not* appear in the
narrative to give an explanation of the (later) laws: it is *not* an etiology for
the Sabbath law.[20] Rather, the later laws are, in fact, theological reflections *on
the reality of the Sabbath*. They clarify the characteristics of God as Creator
(Exod. 20:8–11) and God as Redeemer (Deut. 5:12–14) for Israel in light of
God's role as the Sabbath Lord.[21] The laws provide God's people the space
and time in the normal workweek to reflect on the grandeur of God as well as
the space and time to rest from painful toil in the land of thorns and thistles
(Gen. 3:18).

But in the creation account, the Sabbath day stands as a *timeless* time, with
no evening and no morning, in which thorns and thistles of a broken world
are not present. The Sabbath day is the *culmination* of creation in which God
enjoys his world and his works. It is the time in which God takes up his reign
over his finished, created world. As the divine King ascends to his throne, he
rules over his good world, all in order, all flourishing before him. Later texts
in the Old Testament depict God granting the king of Israel rest from enemies
so that the king can rule the kingdom in peace under God (2 Sam. 7:1–6;
1 Kings 5:4–5; 8:56; 1 Chron. 22:9–10, 18–19; 23:25–26).[22] The Israelite king
enjoys his rule in the land under God, resting in his reign. This point echoes
the rest of God in creation.

God's rest on the seventh day indicates his divine reign over the ordered
world that he has made. In this, there is enjoyment and worship before the
Creator. This reveals that the function of the Sabbath day in Genesis 2:1–4a
is different from that of the others. God made the world in the first six days

20. John Calvin leans toward this interpretation. See John Calvin, *Commentaries on the
First Book of Moses Called Genesis*, vol. 1, Calvin's Commentaries, trans. John King (Grand
Rapids: Eerdmans, 1948), 103–8. See, too, the otherwise beautiful analysis in Dennis T. Olson,
"Sacred Time: The Sabbath and Christian Worship," in *Touching the Altar: The Old Testament
for Christian Worship*, ed. Carol M. Bechtel (Grand Rapids: Eerdmans, 2008), 2–34.

21. So helpfully disclosed in Olson, "Sacred Time," 12–14.

22. Note the discussion in G. K. Beale, *The Temple and the Church's Mission: A Biblical
Theology of the Dwelling Place of God*, NSBT 17 (Downers Grove, IL: InterVarsity, 2004),
62–63.

of creation, but he *sustains* the created world in the seventh day, reigning over the good order and rhythm that he established on days 1–6.[23] He ceases from the creative work of days 1–6 because the world he has established stands as complete, good, ordered, and thriving. Day 7 is reserved for the whole of creation flourishing and enjoying God. So we could say that God's rest has little to do with his cessation from work.

The early church theologian Augustine helps us come to grips with God's rest. As Augustine knew so well, it would be nonsense to think that God the King needs a twenty-four-hour period of leisure for recuperation.[24] Instead, the rest of God indicates that God *causes* the type of godly rest and thriving that he envisions for the seventh day. Augustine appealed to three other scriptural instances to bolster this view: Deuteronomy 13:3; Matthew 24:36; and Romans 8:26. Further, the seventh day is, for Augustine, the indicator of the seventh age of the world.[25] In this way, he thinks the seventh day is prophetic, because it depicts a future day when God will return to set the world aright. This aspect of Augustine's interpretation—linking the seven days of creation with the seven ages of the world—is, to our minds, highly evocative (but not essential). But Augustine's great insight lay in connecting the seventh day with the goal of creation: the divine King reigning over creation.

The real world that is revealed in the seventh day discloses what will come about finally, fully, after the great defeat of sin. As we will see in future chapters, those persons who place their faith in the King of creation (Jesus Christ) will experience the "Sabbath rest" that awaits the whole of creation, nothing less than a new heavens and earth under the reign of Christ (Heb. 4:1–11). The writer of Hebrews views God's rest as being the restoration of all things, the hope of the suffering Christian.

The Sabbath day, then, draws us to reflect on the point that creation is closely linked to the kingdom of God. Everything is ordered and whole, so that all of creation reflects the goodness of its King, God himself. Creation, then, is the arena where God rules. God's kingdom, at the very beginning, is not just in people or in heaven; it is on earth. That is the way God designed

23. "God's rest both at the conclusion of creation in Genesis 1–2 and later in Israel's temple indicates not mere inactivity but that he had demonstrated his sovereignty over the forces of chaos (e.g., the enemies of Israel) and now has assumed a position of kingly rest further revealing his sovereign power." Beale, *Temple and the Church's Mission*, 62.

24. Indeed, it was a Manichaean heresy that he combated. See his discussion on Gen. 2:1–3 and his refutation of the Manichaeans in Augustine, *Saint Augustine on Genesis: "Two Books on Genesis against the Manichees" and "On the Literal Interpretation of Genesis,"* Fathers of the Church 84 (Washington, DC: Catholic University of America Press, 1991), §1.22.33–34, pp. 81–83.

25. Augustine, *Saint Augustine on Genesis*, §1.23.41, p. 88.

it. As we have seen, recent research on Genesis notes the way that Genesis 1 especially links creation to God's enthronement in his temple. If this is the case, then Genesis shows us that creation itself is the arena for God's reign.

Conclusion

"In the beginning God created the heavens and the earth" (Gen. 1:1). We hope this chapter has enriched an understanding of the complexity and extraordinary power of this verse and those that follow. Creation is not a throwaway moment in God's grand story of Scripture. All told, Genesis offers a unique perspective on the good world in which we live. To summarize, creation reveals four things to us: God, God's people, God's commands, and God's kingdom.

We hope this chapter has also shown how God created his people to rule as vice-regents under his rule—with order, justice, and goodness, and for the good of all. When we rule in a way that is pleasing to God, we image our God well and bring glory to him. We have seen that God created his vice-regents to experience deep and abiding communion with God, with one another, and with God's world. In the next chapter, we will see how God's vice-regents spurned the charge of God and experienced deep and abiding fracture with God, with one another, and with God's world. How did this happen? Genesis tells us it happened because of human sin.

2

FALL

Human Sin and Its Aftermath

And the LORD *God commanded the man, "You are free to eat from any tree of the garden, but you must not eat from the tree of the knowledge of good and evil, for on the day you eat from it, you will certainly die."*

Genesis 2:16–17

Introduction

We left the last chapter at the end of the biblical narrative's first plot movement: creation. In that opening act, we were given an account of God's creative activity and a depiction of God's good world as one in which human beings flourished in their relationship with God, with one other, and with the created order. Everything was good in God's world, and humanity was living for the King.

In this chapter, however, we will discover that something went terribly wrong. Throughout the centuries, Christians have referred to this moment as the "fall" of humanity. We call it the fall because Adam and Eve rebelled against God the King, falling out of communion with him and dragging the whole world down with them. No longer could humanity live fully for the King.

Each of us knows intuitively that something is badly wrong with our world. We don't need the Bible to come to grips with that. We are constantly made aware of the great evils committed by humanity, such as terrorism, murder, rape, and abuse. I (Heath) had the terrible experience of having my Bible study leader killed in the Oklahoma City bombing, which was perpetrated by Timothy McVeigh on April 19, 1995. McVeigh parked a bomb-laden truck in front of the Alfred P. Murrah Federal Building, and the bomb went off, killing 168 people, 19 of them children. My Bible study leader was found some days later in the rubble.

We also recognize that pain, suffering, death, and destruction are woven into our experience of the natural world through physical afflictions, mental illness, deaths, and natural disasters. I (Bruce) had the terrible experience of learning that one of my elementary school classmates had been killed by one of a swarm of tornados that ripped through my hometown and, separately, learning that another classmate's father had taken his own life.

Those without a belief in God, known as atheists, are constrained to explain evil as a natural part of life. They are *normalists*, thinking that suffering, death, and evil have always been a normal part of nature. But we, as Christians, are *abnormalists*, knowing that suffering, death, and evil are abnormal.[1] They are alien intruders in the good world that God created. Our experience of these things causes anguish in the silent places of our souls and makes us long for a better world.

In this chapter, we will focus on the theological notion of *sin* and its effect in order to identify and explain what has gone wrong with our world. We will begin with a brief summary of the Bible's teaching about sin before going on to trace sin and its consequences in the biblical narrative. We will focus on the Old Testament stories that depict sin in concrete and vivid ways while drawing on New Testament teaching along the way.

Sin

We have identified sin as the root of what is wrong in the world, but sin is a notion that is understood in myriad and contradictory ways. For that reason, we will briefly foreground some of the Bible's most significant teachings about sin.

First and foremost, the Bible associates sin with humanity. Humans can and do sin. Granite rocks and sequoia trees cannot and do not sin. Neither

---

1. Abraham Kuyper develops this point in his argument against modernism. Kuyper's contention with modernism is that modernists think humanity exists in a normal or natural state of upward development, while Christianity believes that humanity exists in an abnormal or fallen state. Abraham Kuyper, *Lectures on Calvinism* (Grand Rapids: Eerdmans, 1931), 54–59.

do rock badgers and ferrets. So they cannot be identified as evil, which is also a moral category. Only human beings are able to act with moral intention. Sin is something humans do, and when we find ourselves sinning, we should recognize our sinful acts as indicators—like the warning light on the dashboard of an automobile—that something has gone badly wrong in us and needs to be repaired.

Second, sin is multifaceted and can be described in many ways. The Bible describes it as a physical burden (Isa. 1:2–4), a debt (Isa. 40:2), a type of spiritual adultery (Hosea), a rebellion (Josh. 1:18), a transgression (Rom. 4:15), a great lawlessness (1 John 3:4), a disobedience (Rom. 5:19), and a type of false worship (Phil. 3:19). This list is representative but in no way exhaustive. Each of these descriptions is important, so we should take care not to allow our understanding of sin to be reduced to any one of them. Take, for example, sin as a debt. If we reduce our understanding of sin to a debt, we will understand it as a failure but not as a relational breach. Or consider false worship. If we reduce our understanding of sin to false worship, we will grasp that we are idolaters but forget that sin is the breaking of God's law.

Third, any attempt at defining sin should therefore be broad enough to incorporate the Bible's many descriptions of it. Building on Cornelius Plantinga's *Not the Way It's Supposed to Be: A Breviary of Sin*, we define sin as any action (thought, desire, emotion, word, or deed) or disposition that displeases God and deserves blame. The inverse is also true: a sin is the *absence* of an action or disposition that pleases God and so deserves blame.[2] Therefore, there are sins of commission and sins of omission. In other words, we can sin not only by doing or saying something that we shouldn't (commission) but also by not doing or saying something that we should have done or said (omission). Plantinga put it well when he wrote that sin wears a thousand faces.[3]

Based on this definition, we should recognize sin as an affront against God. Even when we sin against other people, we are ultimately sinning against God, who created them in his likeness and image. So when we sin, we sin against God, displeasing him and breaking communion with him.

The Bible explores sin in many ways and from multiple angles. Even though we, as sinful humans, would prefer not to think about our sin, the Bible will not let us off the hook. Consider, for example, the Ten Commandments (Exod. 20:1–17; Deut. 5:6–21). Although they were given to Israel, they still express God's universal moral law for us today. Even in instances in which Israel's

2. This definition is similar to Cornelius Plantinga Jr., *Not the Way It's Supposed to Be: A Breviary of Sin* (Grand Rapids: Eerdmans, 1995), 13.

3. Plantinga, *Not the Way It's Supposed to Be*, 9.

particularity is mixed in with universal moral law, the universal aspect of the law still stands. So even though the command not to covet focuses on ancient Near Eastern Israel's oxen, donkeys, and female servants, the universality extends to contemporary Western automobiles, beach houses, and job contracts. Similarly, even though Israel was told to rest and worship on Saturday, Christians can bypass the particular (Saturday) in order to obey the universal of resting and worshiping (albeit on Sunday).

Or consider the list given in Proverbs 6:16–19:

> The LORD hates six things;
> in fact, seven are detestable to him:
> arrogant eyes, a lying tongue,
> hands that shed innocent blood,
> a heart that plots wicked schemes,
> feet eager to run to evil,
> a lying witness who gives false testimony,
> and one who stirs up trouble among brothers.

In these verses, Scripture identifies pride, lies, murder, evil intentions, evil actions, false witness, and familial divisiveness as things God hates. We may think we are good people saying, "I haven't coveted, murdered, stolen, or taken the Lord's name in vain!" But the Bible deepens and extends the "big ten" (especially commandments five through ten) through passages such as Proverbs 6:16–19 in order to help us recognize and avoid sin in its many manifestations.

Indeed, Jesus deepened and extended the Old Testament teaching on sin. He taught that sin cannot be confined merely to one's outward actions (such as committing adultery or murdering a person) but also extends to the inner thoughts and dispositions that nobody other than God can see (such as lusting for a woman or wishing another person would die). Such things count as sin as well. Think of how many times you have harbored sinful desires or entertained unloving thoughts toward another person. Jesus teaches that *inner* sins are actually the source of *outward* sins. Sin indeed wears a thousand faces.

Fourth, sin deserves blame and incurs guilt. Whether an inner or outward action that displeases God, all sin is blameworthy. What does *blame* mean in our definition? It means that a sinner is responsible for their actions that create disharmony in relationships. Blame can be equated with guilt in a law metaphor: sinners are guilty of crimes that demand punishment. Blame can be equated with manual labor: sin creates a kind of burden that has to be carried. Blame can be equated with debt in an economic metaphor: sin creates a debt that must be paid. Using the economic metaphor for sin, Paul says very clearly, "The wages of sin is death" (Rom. 6:23). In this verse, the blame, or payment, that comes as a result of sin is horrifying: the payment of sin is death.

In sum, human beings sin in many ways, each of which is an affront to God and all of which are blameworthy. This biblical concept of sin seems implausible and even bad to many people whose personal formation has taken place in the secular West. In our Western context, individual autonomy (freedom from external authority) is deified, and thus people do not want to give God his rightful place as deity. In response, we offer that God did indeed give human beings freedom, but good freedom is not a freedom *from* all restraints but rather a freedom *for* a life of flourishing under God's reign and according to his law. We saw this in the last chapter.

Sin in the Garden

Genesis 3 takes a dark turn in the story of Scripture. Everything was good until, all of a sudden, it was not. In the midst of the garden, a serpent—that crafty and cunning beast—tempted the first couple to sin against God. God had instructed them not to eat from the tree of knowledge, but at the serpent's suggestion, they took and ate.

God had given them permission to eat from any other tree in the garden and had prohibited that one tree alone. Why did they disobey? Why did the fruit from the other trees not satisfy them? This is where the interpretation of the story gets really interesting. As we understand it, Adam and Eve disobeyed God (a sin) in an attempt to live apart from him and his rule. God had given them rules to follow in their relationship with him, but Adam and Eve did not want to follow them. Rather, they wanted *autonomy*, freedom from external constraints, even when those constraints had been given by God the King.

Sin's Consequences

What does Adam and Eve's sin of disobedience do? Instead of ascending to be autonomous like God, they fall out of communion with him and, as a result, watch their lives fall apart.

First, their sin exposes them and brings shame on them. After eating the fruit, "the eyes of both of them were opened, and they knew they were naked" (Gen. 3:7). Instead of bringing them the honor they might have wanted as they sought to be autonomous like a god, their action brings shame and exposes them for who they are—sinful earthlings who foolishly tried to subvert God the King.

Second, the first couple's sin corrupts their union and twists God's blessing of sexuality. Sexuality is a unique blessing built into God's design for humanity (Gen. 1:28). Prior to the first couple's sin, their sexuality was an unmitigated blessing. But in the aftermath of the fall, it became the source of competition, guilt, and shame. Indeed, Adam and Eve hide their sexuality from themselves and from each other. They employ fig leaves to cover their shame and to conceal the blessing God had given them in the first place: the blessing of sexuality. In a sinless world, the first couple was freely and unashamedly naked, innocently affirming and delighting in the other's sexuality and individuality before God. The fig-leaf cover-up is a recognition that the freedom they felt when sinning against God was not worth the price they were paying.

Third, their initial sin launches them on a sinful trajectory in which they are continually tempted to live apart from God, to seek salvation apart from him. Notice that, after their sin, they do not turn to God for help. They do not ask him to remove their shame or cover them where they were exposed. Instead, as sinners, they try to cover themselves and conceal their own shame. In a word, they try to save themselves.

Fourth, sin dislocates Adam and Eve from fundamental relationships. After sinning, they experience a break with God. In Genesis 3:8, the first human pair hear the "sound" of the Lord God walking through the garden at dusk. The word for "sound" is the same as the word for "voice" in the Hebrew language. God's voice, or sound, which previously brought delight and goodness (think about God's voice bringing about the good world in Gen. 1–2), now brings fear to the first human pair, causing them to hide from him. The text exposes in shocking detail nothing short of a loss of intimacy and communion with God. God speaks, and humans fear and hide. This is why the Bible speaks of Christ reconciling us to God (2 Cor. 5:19).

Sin's inexorable drive toward dislocation extends to the "self." Sin brings us to the point where we are, in effect, shattered selves. We know what God has created us to be but cannot attain it because of sin. We hide and run away from God and, therefore, from his design for humanity. We run from ourselves. Nothing will remedy our plight except God's act of redemption. This is why, in part, the Bible speaks of Jesus Christ reinstilling our humanity in his salvation. We become renewed selves in Jesus Christ: "So if anyone is in Christ, there is a new creation: everything old has passed away; see, everything has become new!" (2 Cor. 5:17 NRSV).

Sin's dislocating effect extends also to the "other." Adam and Eve were partners in God's garden, naked and unashamed of their differences. They knew each other intimately without shame (Gen. 2:24–25) or threat. But sin shatters the intimacy that bridges the sexes. Their disobedience leads to blame and competition, dishonor and threat. They no longer know each other as partners but as threats. The disordering of their relationship with each other would now extend to all of our relationships with others, for which reason Christ died to reconcile us not only to God but also to one another (Eph. 2:11–18).

Perhaps surprisingly, sin also causes a dislocation between humanity and the rest of the created order. Literally, Adam and Eve have to leave the garden. Metaphorically, they have to leave the perfect relationship they had experienced with the created order in general. Take agriculture, for example. At creation, God designed the land to produce food for humanity. After the fall, the earth still brought forth food, but only through hard labor. Rather than fertility and unbounded productivity, the natural world now exposes us to conflict and hardship.

Fifth, sin brings on humanity a divine curse, whereas previously Adam and Eve had only known God's blessing. In Genesis 1:26, God blesses humanity, but in Genesis 3:14–19, God utters a curse. To understand the full ramifications of sin, we must see not only how Adam and Eve respond to their sin but also what God says in response to their sin.

Structure and Direction

As we have seen, sin changed things for the worse. But we should remember that sin didn't change everything comprehensively. That is because sin doesn't have the power to destroy creation's order, make the natural world evil in itself, or obliterate our humanity. One way to put the situation is to say that God's good world remained good structurally but was corrupted directionally. Although the fundamental ordering of the world remains according to God's good intentions, sinful humanity takes the good world he made and directs it toward sinful ends, causing life to be frustrating and painful.

Reflect again on the responsibilities God gave to humanity before the fall, responsibilities we discussed in the first chapter.

1. Be fruitful and multiply (Gen. 1:28).
2. Fill the earth and subdue it (1:28).
3. Rule over the animal world (1:28).
4. Tend and till the earth (2:5, 2:15).
5. Eat from any tree (2:16).
6. Do not eat from the tree of the knowledge of good and evil (2:17).

God gave these commands and responsibilities for the thriving of his good creation and for the delight of humanity. These commands delighted God. But what happened with Adam and Eve? They disobeyed the last command (sixth) and as a result, all the other commands became deeply complicated by sin (see table 2.1).

Table 2.1: Responsibilities Complicated by Sin

Prefall	Postfall
Be fruitful and multiply (Gen. 1:28)	Have painful, anguished childbirth (3:16)
Fill the earth and subdue it (1:28)	Go back to the earth (3:19)
Rule over the animal world (1:28)	Experience conflict between serpent and seed (3:15)
Tend and till the earth (2:5, 15)	Work cursed ground, thorns, and thistles (3:18)
Eat from any tree (2:16)	Eat by "the sweat of your brow" (3:18–19)

Based on the data in table 2.1, notice how human responsibilities are not abrogated by sin. The only thing abrogated by sin is Adam and Eve's ability to do specific tasks within the garden of Eden; since they are barred from the garden, they can no longer eat from its trees. The other responsibilities, however, remain in place. We should be fruitful and multiply, even if in the postfall world childbearing will be painful. We should continue to till the soil, even though in the fallen world that task will be frustrating. By extension, we should continue to lovingly manage God's good world in a thousand different ways, even though each of those ways will be frustrating or painful in our fallen world.

So our basic human responsibility remains the same structurally, but because of the misdirection caused by sin, we experience great frustration and suffering in carrying out those tasks. This experience of frustration and suffering should serve—as we mentioned earlier—as a warning sign that something has gone wrong in all of us and needs to be made right.

As the apostle Paul explains, all of humanity has fallen into sin, and there is, in fact, a deep connection between Adam's sin and humanity's sins. "So then, as through one trespass [Adam's sin in the garden] there is condemnation for everyone, . . . just as through one man's disobedience the many were made sinners" (Rom. 5:18–19). Indeed, "We all went astray like sheep; we all have turned to our own way" (Isa. 53:6). Each of us has "exchanged the truth of God for a lie, and worshiped and served what has been created instead of the Creator, who is praised forever. Amen" (Rom. 1:25). What does this mean? It means that Adam and Eve's fall into sin corrupted humanity to the point where we choose to sin rather than choosing to follow God. Our sin stains through and through, and we cannot remove the mark. Our sin makes us guilty, and we cannot make ourselves innocent again.

Like Adam and Eve in the garden of Eden, we break God's commands, thinking ourselves to be above God's law. God draws lines, but we blur them, break them, transgress them; when we disregard the lines he has drawn, we commit the same mutinous act of humanity's patriarch and matriarch. We relive the fall again and again like a living nightmare.

In light of what has gone wrong due to human sin, an extraordinary creation-healing action is needed to set it right. We know this action is found in Jesus Christ. But we get to that in the next chapter.

Cain and Abel, Noah and Babel

Immediately after the story of the first couple's fall, the Bible's narrative depicts in vivid detail the corruption and misdirection that sin brings to all of society and culture. The narrative arc of Genesis 4–11 is tragic. Think about it: After the account of the first couple's sin, the very next episode in the narrative portrays a murder that takes place within a family. The second-born son of Adam and Eve, Abel, is tragically murdered by his own brother, Cain. This murder is an ominous portent of the ways of humanity as it moves forward in history.

After Cain's act, life on earth continues in the same dark vein. The first major poem uttered by a human after Adam and Eve's rebellion in the garden of Eden is nothing other than a curse delivered by Lamech (see Gen. 4:23–24). Poetry was meant to bless and delight rather than to curse and destroy. But this is the way of the story after the fall: one sin follows on another in an unending chain of disaster and degradation.

Next in the narrative is the account of Noah, which captures graphically the general degradation and wickedness of humanity. Although humanity continues to "be fruitful and multiply" (Gen. 5), the multiplying population sins against God. Genesis 6 depicts God's world sinning with utter abandon:

> When the LORD saw that human wickedness was widespread on the earth and that every inclination of the human mind was nothing but evil all the time, the LORD regretted that he had made man on the earth, and he was deeply grieved. Then the LORD said, "I will wipe mankind, whom I created, off the face of the earth, together with the animals, creatures that crawl, and birds of the sky—for I regret that I made them." (vv. 5–7)

Did you catch God's perspective on humanity? He sees humans as utterly wicked to the core. Provocatively, the text even indicates that God regrets having created them. God says to Noah in verse 13, "I have decided to put an end to every creature, for the earth is filled with wickedness because of them; therefore I am going to destroy them along with the earth." Humanity has sinned and thereby pervaded the world with wickedness; hence, God will destroy humanity and the wickedness humans precipitate.

In light of the goodness of God's creation, God's judgment should shock us! God, who created the world good and gave humanity a distinctive place, has now determined to *uncreate* his creation and wipe out humanity (Gen. 6:7). Why would God enact this decree of judgment? Because of the seriousness with which he takes sin. The flood is a horrific judgment. In the story of the flood, only the wind, rain, and waves echo outside the boat. All other life outside the boat that needed air to live ceased.

Still, God was not done with his creation. Although he judged the world's sin, it was a purifying judgment. It was intended to wash wickedness from the world. Noah acted as God's agent of blessing in this new, post-flood world. Noah and his family were meant to repopulate the world and be the blessing that God had intended for Adam and his family to be.

But while it took Adam and Eve a chapter to fall into sin, it takes Noah all of two verses! In Genesis 9:20–21, Noah plants a vineyard (good!) but gets drunk off the produce (bad!). Notice how the role of tending and tilling the earth is reaffirmed in Noah's planting a vineyard. But also notice how that good action is once again twisted in sin. A particular story of human sin closes the universal story of divine judgment.

By the time we reach Genesis 11, humanity is once again sinning with abandon. At Babel, the people determine to make a tower to "make a name for [themselves]," lest they be "scattered" all over the earth (Gen. 11:4). This tower is planned in a great city, like a super skyscraper that will be seen for miles around. The underlying motive, Kass reminds us, is idolatrous: "To make a new name for oneself is to remake the meaning of one's life so that it deserves a new name. To change the meaning of human being is to remake the content and character of human life."[4] He continues, "The children of man . . . remake themselves and, thus, their name, in every respect taking the place of God."[5] Setting themselves apart from God, humans want to remake themselves to be like God (perhaps a subtle nod back to Adam and Eve's desire to be like God in Gen. 3).

4. Leon Kass, *The Beginning of Wisdom: Reading Genesis* (Chicago: University of Chicago Press, 2006), 231.
5. Kass, *Beginning of Wisdom*, 231.

Besides the desire to replace their Maker, there is at least one other problem with this endeavor. The whole enterprise of coming together into one place to make a name for themselves directly goes against God's clear command to "fill the earth" in Genesis 1:28 and 9:1. God made humanity to spread out through-out the whole of his creation, filling it with his priest-kings, his ambassadors, rather than localizing in one place. In their desire to refashion themselves and displace their God, humans, as is typical, disobey God's clear commands.

What is the result of disobedience to God? As in the garden of Eden and the days of Noah, disobedience brings God's judgment. So the people of the valley are judged by God. The tower is obliterated, God curses the people with confusion, and their pride is reduced to another fall.

Abraham and His Family

Only God can make things right where Babel went wrong. After Babel, the biblical narrative moves to the story of a man named Abram (whose name is later changed to Abraham) and his wife, Sarai (whose name is later changed to Sarah).[6] The story of Abraham's family is recorded in Genesis 12–50.

Abraham

The story of Abraham and Sarah is, at least on one level, quite a sad tale. They are childless, which means they cannot "be fruitful and multiply." They are also likely people who worship gods other than the one true God. Abraham experiences the death of his brother and becomes the caretaker of his nephew and their extended family. He also experiences war, betrayal, family disputes, death, and famine. By all accounts, he lives a hard life.

But on another level, Abraham's life is extraordinary. In Abraham we find God actively working to heal and redirect life where sin has caused corrup-tion and misdirection. In a number of texts (Gen. 12:1–3; 15:1–21; 17:1–22; 22:15–18), God promises Abraham the following:

a land (a home to call his own)

a great nation (children and family)

a great name (honor among others)

God as his shield and reward (divine relationship and protection)

6. God administers these name changes in Gen. 17 to highlight the surety of his promises to Abram. We will cover these promises in the next chapter. But for ease and clarity in this discussion, we will be using "Abraham" and "Sarah" throughout this section.

These promises cannot and will not be revoked, because God has promised them. More will be said about this in the next chapter, but it is important to ask, Did God expect Abraham to be perfect in order to receive these promises? No. But why is this? God does not choose perfect people to accomplish his purposes or achieve his promises. Abraham and his family are a case in point.

Once again, Kass's description of Abraham is instructive. Abraham is not perfect or fully trained in the ways of God. Rather, Kass suggests that Abraham must "go to school" so he can fully live into the promises that God has given him. He is not worthy in Genesis 12 to receive the fullness of the promises, but God "takes him to school" through his experiences and trials (in Christian theology, we might call this a process of spiritual formation or even sanctification, through which we begin to live into the holy and righteous life that is given to us in Jesus Christ). By Genesis 22, Abraham understands what it means to follow God: it means obeying God's word even if it costs him God's promises. In Abraham, then, we see an inverse of Adam and Eve's disobedience. Abraham obeys, even if it costs God's promises. Of course, from Abraham's story, we learn that he is a sinner like the rest of us, and for that reason, God had to "school" him in the ways of God. Consider a few of Abraham's foibles.

As soon as Abraham gets to the land where God instructed him to go, we find that he is not quite the paragon of piety that we hoped he would be. In fact, soon after arriving, he up and leaves to go to Egypt. His excuse for leaving is to escape a famine (Gen. 12:10–20). When he arrives in Egypt, he is fearful that he will be harmed because his wife, Sarah, is stunningly beautiful. He fears that he will be killed so a more powerful man can have his wife. Thus, in order to avoid the scenario he imagines, he lies to Pharaoh, the king of Egypt, telling Pharaoh that Sarah is his sister. He even profits from his lie (v. 16). What's more, he does this twice, lying about Sarah to King Abimelech in Genesis 20. Along the way, Abraham sins in other ways, for example, by throwing his son Ishmael out of the house (Gen. 21).

We get the point, right? Abraham is not a perfect person. He battles with sin throughout his life. His children will be a blessing to the nations, but Abraham is still living in the land of thorns and thistles, east of Eden. Abraham sinned.

Abraham's Family

What is true of Abraham is also true of his family. Throughout the remainder of Genesis, we learn of his family's sins and foibles. Indeed, these chapters in Genesis highlight the fundamental breakdown of family relationships because of sin.

Abraham's son Isaac marries, but just like his father, when faced with a scary situation, he lies and says his wife, Rebekah, is his sister (see Gen. 26:7–11; cf. 12:10–20). Isaac has two children: Jacob and Esau. Esau is the eldest son, but Jacob is the more devious of the two. Esau marries women who bring his parents grief (26:34–35), and Jacob unethically strives for power, influence, and control in his family. He tricks his brother into selling his birthright to him (a *birthright* is the rights of the firstborn son in the family; see 25:29–34). Jacob then tricks his own father into giving him the patriarchal blessing instead of giving it to the rightful recipient, Esau (27:1–40). And the problems between Jacob and Esau are matched by the problems of their parents: "Isaac loved Esau because he had a taste for wild game, but Rebekah loved Jacob" (25:28). The narrative of Genesis, then, reveals the family competing and broken. When a family plays favorites with the children, no one wins. As with Adam and Eve, the children and grandchildren of Abraham experience the ravaging effects of sin.

Things get worse with the children of Jacob. Jacob has twelve sons and at least one daughter named Dinah. Dinah is raped by a man named Shechem, and her father does . . . nothing. Dinah's brothers, however, rouse in anger to avenge the violation of their sister. What do they do? They lie, deceive, and use God's sign of blessing (circumcision) as a front to incapacitate both Shechem and his people. While they are laid up (circumcision understandably puts adult males out of commission for a while), the brothers murder the entire company. The whole sordid account appears in Genesis 34, a terrifying story that highlights family dysfunction, violation, and sin. Sadly, Dinah's voice is not heard again. We know her last as a violated woman who does not experience the rights she deserves. Jacob's sons, however, do not stop there. One son, Judah, sleeps with his daughter-in-law (Tamar) after she disguises herself as a prostitute (Gen. 38). It is also Judah who leads his brothers to sell one of the younger brothers (Joseph) into slavery (37:26–27).

All told, the story of Abraham's family is in many ways a tragic tale of how sin corrupts and misdirects society's foundational institution—the family. As discussed above, sin breaks communion with God, self, and others. In the case of Abraham's children and family, it is apparent that sin does just that. Note the pervasive sin present in the narrative thus far: lying, murder, selfishness, greed, deception, rape, revenge, illicit sex, and sexual deviance. Astonishing!

You may be thinking that the stories in Genesis sound a bit too modern to be in the Bible. Sex, deception, perversion, greed, murder—this is the stuff of reality television but not of the Bible, surely! But as surely as humans make decisions, we tend to make bad ones that displease God and are blameworthy.

This is true in every age. Perhaps it is better to say that Abraham's sinful family is not *extraordinary* in their sin but horrifically *ordinary*.

God's People in God's Land

Genesis concludes with Abraham's family in Egypt. Will they ever get to the land that God promised Abraham (the "promised land")? If so, how will they get there? And how will they live when they arrive?

These questions find their answers as the story progresses. The story picks up in the book after Genesis, the book of Exodus. Then it carries through Leviticus and Deuteronomy.[7] Deuteronomy's setting is just on the western border of the promised land. The books of Joshua, Judges, Ruth, 1–2 Samuel, and 1–2 Kings tell the story of what happens after God's people have entered the land and while they are living there. As we will see, it is not the happiest of stories because it highlights the prevalence of Israel's sin.

Exodus

Hollywood movies attempt to retell and recast the biblical story of the exodus in various ways. In Cecil B. DeMille's *The Ten Commandments* (1956), Charlton Heston is cast as Moses, and the story is used to smuggle objectionable sexual themes and content into theaters.[8] More recently, Disney studios picked up the story and retold it in the animated film *The Prince of Egypt* (1998). Even more recently, Ridley Scott directed the epic, high-budget action film *Exodus: Gods and Kings* (2014), which contrasts the experience of Moses with that of the Egyptian pharaoh. Hollywood directors know a good story when they read one!

The story of Exodus is about God's people, Israel, who are the descendants of Abraham and his family, living as slaves in Egypt and making their escape (or exodus) into the desert on their way to the land that God had promised to Abraham. The significance of the exodus is that it is the foundational story to which God's people return again and again to understand their God, themselves, and their world. The exodus teaches that Israel's God loves and

7. Genesis, Exodus, Leviticus, Numbers, and Deuteronomy are the Five Books of Moses, also called the Pentateuch. These books introduce the world, what's gone wrong, and what God is doing to set it right. We are focusing on "what's gone wrong" in this chapter.

8. Interestingly, this was the second time DeMille told this story. His first portrayal of the exodus was thirty-three years earlier than his 1956 film. He first told the exodus story in the silent film *The Ten Commandments* (1923). The two films are quite different, but both are worth watching.

saves, he gives his people purpose, and that through them he will set the world right. But the book of Exodus teaches that God's people have a serious sin problem as well.

God's people are in the land of Egypt, suffering as slaves. These slaves are the children of Abraham, Isaac, and Jacob. Jacob had twelve sons who eventually made up the twelve tribes that suffered in Egypt. (Remember this point about the twelve tribes of Israel. It will prove important in one of the later chapters.) In Egypt, the great antagonist is Pharaoh, the Egyptian king who stands as a rival to God the King and as an obstacle to God's promises (a land, a great nation, a great name, and a unique relationship with God). In the story, we learn that the people of Israel are being held by the Egyptians as slaves without honor, as a people without a place. Still, even Pharaoh cannot prevent the people of Israel from multiplying, as God had promised (Gen. 1:28; 12:2–3; 15:5; 17:6; 22:17–18; 26:4; 28:14; Exod. 1:7, 12, 20), or from showing allegiance to God the King rather than to Pharaoh the king (Exod. 1:17, 21).

In the midst of Israel's retention of its allegiance to God and its rapid multiplication, God works to fulfill his other promises. As the story unfolds, we learn that God raises up Moses to be his spokesman to the wicked pharaoh. Moses is significant in the story of Israel, and his profile increases as we move from Exodus to Deuteronomy. He is Israel's leader, their prophet, and their lawgiver (especially in Deuteronomy). He occupies the role of a great prophet as he encounters the pagan king of Egypt.

On God's cue, Moses tells Pharaoh to let God's people go to worship God at Sinai. If the Egyptian king will acquiesce to God's demand, Moses prophesies, then things will go well for him. But if he does not, Moses declares, then he and all of Egypt will be afflicted by a series of ten plagues. In response, Pharaoh refuses to release Israel, and God reveals his divine power by judging Pharaoh for his recalcitrance. After the tenth plague, Pharaoh finally relents and gives God's people the freedom to worship their God and go to their land. Once they have departed, however, he changes his mind and attempts to recapture them. Again, God steps in to show his power and judge the Egyptians, and he does so by drowning Pharaoh's armies (Exod. 14).

The Law for God's People at Sinai

After granting the Israelites their freedom, God brings them to Mount Sinai, where he gives them his law (Exod. 19–31; esp. Exod. 20). What is the purpose of this law? Its purpose is twofold. Positively, the law is the way he lets his people know his demands, his virtues, and his values as they move into the promised land. Just as Adam and Eve had responsibilities in the garden of Eden (both dos and don'ts), so Israel has laws that show them the "dos" and "don'ts" as they move into the land. Adherence to this law will enable the Israelites to be a light to the nations and to flourish in their relationship with God, with one another, and with the created order.

Negatively, the law exposes the deep sin problem rooted in the hearts of God's people. In the law God gives at Sinai, we encounter an extensive list of punishments for breaking it. Why does Israel need an articulated law declaring the wrongness of lying, adultery, cheating, deception, or murder? Because God's articulation of his law exposes the pervasive presence of sin in Israel. They need to be told not to sin because they are a sinful people.

Even the worship laws expose the problem of sin.[9] Although not all sacrifices offered in Israel's worship are given to alleviate sin, three of them are designed to deal with sin. These are the *'olah* ("burnt"), *'asham* ("guilt") and *khatta'th* ("sin") offerings. The instructions regarding these sacrifices are very specific and remind God's people that sin must be addressed for God's people to relate rightly to God, one another, and the land. Israel's laws reveal the deep problem of sin among God's people.

This point gains terrible clarity in the narrative of Exodus, because just as soon as the people receive God's law, they break it. Exodus 32 is a story of Israel's rebellion against God. While God meets with Moses on the mountain, Aaron, Moses's brother and the priest of Israel, leads God's people to build an idol (a golden calf, to be precise) and worship it. God's people break the primary commandments that God gave them in the Ten Commandments. Exodus 32 reveals the following:

- God's people make an idol of another god (specifically, a golden calf).
- They build the idol out of the gold that God provided for them through the Egyptians.
- They call the idol by God's name (Yahweh).
- They worship the idol and give glory to a bull rather than to the Lord of the universe.

This episode shows that no one escapes humanity's fall into sin. All fall short of God's standards and sin against him. Even at its inception as a national and political body, Israel has a sin problem.

After leaving the mountain of God and being disciplined for building the golden calf, the Israelites persist in their lack of faith and trust in God. As a

9. See Lev. 1–16.

result of their unrepentant sin, the older generation of Israelites—who had seen the signs and wonders of God in Egypt, at the crossing of the sea, and even at Mount Sinai—is not allowed to see the land that God promised to Abraham.

Life in the Promised Land

Even Moses dies outside the land. The entire book of Deuteronomy is set on the plains of Moab, which is the geographical region just on the west side of the Jordan River, west of Canaan. At this spot, Moses delivers three farewell sermons to God's people as they are going to enter the land. Moses will not be with them, so his sermons are designed to persuade the people to be faithful to God, but they are also designed to highlight Israel's perpetual sin problem. Because of their sin, God's people will incur guilt and blame; their punishment is that they will forfeit the right to live in God's land and will become slaves once again, just as they had been in Egypt (Deut. 28–29). Nonetheless, they enter the promised land, fulfilling not only the promise of a great land but the other promises also: they have a great name because of God, they are a large nation because of God, and they have a unique relationship with God (through a covenant, which we will explore in the next chapter).

Once the Israelites arrive in the promised land, they continue to sin and to experience the consequences of their sin. In fact, the book of Judges identifies Israel's sin as a vicious cycle of disobedience and judgment. In Judges 2:11–19, the cycle is outlined in four phases:

1. The Israelites rebel and sin against God.
2. God raises up an oppressor.
3. The Israelites cry out to God.
4. God raises up a deliverer (judge).

Scholars identify this process as a *cycle* because it occurs repeatedly (see Judg. 3:7, 12; 4:1; 6:1; 10:6; 13:1). Note the problem: God's people continue to sin against him even after he delivers them. This doesn't happen just once but over and over again. Why? Because the propensity for sin is pervasive for God's people—indeed, for *all* people.

Even Israel's greatest leaders sin boldly. Consider, for example, the sins of Israel's priests. Eli is a high priest, and his sons, Hophni and Phinehas, are also priests (1 Sam. 1:1–4:18). Hophni and Phinehas are described as "wicked men" who "did not respect the LORD or the priests' share of the sacrifices from the people" (2:12–13). Their sin is "very great in the sight of the LORD"

(2:17 NRSV). Because of their sin, God declares that the duties of the high priesthood will be taken from Eli's family. Eli will die, his sons will die, and that will be the end of their priestly duties before God.

What about prophets, or the people who speak for God? Surely they are better than the priests! Yet the Old Testament reminds its readers that, while there were some good prophets (and there were some good priests), by and large the overwhelming problem of sin among God's people remained. One of the major problems is with *false* prophets, who say they speak for the true God but do not. Rather, they speak for themselves or lead the people away from their God. False prophets told God's people that God would never judge them and that they would always remain in the land that God had promised to Abraham and that he had given to Israel (see Jer. 23:16–22). God, however, told a different story.

God's King and Exile

By the end of the sixth century BC, it became clear that God was going to send his people into a foreign land under foreign rule as a punishment for their sins. In the Bible, this punishment for sin is called *exile*. Instead of being delivered out of slavery and into the promised land (as in the exodus), God's people are now being delivered into slavery and out of the promised land. Why? Because of sin. The poetry of Lamentations gives one reason (there are many) for exile: "Because of the sins of [Israel's] prophets and the iniquities of her priests" (4:13).

And as we will see, Israel's kings are implicated in sin just as Israel's priests and prophets were. God intended for Israel's kings to be the exemplars for God's people, leading them in the right ways, obeying God's laws, administering true justice, and leading God's people in worship. Unfortunately, the hearts of Israel's kings are wayward also. In fact, the entirety of the book of Kings testifies to sin's pervasive hold on Israel's monarchs. In that book, the reason for exile is precisely because of the sins of one king, King Manasseh (2 Kings 23:26–27).

Just as the leaders of Israel sin, so do the people of Israel. Psalm 106 is an especially poignant testimony to the persistent problem of sin among God's people from the time of the exodus through their entry into the promised land. How does the psalmist describe their sin? He describes it not only as wickedness but also as forgetfulness. Israel forgot God by forgetting his goodness and the goodness of his law.

Even in exile, we see sin recur: God's people are dislocated from God, self, others, and the world. God's people choose sin, and honor turns to shame.

Or as the poet of Lamentations writes late in the exilic age (ca. 587–539 BC), "The crown has fallen from our head. / Woe to us, for we have sinned" (5:16).

During this time and later, God's people begin to look for the one who will take the pain of sin and exile away. The prophecies of Daniel speak about one who will come. This one is called "one like a son of man" (7:13). Another way to translate this is "one like a human being" (so the NRSV). The comparative particle "like" is important. This is one who is "like" a human being and one who is also, then, "unlike" a human being. On the one hand, he comes in human form and rules as God's king, the king of Israel. On the other hand, he rides on clouds. Only *divine* beings do that.

Thus, in Daniel's vision, the son of man comes into the broken, sinful world as a divine and human being. God gives authority and power to this one, and all creation celebrates as a result. Not only that, but this son of man ushers in the reign of God, otherwise known as the kingdom of God. As Daniel describes it:

> He was given dominion
> and glory, and a kingdom;
> so that those of every people,
> nation, and language
> should serve him.
> His dominion is an everlasting dominion
> that will not pass away,
> and his kingdom is one
> that will not be destroyed. (7:14)

This coming of the son of man is vitally important because it testifies to hope beyond Israel's sin, the end of idolatrous and unjust nations, and the coming of the kingdom of God. God's future King will come, but he will be like *and* unlike any king that came before him. When will this happen? It arrives in the coming of Jesus, but we will get to that in a couple of chapters.

After the exile, when God returns his people to the land, the problem of sin remains. During the postexilic age (ca. 538–200 BC), a new genre of prayer begins to appear in earnest: penitential prayer (see Lam. 3:21–42; Dan. 9; Ezra 9; Neh. 9). In those prayers, it is common for God's people to express penitence for their sin. Ezra's prayer is indicative: "My God, I am ashamed and embarrassed to lift my face toward you, my God, because our iniquities are higher than our heads and our guilt is as high as the heavens" (9:6).

The problem of sin persists to the time of Jesus (in the first century AD) and after in the New Testament church (AD 100–300). The premier prophet who preceded Jesus, who was called John the Baptist, preaches the need for repentance and the forgiveness of sins (Luke 3:3). The apostle Paul, who lived just after Jesus and was one of the founders of the Christian church, testifies to the same problem. God's people, indeed all people, are bound up in sin: "All have sinned and fall short of the glory of God" (Rom. 3:23). What is the point? All preached the problem of persistent sin. And as we have seen, all sin is blameworthy.

Conclusion

The history books and newspapers are chock-full of evidence of sin and evil. That is because we as humans are thoroughgoing sinners. We sin by what we do and say; likewise, we sin by what we neglect to do and say. None of us is without sin. Non-Christians often speak about the hypocrisy of the Christian church: that it is full of sin just as much as any other place. This, of course, is sad but true. It is also not surprising. There is no moral high ground in the story of sin. The fall affects us all. Inside the church. Outside the church. It does not matter because, as says the 1777 edition of *The New England Primer*, "in Adam's fall, we sinned all."[10]

What a sad and tragic tale. There is no escape from the story of sin, because we are complicit in it. We have committed high treason against our King. We have rebelled against his rule and tried to make our own kingdoms. But these faulty kingdoms are built on sand. They will fall. This is because kingdoms built on sin are blameworthy. They will incur their guilt, bear their own shame, and undergo God's punishment. Remember what the apostle Paul said? "The wages of sin is death" (Rom. 6:23). Is there any hope in this terrible account? Is there any way to break the fall? In the next chapter we explore the Bible's response to what went wrong by looking at God's work in redemption.

10. John Cotton, *The New England Primer Improved: For the More Easy Attaining the True Reading of English: to which Is Added the Assembly of Divines, and Mr. Cotton's Catechism* (Boston: Edward Draper, 1777), 8.

3

REDEMPTION

Covenant and Kingdom

I am the LORD, and I will bring you out from the forced labor of the Egyptians and rescue you from slavery to them. I will redeem you with an outstretched arm and great acts of judgment. I will take you as my people, and I will be your God.

Exodus 6:6–7

Introduction

In the 1930s, the city of New York built a set of railroad tracks called the High Line that ran out of the meat-packing district to other parts of the city. Architects and engineers designed the tracks so they would rise thirty feet above the streets, far above the hustle and bustle and traffic of the city (hence its name). As you can imagine, the tracks were large, wide, and extensive. In fact, the tracks ran for over a mile from 34th Street to St. John's Park Terminal at Spring Street. Trains supplied the city with meat, agricultural goods, and mail for nearly fifty years. But the tracks, as with many things, became more and more obsolete with the changes in the city. They went into disrepair, and the last trains ran on the line in the 1980s.

What was the city to do with the tracks after they were broken, stained, and without purpose any longer? Some suggested that the city demolish the

High Line. After all, little bits had been destroyed here and there since the 1960s. The city might as well level the whole thing. However, a group in the city had a different idea. They wanted to see the High Line reclaimed.

And that is what happened. Members of the High Line community worked to see the tracks redeemed as something beautiful, as public space. Over the course of a decade, the High Line tracks were created anew into a public park. It is now High Line Park, a 1.5-mile greenway that runs down Manhattan's West Side. It is a serene space that boasts trees and gardens, sitting areas and a walking path. It is an oasis of flora in the midst of a concrete jungle. It is a reclamation project done right.

What Is Redemption?

The High Line project illustrates the logic of redemption. The King went on a reclamation project to set right what went wrong in the world. In light of chapter 2, it would be easy for us to see our world, even humanity, as a failed project wrecked by sin. Sin stained the kingdom of God so that God's rule became twisted and turned to all sorts of perversion. What would God do with his broken world, his broken humanity? He could have demolished the whole sin-riddled project, but he would not allow his hand to be forced by the evil one. Not even the evil one could make bad what God had made good. Instead of abandoning or annihilating his creation, God would reclaim, restore, and renew it. If the seventh day—in which God's kingdom enjoyed his rule and everything was in order—was the goal of creation, God would see to it that the seventh day (his promised "rest") would come.

And that is what we learn as the Bible's narrative unfolds. The King works to see his kingdom redeemed as something beautiful, as testimony to his goodness and kindness. Over the course of thousands of years, God implements his redemptive plan to "reconcile everything to himself" (Col. 1:15–20). Each stage in the redemption plan gave further insight into what he was ultimately going to do to make all things new. As we will learn in the next chapter, his ultimate goal in redemption is to establish a "new heavens and a new earth," or to renew his originally created heavens and earth. In this renewed heavens and earth, Jesus Christ rules on the throne and all of creation worships him (Isa. 65:17; Rev. 21:1, 5). In the present chapter, however, we will explore the initial stages of this redemptive project.

In the Scriptures, *redemption* is a way of talking about God restoring what is broken in his kingdom. Understood properly, it is a way of talking about how God sets things right in his world. "Setting things right" is important because those who are "not right" are people like us—both the writers of this book and the readers. Christian theology affirms that redemption is accomplished in the work of Jesus Christ, which is recorded in the New Testament. Particularly through Jesus's sacrifice on the cross, broken and sinful humans find forgiveness of sin and reconnection with our Maker in his world (see Eph. 1:7–14). Jesus, as we will see, is God's answer to the fall because he redeems a lost and broken humanity back to himself.

Long before the New Testament was written, Old Testament authors wrote extensively about God's great redemption. The term *redeem* occurs in a variety of contexts and describes God doing something great to save and deliver his people.[1] In fact, as Ronald Youngblood argues, the concept of redemption "helpfully sums up the ultimate goal of the biblical narrative from Genesis to Malachi" and "deserves a prominent place among the subjects that lie closest to the heart of the Old Testament."[2]

The Old Testament connects redemption to God delivering his people from Egypt and bringing them into the promised land. In Exodus, God tells Moses to instruct the Israelites on his divine identity and activity:

I am the LORD, and I will bring you out from the forced labor of the Egyptians and rescue you from slavery to them. I will *redeem* you with an outstretched arm and great acts of judgment. I will take you as my people, and I will be your God. You will know that I am the LORD your God, who brought you out from the forced labor of the Egyptians. I will bring you to the land that I swore to give to Abraham, Isaac, and Jacob, and I will give it to you as a possession. I am the LORD. (Exod. 6:6–8)

In these verses, redemption is richly textured: God's redemption provides freedom from slavery, deliverance from oppression, relationship with God, knowledge of God, release from burdens, and a place to call home. In fact, Israel celebrates God's work of deliverance in a beautiful hymn, the end of which states:

You will bring them in and plant them
on the mountain of your possession;

1. What once was distressed and oppressed is now delivered. What once was indebted is now released from debt by means of payment. What once was lost is found. What once was broken is fixed. What once was stained is pure again. What once was cursed is now blessed. What once was bound in sin is now covered and released in the mercy and forgiveness of God. Classic works that deal with the concept of redemption are H. Ringgren, "גאל, ga'al," in *TWOT* 2, ed. G. J. Botterweck and H. Ringgren (Grand Rapids: Eerdmans, 1977), 350–55; Walther Zimmerli, *Old Testament Theology in Outline* (Edinburgh: T&T Clark, 1978), 217–18.

2. Ronald Youngblood, *The Heart of the Old Testament: A Survey of Key Theological Themes*, 2nd ed. (Grand Rapids: Baker, 1998), 102.

> Lᴏʀᴅ, you have prepared the place
> for your dwelling;
> Lᴏʀᴅ, your hands have established the sanctuary.
> The Lord will reign forever and ever! (Exod. 15:17–18)

Redemption is God's way to bring God's people to God's land under God's rule. Redemption here is closely related to the restoration of God's kingdom.

Similarly, the book of Isaiah reveals the richness and profundity of God's redemption. God is called the Redeemer.[3] In these texts, God does something for his *people*, to be sure, but God does something for the land and sky as well: the sky drops rain in its season and makes the land productive, restoring God's creation design (Isa. 45:8–13). To know God is to know his redemption. Redemption, then, is a really great thing and something only God can do. Israel cannot earn its redemption, and no one (other than God) guarantees it. Redemption is the sure work of God, and God alone.

In other texts, redemption conceptualizes the act of wiping debt from a record sheet.[4] We see this, for instance, in Psalm 130. In the first part of the psalm, the petitioner acknowledges the blameworthiness of sin, that it creates a kind of debt that cannot but condemn the sinner: "If you kept a record of iniquities, O Lᴏʀᴅ, who could stand?" (v. 3, authors' translation).[5] The point is that no one could stand before God if God kept a record of sins. The psalmist, however, affirms that God is *not* like that. He keeps no record of wrongs. Rather, God forgives (v. 4), and the psalmist connects that idea with the concept of redemption. God's redemption wipes sin off Israel's record sheet: "He will redeem Israel from all its iniquities" (v. 8, authors' translation). God's redemption wipes away the blame of sin and makes it possible to regain communion with him.

God himself says something similar in the restoration prophecy given in the book of Isaiah. Note God's statement to sinful Israel there:

> I have swept away your transgressions like a cloud,
> and your sins like mist.

---

3. See Isa. 41:14; 43:14; 44:6, 24; 47:4; 48:17; 49:7, 26; 54:5, 8; 59:20; 60:16; 63:16.

4. This occurs, for instance, in Old Testament legal material in which a relative can "redeem" land or possessions that have been lost to forfeiture. Redemption of this lost material means paying something to clear the debt and restore the forfeited property back to its rightful owner (see, e.g., Lev. 25:25–28).

5. The name for God in the Hebrew here is "Yah," which we have rendered as "the Lᴏʀᴅ." The verb in verse 3, which we have rendered "kept a record," is the Hebrew root *shamar* and seems to conceptualize God as a kind of scribe who is marking down the iniquities in a kind of ledger. See the explanation in Mitchell Dahood, *Psalms III: 101–150*, AYBC (Garden City, NY: Doubleday, 1970), 235.

Return to me,
for I have redeemed you.
Rejoice, heavens, for the LORD has acted;
shout, depths of the earth.
Break out into singing, mountains,
forest, and every tree in it.
For the LORD has redeemed Jacob,
and glorifies himself through Israel. (44:22–23)

In these verses, God's mighty work of redemption means wiping transgression and sin away, or canceling sin's debt. And yet, verse 23 provides another angle to God's redemption. His work for *his people* drives *all of creation* to shout and sing. Why? Because of the close relationship between humanity and the rest of creation, as we saw in chapter 1 on creation.

Significantly, the Bible "orders" or "unfolds" redemption in a very particular manner. Overall, the story of redemption in the Old Testament is one of promise (with bits of fulfillment along the way), while in the New Testament, it is one of fulfillment (with bits of promise along the way). As Paul says in Romans 8:19, the created world *awaits* future freedom that it has not yet experienced in full. But in the Old Testament, the promise of future redemption is clear.

Redemption is key because it describes how human beings might be brought back into proper relationship with the King so that we can once again live for the King. Without redemption, humanity is adrift, aimless, lost, broken, and listless. But redemption shows us that we can be made new and set right. How?

In the New Testament, redemption finds a name: Jesus the Messiah. He is the center of the redemption story. He is the firstborn over all creation. He is the second Adam. He is the fulfillment of the promises that God made to Abraham. He is the perfect, faithful Israelite. He is the good King whom Israel hoped for. He is the great Redeemer of all things and the King over God's kingdom. He is the atoning sacrifice that satisfies the payment for sin. He is all of this and more as the center of Scripture. But to understand redemption fully, we need to turn back to the beginning and unpack the relationship between redemption and covenant.

Redemption and Covenant

Redemption is revealed through the unfolding of God's covenants with his people. But this begs a question: What is a covenant? When we think of a covenant today, perhaps we consider it to be like a contract. Contracts are arrangements between two parties in which goods and services are agreed on and supplied, with certain stipulations (e.g., pay money and receive a certain service). Take a mobile telephone contract as an example. If you want to buy a mobile telephone, then you journey to your local mobile telephone store, set up a contract, and walk out with your new phone. You had no relationship with that business prior to the contract, and if you forfeit the contract, then the services to your mobile phone are cut off. The relationship, as defined by the contract, is terminated.

God's covenants, however, are not contracts.[6] Covenants that are made by God are different because (1) God's covenants are not impersonal like a business contract but personal and even familial in that God's covenants incorporate human beings into his family; (2) God's covenants are guaranteed by God himself—that is, God initiates his covenants and guarantees their efficacy; and (3) God's covenants are rooted in his creative activity, as we will see. So the concept of covenant is quite significant, being present at creation (as we will explain below) and providing structure for the story of redemption.

The Bible's (major) covenants, listed in figure 3.1, structure the story of God's redemption in Scripture.

Figure 3.1
Progression of Divine Covenants

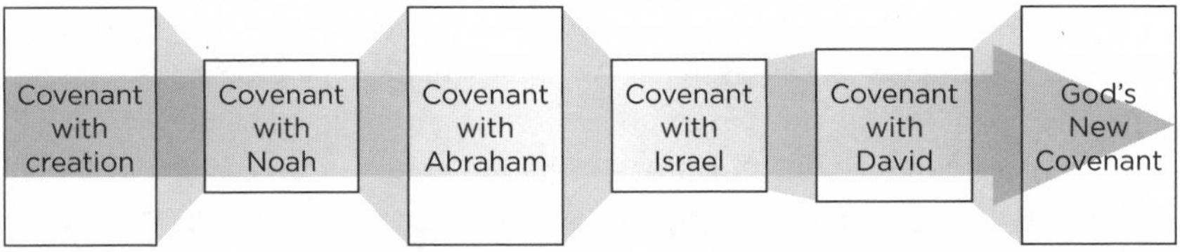

Covenant with creation	Covenant with Noah	Covenant with Abraham	Covenant with Israel	Covenant with David	God's New Covenant

Even though we did not emphasize the concept of covenant in chapter 1's treatment of God's creative activity, we will make clear in this chapter that God "covenanted" creation into existence. As William Dumbrell has argued convincingly, all the Bible's later covenants depend on the creation covenant

6. For human covenants, see Paul Kalluveettil, *Declaration and Covenant: A Comprehensive Review of Covenant Formulae from the Old Testament and the Ancient Near East*, AnBib 88 (Rome: Biblical Institute Press, 1982). A recent exploration of covenant appears in the comprehensive work of Scott Hahn, *Kinship by Covenant: A Canonical Approach to the Fulfillment of God's Saving Promises*, AYBRL (New Haven: Yale University Press, 2009). For classic exposition of the covenants mentioned in fig. 3.1 see William J. Dumbrell, *Covenant and Creation: An Old Testament Covenant Theology*, rev. ed. (Milton Keynes, UK: Paternoster, 2013).

and share with it the expectation that God would renew the heavens and earth.[7] Creation sets the framework for God's redemption, which climaxes in the New Covenant.

The story of these many covenants is really the story of one unfolding covenant. To summarize this progression:

- In the covenant with *creation*, God provides the foundation on which all the other covenants will grow. This is unsurprising and logical. All the other covenants would be nonsensical if there were no *world* in which they could exist.

- In the covenant with *Noah*, God specifies how he will relate to his creation in the face of continued and persistent sin.

- In the covenant with *Abraham*, God identifies the family through which the whole world will be blessed, particularly through the theme of election and the gifts of land, seed, and name.

- In the covenant with *Israel*, God discloses his salvation and his desire for a nation to be a holy priesthood to the world. His instruction is given a nationalistic flavor as God's people live in God's land under God's rule.

- In the covenant with *David*, God reveals the anointed King as the leader of his holy nation, whose rule will be forever in Zion. Although Israel is God's firstborn son (Exod. 4:22; Hosea 11:1), the Davidic covenant highlights the messianic, Davidic king as the pinnacle of Israel's sonship: the King is the exemplar and the leader of God's people. He is thus the individual Son of God, whose reign will emulate the reign of his Father, God himself. God's king will reign under God over God's people in God's land.

- In the *New Covenant*, God reveals how his redeemed people will worship him faithfully from forgiven hearts. God also reveals how this forgiven

7. Dumbrell, *Covenant and Creation*, 8. Peter Gentry and Stephen Wellum agree with Dumbrell on a covenant at creation. Their words concerning Jer. 31:35–37 provide a good example of their understanding of a covenant at creation. They state that Jer. 31:35–37 "refers to creation and indicates that God's commitment to Israel is as certain as his commitment to creation. The reason for this is that Israel's doctrine of *salvation* is based on her doctrine of *creation*" (Peter J. Gentry and Stephen J. Wellum, *Kingdom through Covenant: A Biblical-Theological Understanding of the Covenants*, 2nd ed. [Wheaton: Crossway, 2018], 258). Not all biblical scholars agree about the existence of a creation covenant. For example, see John H. Stek, "'Covenant' Overload in Reformed Theology," *CTJ* 29 (1994): 12–41. For a thorough critique of Stek, see Craig G. Bartholomew, "Covenant and Creation: Covenant Overload or Covenantal Deconstruction," *CTJ* 30 (1995): 11–33.

people (now Israel and the nations) will follow God's instruction faithfully under the rule of the messianic King.[8]

Significant points in God's covenant story of redemption emerge in the creation, Abrahamic, Davidic, and New covenants. However, even the Noachian and Israelite covenants have distinct and important parts to play as well: both of them negotiate explicitly the reality of human sinfulness and provide ways for God to manage sin among his people.

Certain characteristics are shared by all the covenants. These characteristics speak volumes about God's character and the nature of the salvation he offers to humanity.

The most significant characteristic, and the one on which all the others depend, is that God's covenants are based on his grace and provision. God takes the initiative in each of the covenants as a way of blessing humanity. Just as he blessed humanity at creation, he now extends his blessing even in the aftermath of the fall. God gives blessing at creation, and God guarantees that the blessing of humanity continues (even in the face of human sin). Consider the fact that God speaks about blessing in the narratives about Noah (e.g., Gen. 9:1), Abraham (e.g., 12:2–3), Abraham's family (e.g., 25:11), King David and his royal house (e.g., 2 Sam. 7:28–29), and the promise of the New Covenant (e.g., Ezek. 37:26). In each instance, God is revealing his grace as something that we could never earn but instead must receive with gratitude and faith.

In addition to extending God's grace, the covenants call God's people to obedience. Just as God graciously offered for human beings to be reconciled into his family, so he lays down some "rules of the house" for their good and the good of the family. Why would God's people follow God's commands? Because they love him. He has been good in the past, and his love fuels their obedience to him. The covenants give the context in which to live for the King.

Significantly, the covenants make certain promises contingent on obedience or disobedience to God's commands. Just as God promised Adam and Eve a long and good life if they followed his commands and death if they did not, so the Bible's later covenants offer promises contingent, respectively, on obedience or disobedience. These promises remind God's people of the certainty of God's word and show them the nature of faith: believing in the promises of God and living in accord with his standards.

8. Bernhard Anderson offers different nuances of these covenants on the basis of divine names and divine promises. He focuses on three periods of covenant: creation to the end of primeval history, Abraham to Moses, and the Mosaic period. See Bernhard W. Anderson, *Contours of Old Testament Theology* (Minneapolis: Fortress, 1999), 81–86.

Another defining characteristic is that the covenants reveal God's loving determination to bring a broken and wayward people back into his family. He does not simply wait for his family to be reconciled to him; he goes to the distant country to find his wandering family and bring them home. Scott Hahn says that to "get to the heart of Scripture, think *covenant* not contract, *father* not judge, *family room* not courtroom; God's laws and judgments are meant to be interpreted as signs of his fatherly love, wisdom and authority."[9]

Two Caveats

In the remainder of this chapter, we will explore the unfolding of these covenants, progressively, through the Scriptures from creation to new creation. There are a couple of dangers in doing this. The first danger is to think that, by organizing the redemption story on the foundation of covenants and understanding it in those terms, we now have mastered the biblical narrative. To think in that manner would be naive and reductionist. While the covenants are vital to the biblical narrative and help orient us to God's redemptive work, we should not presume to replace Scripture with the covenant story. Instead, the covenants should serve as helpful heuristic devices that lead us more deeply into the full story of redemption, recorded in the full testimony of Scripture.

The second danger is to explore the covenants seeking only to understand what they can do for us. To do so would be a violation of God's purposes in giving the covenants. The story of redemption is about God and humanity, and *God*, rather than *us*, gets the emphasis. The main reason we seek to understand the redemption story through God's covenants is so that we can know and love God himself. In fact, the redemption story testifies not only that we can know and love God but also, more importantly, that God has already known and loved us. Our response should be the response of those who receive the body and blood of Jesus in Eucharist celebration: "Thanks be to God!"

In the Beginning

As we learned in chapter 1, the creation account reveals God as the Creator-King, all of creation as his kingdom, and humans as his vice-regents who are to lovingly practice dominion over creation. What we did not mention

9. Scott Hahn, *A Father Who Keeps His Promises: God's Covenant Love in Scripture* (Cincinnati: Servant Books, 1998), 27, italics original.

in chapter 1 is the Genesis account's suggestion that the Creator-King "covenanted" the world into existence and that this covenantal relationship remains today. Thus the Bible's opening narrative provides our first peek at the dual thread of covenant/kingdom that weaves through the remainder of the biblical narrative.

For good reason, the Genesis account is suggestive regarding covenant and kingdom. Indeed, the pervasiveness of the Bible's covenant/kingdom teaching causes us to compare it to the main entrance of a cathedral. If Christian theology could be compared to a grand cathedral, we could say that covenant/kingdom forms a double-door entrance that opens up into a captivating view of the inside of the cathedral. God the Creator is King over his created kingdom. As King, he covenants with his creation. Taken together, covenant and kingdom reveal God's character: the notion of kingdom reveals his power and authority as Lord, while the notion of covenant reveals his faithfulness and relationality as Father.

But where, you ask, is the word *covenant* found in the Genesis creation account? The answer is nowhere. Even though the Hebrew word for covenant, *berit*, does not appear in Genesis 1–2, the concept is nonetheless present in the text.[10] Significant features of ancient Near Eastern covenants appear in the text. For instance, the Genesis account contains a preamble ("In the beginning God") that introduces the King in his relationship to the subjects of the covenant. The King gives promises and obligations, which define the covenantal community, as well as blessings and curses. Even if the term *berith* is not present in the text, the concepts are evident. As Walter Eichrodt recognized in his now classic Old Testament theology: "The crucial point is not—as an all too naive criticism sometimes seems to think—the occurrence or absence of the Hebrew word *berith* [covenant]," since that term "is only the code-word for something more far-reaching than the word itself."[11]

Other biblical texts reinforce the point about creation's covenantal nature. For instance, Jeremiah says that God made a covenant with the day and the night, with heaven and earth, and with Jacob and David (33:20–21, 25–26).[12] Or consider Genesis 6:18. There God says he will "establish" his covenant with Noah. The Hebrew word for "establish" makes it sound, at least to English

10. For further discussion on the covenant features in Gen. 1–2, see the work of Meredith Kline, *Kingdom Prologue: Genesis Foundations for a Covenantal Worldview* (Eugene, OR: Wipf & Stock, 2006), 14–61.

11. Walther Eichrodt, *Theology of the Old Testament*, Volume 1, Old Testament Library (Philadelphia: Westminster Press, 1960), 17–18.

12. For an exposition and defense of the covenantal view of creation, see Gentry and Wellum, *Kingdom through Covenant*. Also see Dumbrell, *Covenant and Creation*.

speakers' ears, like God is going to start something *new*, like God is going to inaugurate a wholly new covenant with Noah after the flood. However, as Dumbrell has argued, the better translation is, "I will *maintain* my covenant with you" (Gen. 6:18).[13] The idea here is not that God will create a brand-new covenant with Noah but rather that God will continue a pre-existing covenant through Noah and his family.

The covenantal nature of God's creative activity explains the regularity of the world. "The entire created order," writes Gordon Spykman, "is anchored securely in God's mediating covenantal Word, by which he called the world into existence, by which he also continually calls it (back) to order. This lends a solid constancy, even a certain predictability, to the affairs of daily experience."[14]

It also sets the stage, as we have mentioned, for the remainder of the biblical narrative. Genesis 1–2 is God's way of kicking off the best story ever told. He begins by covenanting the creation into existence. This creation serves as a stage on which the rest of the Bible's dramatic narrative is to take place. Thomas Oden writes, "The drama is all about a relationship. It is the thorny, conflicted, seductive, unpredictable unfolding epic of a covenant relationship between Yahweh and Adam, Yahweh and Abraham, Yahweh and Israel, Yahweh and humanity. The real story concerning creation is about the creature/Creator relationship, not about creatures as such as if creation were to be considered a detached occurrence or autonomous event."[15]

The covenant is one sided in its origin but two sided in its continuation. It is initiated by our gracious God, but it carries with it responsibilities for God's people. "God came out to us . . . in his covenant Word," Spykman writes, "to meet us where we are and to draw us into a bond of fellowship with himself. He made the first move, and continues to do so. . . . Along the way, however, once the covenant is inaugurated, . . . we as human beings are now called irresistibly to play our decisive roles."[16] God initiated the covenant by himself, but we are called into redemptive history in order to play a significant role alongside God and under his reign.

Significantly, covenantal history reveals God's faithfulness. Despite the fact that God's imagers repeatedly break covenant, God himself never does. God

13. Dumbrell, *Covenant and Creation*, 1–20; see his earlier and more extensive argument on v. 18 in William J. Dumbrell, *Covenant and Creation: A Theology of the Old Testament Covenants*, BTCL (Carlisle, UK: Paternoster, 1984), 1–33.

14. Gordon Spykman, *Reformational Theology: A New Paradigm for Doing Dogmatics* (Grand Rapids: Eerdmans, 1992), 259.

15. Thomas C. Oden, *Classic Christianity: A Systematic Theology* (New York: HarperOne, 2009), 129. Oden cites Irenaeus, *Against Heresies* 2.10.1–4, ANF 1:369–70.

16. Spykman, *Reformational Theology*, 264.

continually steps in to renew the covenant in the aftermath of human sin and rebellion. In fact, one way to view all of humanity is through the lens of covenant keeping and covenant breaking. Every human being is either a covenant keeper or a covenant breaker. Because of the fall, all of us suffer under the curse of the broken covenant. However, Christ Jesus kept the covenant on our behalf. Through his atonement, we are now recognized as covenant keepers in fellowship with God. Our covenant keeping is "already" and "not yet." We are already covenant keepers (in principle) and not yet covenant keepers (in perfection).

Covenant keeping, as the Genesis account suggests and the biblical narrative makes clear, is a robust and holistic way of life that involves bringing everything in our lives under submission to God's lordship. The creation account signifies this reality when it reveals God's desire for humans to practice dominion, to be fruitful and multiply, and to till the soil. Old Testament law shows how godly living extends beyond our inner spirituality and into the social and cultural dimensions of life. Old Testament wisdom and prophecy likewise portray covenant keeping as holistic. Finally, the New Testament confirms its holistic nature but enhances our understanding of it by showing how the gospel fuels such covenant keeping. God's lordship is as wide as creation, and therefore our covenant keeping (and by implication, all our theological, social, and cultural doings) is as wide as creation.

Noah and His Family

Immediately after Genesis's account of the fall, we learn that God provides another son to Eve, whose name is Seth (Gen. 4:25). The descendants of Seth begin to call on God's name and worship him (4:26). God preserves Adam and Eve's family as they populate the world, and God's divine preservation once again reaffirms his commitment to his creation.

One of Seth's descendants, called Lamech, has a son, whom he calls Noah. We learned about Noah in the last chapter, but it is significant that Lamech gives his son the name Noah, which means "rest." Lamech says, "This one will bring us relief from the agonizing labor of our hands, caused by the ground the Lord has cursed" (5:29). Lamech's words echo the goal of creation: rest on the seventh day. Lamech's statement also draws us back to the curse in Genesis 3 and hints to us that the curse will not last forever. God's promised rest will come, and Lamech thinks that the curse will be reversed through Noah.

But as the biblical narrative unfolds, we learn that the story of Noah points us forward to *another* child who will come—one who will defeat sin, the curse, and death and will draw all things together in heaven and earth. Ephesians 1:7–10 says, "In him [Jesus] we have redemption through his blood, the forgiveness of our trespasses, according to the riches of his grace that he richly poured out on us with all wisdom and understanding. He made known to us the mystery of his will, according to his good pleasure that he purposed in Christ as a plan for the right time—to bring everything together in Christ, both things in heaven and things on earth in him."

But Noah is significant and not just as a signpost for the future. Noah's narrative gives us a glimpse of the graciousness of God. The entire narrative of Genesis 6–9 is a unit whose center is Genesis 8:1: "God remembered Noah, as well as all the wildlife and all the livestock that were with him in the ark." The fact that God remembered the animals is important because it provides a picture of God's commitment to his creation. Redemption is God's act of setting right what went wrong, and the flood narrative reminds readers that God enacts judgment so that creation might be preserved anew. The narrative of Noah reveals a God who loves the created world but purifies it of sin. God's promised rest means nothing less than the redemption of the *entire* world (animals, land, plants, and people). Redemption, as we have discovered, comes by way of God's purification. The flood becomes God's way of dealing with humanity's sin.

God remembering Noah and his family is also important because through him God's blessing flows. Noah becomes a kind of second Adam after the flood. The promised seed of the woman will now come through the line of Noah. The same originating blessing that God gave to humanity in Genesis 1 is how God blesses Noah: to be fruitful and multiply, to fill the earth, to tend and till it. We see this clearly in Genesis 9:1: "God blessed Noah and his sons and said to them, 'Be fruitful and multiply and fill the earth.'" We also see that Noah obeys the original command that God gave to Adam in the garden of Eden to tend and till the earth. After coming out of the ark, Noah does a good thing and tends and tills the earth by cultivating a vineyard (Gen. 9:20). Humanity's responsibilities at creation are not abrogated by the fall or by the flood.

Abraham and His Family

Following the narrative of Noah, Genesis 6–9 reveals that the seed of the woman will flow through the line of Noah to Noah's son Shem. Genesis 10–12 reveal that Shem's descendant is Abram (which means "exalted father"), whose name God changes to Abraham (which means "father of many nations") in Genesis 17:5. God establishes his covenant with Abraham in Genesis 12–22. It is probably best to see this narrative as revealing, progressively, the full context of the Abrahamic covenant. This is because Genesis 12:1–7 provides God's promises, Genesis 15 enacts a covenant ceremony, Genesis 17 reveals the covenant stipulations, and Genesis 22 serves to "ratify" the covenant through God's testing of Abraham (see esp. Gen. 22:17–18). Tearing each of these texts from the story of Abraham is difficult, however, as they work together and build on one another in Abraham's ongoing discovery of God and developing relationship with him. As we saw in the last chapter, in Genesis, God promises Abraham four things:[17]

> a land (a home to call his own)
> a great nation (children and family)
> a great name (honor among others)
> God as his shield and reward (divine relationship and protection)

Abraham's *name* will be great because Abraham's *seed* will bless the nations, and Abraham will have a *land* to call home. All those who bless Abraham and his descendants will be blessed, and all those who curse them will be cursed. God then affirms that "all the peoples on earth will be blessed through you" (Gen. 12:3). The phrase is significant because it testifies that Abraham and his family will be the line through which *all* will experience the blessing God promised at creation and reaffirmed in Noah. To use Richard Bauckham's pregnant language, the "particular" (Abraham) is God's means of blessing the "universal" (the world).[18] God's kingdom will come through the line of Abraham. Those who live in Abraham's family will live *for the King* and draw the rest of humanity to do the same.

Abraham has to live in a certain way for those blessings to continue to his children. The command for Abraham and his descendants to practice circumcision is not an option but an imperative. Incidentally, if Abraham or his children would have rejected the command, then they would have been cut off from God's redemption plan (Gen. 17:14). What does circumcision do? It sets Abraham and his family off on mission: it reminds them that they are not just Abraham's family but God's representatives on earth through whom God will bring about his blessing of the world. It reminds them that they are to live for the King. And, based on the New Testament, we know (even if they did not) that the seed of Abraham that will bring blessing to the world

17. Specifically, see Gen. 12:1–3; 15:1–21; 17:1–22; 22:15–18.
18. Richard Bauckham, *The Bible and Mission* (Grand Rapids: Eerdmans, 2003), 27–36.

is none other than Jesus. He is Abraham's seed, in the Davidic line, and the only begotten of God the Father.

It is a good thing that human holiness never qualified anyone for God's redemption. If that were the case, each of us, including the people who seem exemplary in the Bible, would be in dire straits. As we saw in the last chapter, Abraham was a scoundrel, and his children were no better. Still, God promised blessing through the line of Abraham. Despite the frailty of Abraham and his family, God persevered with his plan. The covenant with Abraham, including its language, reappears in God's dealings with Abraham's children (Gen. 26:2–5, 24; 28:13–15; 35:11–13; 48:3–6, 15–20). Genesis carries forward the point, then, that God continues his covenant, attendant with promises and stipulations, through Abraham's family. They will be a community for the King.

The Community for the King

The books of Exodus, Leviticus, Numbers, and Deuteronomy help us understand that God's redemptive work continues through his covenant with Abraham's descendants, the people of Israel. Israel is Abraham's family, which means that the covenant with Abraham governs God's covenant with Israel. The creation accounts (Gen. 1–2) and the story of Israel (Gen. 12–Deut. 34) come together in the books from Genesis to Deuteronomy (often called the Pentateuch because there are five books in this collection). These texts show that God makes Israel thrive and multiply wherever it is: in Egypt (Exod. 1:7, 12, 20), in the wilderness (Deut. 1:10), or in the promised land (Lev. 26:9). Israel's prolific multiplication echoes and fulfills God's command to humanity at creation: "Be fruitful, multiply" (Gen. 1:28).[19] God's gift of multiplication for Israel is such that its number might be compared to the number of the "stars of the sky" (Exod. 32:13; Deut. 1:10; 10:22), a phrase that resonates with God's promise to the patriarchs in Genesis 15:5; 22:17; and 26:4. Note how this phrase draws the Pentateuchal narrative together, from the primeval history to the patriarchal stories to the story of Israel.

The book of Exodus provides the first telling of God's covenant with Israel while God's people are at Sinai, and the book of Deuteronomy records the second telling of the (same) covenant with Israel on the plains of Moab. For the geographical locations, see figure 3.2. Moses gives his instructions to Israel (recorded in Deuteronomy) just north of the Dead Sea, on the eastern side of the Jordan River.

19. The language that describes Israel's fertility is quite precise: *Yahweh* has multiplied Israel. See Deut. 1:10; 7:13.

Figure 3.2

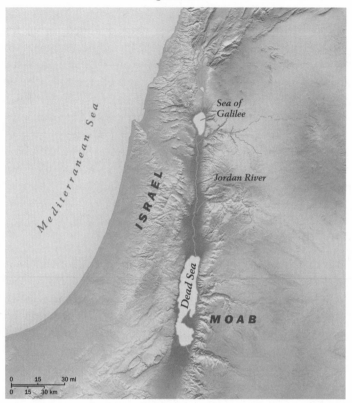

The promised land is significant theologically and helps tie God's redemptive story to the language of "blessing" and "multiplication," which we explored above. The promised land is God's Edenic paradise for Abraham's family to enjoy. God's land provides rich foodstuffs for the Israelites' livelihood (Num. 24:5–9), causing us to remember the Bible's description of the garden of Eden. Similarly, Deuteronomy describes the promised land as a place of divine provision and abundance, which should cause Israel to worship: "When you eat and are full, you will bless the LORD your God for the good land he has given you" (Deut. 8:10). Canaan is the place where Eden will be modeled once again in God's world.

In the books of Numbers, Deuteronomy, and Joshua, several significant points are made. First and foremost, God is gracious even in the face of Israel's continual sin. Even though the first generation, whom God had delivered from Egypt, died in the wilderness over a forty-year period, God paved the way for the second generation (the Joshua and Caleb generation) to prosper in the land that God would give them. The book of Deuteronomy testifies to the anticipation of the moment: they are on the cusp of receiving the land of promise! Their "Eden" is within their reach because God is giving it to them. From there, God's people will serve God for his glory.

Israel is even "baptized" into service, as the book of Joshua indicates. Just as the first generation of Israelites experienced God's deliverance through the Red Sea, so the second generation experiences it through the waters of the Jordan River. Just like at the sea, God goes before the people, and the waters part so that God's people can cross the Jordan on dry land. They are, in a sense, baptized into their vocation in the promised land. This baptism shows up again in the life of Jesus, but for now, it is important simply to understand that God brings them into the promised land and baptizes them for service. What will their service look like? How will they live? To answer those questions, we turn to God's law for God's people in the Israelite covenant.

The Law and Covenant of the King

The life that God's people experience in the land is organized around a covenant with Israel that extends from the Abrahamic covenant. Even though this covenant is often called the Mosaic covenant, we prefer to call it the covenant with Israel or the Sinai covenant simply because Moses did not establish the covenant, nor was it with Moses exclusively. Rather, God established the covenant with Israel at Sinai as an extension of God's covenant with Abraham. God's divine favor and blessing on Israel derive neither from its power (Deut. 7:7) nor from its righteousness (9:4–5) but rather from God's faithful love to the patriarchs and matriarchs and his promise to them (7:6–8). The people are called on to live well before the Lord in the land that God has granted them. How were they to live well? By obeying his commands.[20]

The covenant with Israel is recorded in the book of Exodus but continues all the way through Leviticus to Numbers 10. God delivered the Israelites from Egypt in order for them to be a blessing to the whole world or, as Isaiah would later say, "a light for the nations" (Isa. 49:6).

So, the question for Israel becomes, "In light of God's call to us as a people, how then shall we live?" The Sinai covenant answers that question by giving God's people the instruction they need to live well in the land. In Exodus, Leviticus, and Numbers, God's law is divided into sections:

---

20. See Heath A. Thomas, "Law and Life in Deuteronomy," in *Interpreting Deuteronomy: Issues and Approaches*, ed. David G. Firth and Philip S. Johnston (Nottingham, UK: Apollos, 2012), 177–93, esp. 178–88.

1. The prologue to the law (Exod. 19:3–6)
2. The Decalogue (Ten Commandments; 20:1–17)
3. The other laws (21:1–23:33)
4. Worship laws regarding the tabernacle (25:1–31:18)
5. Laws concerning priests and sacrifice, and ritual practices (Lev.; Num.)
6. What will happen to the people of Israel if they disobey God's instruction (Lev. 26)

In Deuteronomy, God's law is reiterated and somewhat reconfigured:

1. The prologue to the law (Deut. 1:1–5:5)
2. The Decalogue (Ten Commandments; 5:6–21)
3. The other laws (12–26)
4. Blessings for obedience and curses for disobedience (28–29)
5. What will happen to Israel if they disobey God's instruction (30–32)

God gives the first iteration of his law (recorded in Exodus) to the first generation of Israelites, whom God delivered from Egypt and who wandered in the wilderness and ultimately died there. He gives the second iteration of his law (Deuteronomy) to the second generation of Israelites, those who did not die in the wilderness. The two sets of law are not identical, but they are related to each other and build on each other, giving a larger framework within which to answer the question, How shall Israel live well before God in the land?

Exodus 19:3–6 is important in this regard because it helps to clarify Israel's identity and vocation in the land as the people serve God. In this passage, God identifies the Israelites as the "house of Jacob," which is the family name of Abraham's grandson. In so doing, the "my covenant" in verse 5 reminds us of the covenant with Abraham but also applies to the house of Jacob standing at the mountain. As Fretheim puts it, *The covenant at Sinai is a specific covenant within the context of the Abrahamic covenant.*[21] The purpose of the Israelite covenant, then, is to continue God's purposes with Abraham's family but to contextualize his plan with Israel as the people live in the land as a nation. It provides the people of God a way to answer the question, How shall we live for the King?

21. Terence Fretheim, *Exodus*, Interpretation (Louisville: Westminster John Knox, 1991), 209, italics original.

Like God's covenant with Abraham, his covenant with Israel is imbued with his grace. God's covenant faithfulness does not depend on Israel's obedience but on God's grace. That is good news for Israel, who, as we will see, continuously sinned against God.

In the Sinai covenant, God clarifies the nature of Israel's relationship with him in the land: "And now, if you indeed hearken unto my voice and keep my covenant, you will be for me a treasured possession from all the peoples; for all of the earth is mine. And you, you will be for me a kingdom of priests and a holy nation" (Exod. 19:5–6, authors' translation). The point is that God desires obedience so that God's people will enjoy a special relationship with him as a priestly kingdom in God's land amid all the other nations. This means two things:

1. Israel will enjoy a special status as a treasured possession.
2. Israel's special status is a blessing, for the purpose of being a blessing to the other nations!

Or, as Chris Wright says, these verses indicate that Israel's "*status* is to be a special treasured possession. Their *role* is to be a priestly and holy community in the midst of the nations."[22] Israel will be the vehicle through whom all the earth will be blessed—that is, through God's work with Israel all the earth will know who Yahweh is. At Sinai, when God calls Israel to be a special possession and a holy, priestly kingdom, he is calling them "to a mission that encompasses God's purposes for the entire world. *Israel is commissioned to be God's people on behalf of the earth which is God's.*"[23] If Israel does *not* live in obedience to God's voice, then they forsake their opportunity to make the King known to the gentile nations, to "love their neighbors," and will experience God's discipline for their disobedience (through covenant curse).

Now, as one can imagine, life in the land for an entire nation is different from life in the land for a nomadic family group like Abraham's. First, there are a lot more people. Second, twelve different families (tribes) descended from the twelve children of Jacob (see Gen. 49). Third, the people need to know how and where to worship their King and what that looks like in practice. They need to know what laws need to be set in place so that God's people can live well in the land that the King has given them. Also, what about the

22. Christopher J. H. Wright, *The Mission of God: Unlocking the Bible's Grand Narrative* (Downers Grove, IL: InterVarsity, 2006), 256, italics original.
23. Fretheim, *Exodus*, 212, italics original. For an especially helpful exploration of this theme, see Michael W. Goheen, *A Light to the Nations: The Missional Church and the Biblical Story* (Grand Rapids: Baker Academic, 2011).

people who already live in the land or outsiders who immigrate into the land because of war or famine? How should the Israelites live with them? The law answers these questions, providing direction for God's people to live in God's land under God's rule.

Christians often explain Old Testament law by dividing it into three categories: *moral* law (which is eternal and binding today, such as the Ten Commandments), *civil* law (which has to do with Israel's national life and is not binding for Christians today), and *ceremonial* law (which has to do with Israel's worship and thereby is not binding for Christians today). This threefold division is helpful, in so far as it notes that *something* in the law persists for Christians today, which is typically understood to be the moral law. It is also helpful in revealing to us the broad relevance of God's revelation for every sector of society and sphere of culture and in preparing us for the future work of Jesus Christ, who fulfills the law in his own person.

But readers should be careful not to replace the rich biblical teaching with a reductionist belief, such as that the moral law is the only thing we need to follow to live well for the King. We must understand that the Bible's exposition of the law is rich and multifaceted, covering family laws, property laws, laws regulating borders, laws regulating farming, laws regulating and organizing cities, laws that give prescription for religious (i.e., cultic) life, laws for kings and priests and prophets and judges, laws regarding sexual norms and marriage, laws regarding immigration, and more besides. Each of these laws provides an indicator as to how those who follow the King today might live well before him. In these laws, we see both legal norms and punitive measures taken when laws are broken.

The law, in all its richness and breadth, instructs the Israelites in how to live as inhabitants of the kingdom in God's land under God's rule. The people's adherence to this way of life will benefit not only their own nation but also the gentile nations, as their obedience "transcribes" God's character into the world.[24] As Goheen writes, "This is why the law's instruction to Israel covers the whole scope of human life. The people of Israel now serve a new covenant Lord, the God of creation. They owe him their undivided loyalty and must consecrate their social, economic, familial, and political structures—indeed, the whole of their personal, social, and cultural lives—to him. . . . [Because of its holistic nature,] Israel's life of obedience is to be lived as a missionary encounter with the pagan religious spirit of Canaanite culture."[25]

24. Michael D. Williams, *Far as the Curse Is Found: The Covenant Story of Redemption* (Phillipsburg, NJ: P&R, 2005), 148.
25. Goheen, *Light to the Nations*, 40–41.

As God's people obey God's law in God's land, they give a picture to a lost and broken world of their redemptive and gracious God: his virtues and values, his desires and plans. Israel's adherence to the law is God's way to show the nations around Israel what God is like.

And finally, as the people obey God's law, they are fit for service before the Lord. Israel's law does not save God's people, but it does make them fit for service in God's kingdom. Through their obedience to God's law in the covenant, God's people are fit to serve as his royal priesthood and holy kingdom among the nations. Priestly holiness marks a people who is set apart and fit for the King to use.

Was Israel expected to maintain perfect obedience? Well, perfect obedience was the ideal! But the biblical portrait is a bit more nuanced. Considering the fall and the description of the sacrificial system, as we will see, it becomes apparent that God knew his people would imperfectly follow his law. The more they sinned against God and broke his law, the more they were shown to be imperfect instruments in the Redeemer's hands: they were unable to meet God's perfect standards of holiness, they were unable to imitate God's virtues, and they were unable to embrace God's values. They had a serious sin problem. And many had serious heart problems. They exhibited neither inner nor outward devotion to God. This is why later the apostle Paul says that the law exposes sin (Rom. 3:19–20). The seventh day of the promised rest of creation would not be met in Israel, at least not at that time.

Sin and Sacrifice

God knows humanity's persistence in sin (see chapter 2 on the fall), and so he builds redemptive grace into the very fabric of the law of the Israelite covenant. The book of Leviticus is chock-full of regulations regarding worship and sacrifice to deal with Israel's sins (esp. Lev. 1–16). God gives his people sacrifice and ablution (ritual cleansing) as ways they can be reconciled with God and set apart as holy once again, after they have sinned. When they have been set right with God once again, then they are fit for service as God's royal priesthood and holy nation. Seen in this light, the entire sacrificial system is God's gracious response to sin. The sacrificial laws prescribe a way for Israel's sin to be *managed*.[26]

Key to the management of sin is sacrifice, particularly the killing of a sacrificial animal, shedding its blood, and placing it on the altar as an offering.

---

26. See the helpful work of Mark J. Boda, *A Severe Mercy: Sin and Its Remedy in the Old Testament*, Siphrut 1 (Winona Lake, IN: Eisenbrauns, 2009).

The shedding of the blood is very important. "For the life of a creature is in the blood, and I have appointed it to you to make atonement on the altar for your lives, since it is the lifeblood that makes atonement" (Lev. 17:11). The word *atonement* in this translation could also be translated as "ransom." So the verse could be paraphrased, "I have given it to you to ransom your lives on the altar; for, as life, it is the blood that is the price of ransom."[27] Shed blood pays the price for sin so that human beings can enjoy renewed life with God in his world. The problem with this kind of sacrifice, however, is that it needs to be offered again and again and again without end.

This is why we say that the sacrificial laws *manage* sin but do not *eradicate* it. This is an important point. Nowhere in the Old Testament sacrificial law does Israel experience the eradication of its sin. Instead, it is managed year to year, sacrifice by sacrifice. Because God's people were broken in sin, God provided sacrifices and a sacrificial system to manage their sin and sanctify or set them apart as holy, fit for God to use. Their sanctification was necessary for them to live for their King.

Did God expect his people to follow the law, despite the recognition of their sin problem? He did, but he expected a very specific kind of obedience. The songs of Israel give us a glimpse of the kind of obedience that was expected. Notice the words of Psalm 40:8: "I delight to do your will, my God, / and your instruction is deep within me." The Psalms regularly depict obedience to God's law as being a delight that comes from the law being implanted in the heart of the faithful (cf. Pss. 1:2; 19:8; 40:8; 119:16, 69–70, 77, 80, 92, 111, 143; see also 2 Chron. 34:31; Ezra 7:10).

God expected Israel to exhibit an inner devotion (faith) that expressed itself in outward devotion (faithfulness/obedience). This inner devotion to God was more than merely following the rules. God expected obedience but more than obedience. He expected his people to love him, and out of that love they would obey his commandments. Because of this foundation for obedience, Israel's prophets could denounce God's people when they followed the letter of the law but their hearts were far from God (1 Sam. 15:18–23; Isa. 1:10–17; Hosea 6:5–6; Mic. 6:6–8).

What can be said, in summary, about the law, covenant, and the story of redemption? God redeems his covenant people (by virtue of the fact that they are the children of Abraham) and brings them to the land. He gives them their identity (a royal priesthood and a holy nation) and the law (by which they will live in the land). The law, then, is the way God's people can live for

27. See the discussion in Gordon J. Wenham, *The Book of Leviticus*, NICOT (Grand Rapids: Eerdmans, 1978), 245.

their King. God is the source of their salvation as they live out their priestly vocation in his kingdom.

The Davidic Covenant

Who is Israel's king in the kingdom? As we saw in creation, there really is only one true King: God himself. However, as we saw, Israel displayed a tendency to reject God's kingship over them. For that reason, God installed an earthly king to rule over them, with the intention that the earthly king would urge them to love and obey their heavenly King. Deuteronomy 17:14–20 presents how God's king should rule over his people. He should be an Israelite who relies completely on the Lord, who neither intermarries nor establishes large armies. He should not amass wealth and gold but rather enrich himself by meditating on the law of the Lord. In short, he should be a devoted worshiper who rules at God's behest and under God's command.

In 1–2 Samuel, we learn that God gave Israel a king named David who was indeed a king "after [God's] own heart" (1 Sam. 13:14). Under David's kingship, God gave the people of Israel an everlasting covenant, which we call the Davidic covenant (2 Sam. 7:8–16; 23:5). The Davidic covenant builds on the Abrahamic and Israelite covenants. Consider the similarities, depicted in table 3.1.

Table 3.1: Similarities between Covenants

Abrahamic Covenant	Davidic Covenant
A land (Gen. 15:7)	A land (2 Sam. 7:10)
A great nation (children and family) (12:2–3)	Dynastic succession (7:12)
A great name (12:2)	A great name (7:9)

Israelite Covenant	Davidic Covenant
God's firstborn son (Exod. 4:22)	God's son (7:14)
Royal priesthood, holy nation (19:4–6)	Priest-King (Ps. 110:2, 4)
Stipulations (20:2–17)	Stipulations (Deut. 17:14–20)
Divine promises (23:20–33)	Divine promises (2 Sam. 7:8–20)

The Davidic covenant, then, continues the story of God's redemption. God's kingdom will be manifested most clearly under the rule of the Davidic king. God promises David, "When your time comes and you rest with your fathers, I will raise up after you your descendant, who will come from your body, and I will establish his kingdom. He is the one who will build a house for my name, and I will establish the throne of his kingdom forever. I will be his father, and he will be my son" (2 Sam. 7:12–14).

God's people in God's land under God's rule will find its fulfillment in the line of the Davidic king. The Davidic covenant shows that *God* will enact his rule through the Davidic line.

The king will be successful only in so far as he rules in accordance with and under the rule of the divine King. For this reason, David inquires with the prophet Nathan about building a place of worship so that all can gather to adore God the King. "Look, I am living in a cedar house while the ark of God sits inside tent curtains" (2 Sam. 7:2). King David understands "that his own kingdom will not be established nor will his own line endure, unless divine rule is acknowledged appropriately within Israel."[28] So the Davidic king becomes, at his best, an exemplar for worship and piety among God's people. Moreover, when he is successful, the Davidic king drives God's people to worship the true God of the universe. It is not surprising, therefore, that the Psalms regularly point to Israel's Davidic king as a leader in worship of God.

The Psalms also emphasize the rule of the Davidic king over *all* nations with justice and equity. This international flavor of the Davidic covenant is best seen in Psalm 2 (specifically vv. 7–11), but it appears throughout the Psalter as well (see Pss. 18:40, 43–49; 72:8; 89:35–36; 132:11–12).[29] The Davidic reign over Israel and the nations represents nothing less than the reign of God (or the kingdom of God). As McCann summarizes, "The Psalms proclaim God's reign and invite persons to live under God's rule."[30] The Davidic covenant is God's way to achieve his kingdom among all nations. God appoints David as a "prince" (2 Sam. 7:8 NRSV) who rules over all peoples under the authority of the great King, God himself (Ps. 48:2).

One of the key terms that God uses to describe the Davidic king is the word *messiah* (from the Hebrew verb *mashakh*), which means "anointed one." It stems from David's anointing in the shepherds' fields near Bethlehem (1 Sam. 16). There God anointed David (through the prophet Samuel) for kingship (see also 2 Sam. 12:7). The anointed king of Israel has a sacred role among God's people as their leader and exemplar in fidelity to God (see 1 Sam. 24:6, 10; 26:9–23). The special role of the messiah-king is captured in David's words: "Great salvation he [God] brings to his king, and shows steadfast love to his

28. Dumbrell, *Covenant and Creation*, 219.

29. See the discussion in Gordon J. Wenham, *The Psalter Reclaimed: Praying and Praising with the Psalms* (Wheaton: Crossway, 2013), 161–86.

30. J. Clinton McCann Jr., *A Theological Introduction to the Book of Psalms* (Nashville: Abingdon, 1993), 49.

anointed, to David and his offspring forever" (2 Sam. 22:51 ESV). David's words echo the Davidic and Israelite covenants, but they highlight the special place of Israel's messiah, who stands in relationship with God.

Israel's messiah brings the promised rest of creation to fruition. It is interesting, even significant, that God promises David rest in the land of promise (2 Sam. 7:10–11). The importance of this connection lies in the fact that the goal of the seventh day (the kingdom of God) will come to fruition *at least in part* through David and the Davidic line. God is committed to bringing the kingdom to bear through David's lineage, which we will see is fulfilled in Jesus Christ (Heb. 4).

But until the advent of Jesus, how did the Davidic kings do? Overall, not so well, as we saw in the previous chapter. By the mid-sixth century BC, no Davidic king sat on the throne—a terrible reality. The writers of 1–2 Samuel and 1–2 Kings suggest that the failure of the Davidic line was not the failure of God but rather the failure of the human kings to live faithfully before God the King. Despite this, God preserves the Davidic line well into the future; just as David served as a shepherd before serving as Israel's king, so the future messiah will shepherd God's people in his role as suffering servant and perfect king.

In later books such as 1–2 Chronicles, the biblical writers anticipate that there will be a king who will not be like the old kings. He will be, true to the Davidic covenant, in the line of David. But he will not be like David or Solomon. He will be a good king who lives to pray, to worship, and to lead God's people with justice and equity. The good king will be like all God's people who know and love and worship God in his kingdom. This king will rule over Israel and, indeed, over all the nations. Together, both Israelite and non-Israelite will serve the Lord with gladness.[31]

As time goes by, the Davidic king becomes more and more important for Israel, likely because no king was perfect in justice and righteousness and so God's people looked for a king who would meet God's requirements for justice and righteousness. Indeed, God's people began to anticipate a coming king who would deliver them from oppression, even from their sin.

Conclusion

We explored God's redemption in this chapter, but we only got as far as the Davidic covenant. We still need to flesh out the New Covenant, which we will

---

31. See Scott Hahn's wonderful discussion in *The Kingdom of God as Liturgical Empire: A Theological Commentary on 1–2 Chronicles* (Grand Rapids: Baker Academic, 2012), 23–41.

do in the next chapter. We will do so for two reasons. First, the New Covenant is the climax of all the covenants that came before it. And second, the New Covenant is fulfilled in Jesus Christ, where the story of redemption unfolds. As we understand how Jesus fulfills the New Covenant, we can begin to find our footing regarding what living for the King really means.

4

RESTORATION

New Covenant and Consummated Kingdom

Jesus went to Galilee, proclaiming the good news [gospel] of God: "The time is fulfilled, and the kingdom of God has come near. Repent and believe the good news!"

Mark 1:14–15

Introduction

I (Heath) remember my first trip to the Grand Canyon in the United States. My father dutifully drove the family all the way from south Texas to Arizona. I was amazed at how the landscape changed during the journey. The family made the traverse from humid, green climes to flat, west-Texas oil country to the mountainous, arid land of New Mexico to the deserts of Arizona. We finally arrived at Grand Canyon National Park. We had come a long way!

We parked the car at one of the provided stops that opened up into a viewing area for the Grand Canyon. The journey brought us to the place where we longed to stand, to gaze on the overwhelming expanse that is known as the largest canyon in the world. We exited the vehicle with great excitement, with anticipation for the grandeur of it all. We walked to the precipice of the canyon . . . and there it was—miles of red and yellow, beige and gold in a canyon that is impossibly deep and wide. Colors layered on top of one another contrasted against the crystal blue sky above and the whiteness of the clouds. Undulations and shapes of the canyon appeared that cannot be captured with words. And in the bottom lay the little blue-green ribbon winding this way and that, with millions of diamonds reflecting the sunset in the thread: a river that carries vast quantities of water tumbling through the canyon out to the sea miles and miles away. The sheer scale of everything was incomprehensible, overwhelming. Peering over the edge, the lip, of the canyon, I was exhilarated by the wonder of it all. The canyon's magnificence takes your breath away and opens your senses.

The same anticipation is felt in God's story of redemption. At this stage in our journey, we stand at the edge, so to speak, longing to glimpse the overwhelming horizon of the King's climactic work in the New Covenant. And it is here that we see the sheer scale of God's redemption plan. The last chapter brought us through the changing terrain of God's covenant story of redemption. We have come from the beginning of creation through Noah to God's work with the family of Abraham. We have passed through the covenants with Israel and David. Each step along the way opened us up further and further to God's redemption. Each step showed how many in the past did not fully live for the King. But the story has brought us here . . . to the *New* Covenant that comes in Jesus Christ. We will see that Jesus faithfully lives for the King and invites us to join in that same mission.

It is easy to reduce Jesus to a one-dimensional character: he is *either* this or that, one or the other. But this is a mistake. One of the great challenges of understanding and embracing Jesus comes from the diverse way he is presented in the New Testament: he is a prophet, a priest, a king, a sacrifice, the temple, Israel, Moses, Adam. He is so many things! This is because Jesus is the fulfillment of the grand story of redemption. To embrace Jesus in *all* the ways he fulfills this story is to learn to call him Lord and Savior.

Jesus, the Center of Scripture

As we saw in the introduction of this book, Dietrich Bonhoeffer identifies Jesus as the "center" of Scripture.[1] Jesus is the full realization of all the major symbols and stories of the Old Testament. It would take us beyond what we can cover here to unpack fully how Jesus opens up the totality of the biblical story. However, we will note a few key features that demonstrate the point.

1. Dietrich Bonhoeffer, *Ethics*, trans. N. H. Smith (New York: Macmillan, 1965), 56.

Jesus is the Creator. In Paul's letter to the church at Colossae, he argues that Jesus is the agent of creation and the glue that holds all things together:

> He is the image of the invisible God,
> the firstborn over all creation.
> For everything was created by him,
> in heaven and on earth,
> the visible and the invisible,
> whether thrones or dominions
> or rulers or authorities—
> all things have been created through him and for him.
> He is before all things,
> and by him all things hold together.
> He is also the head of the body, the church;
> he is the beginning,
> the firstborn from the dead,
> so that he might come to have
> first place in everything.
> For God was pleased to have
> all his fullness dwell in him,
> and through him to reconcile
> everything to himself,
> whether things on earth or things in heaven,
> by making peace
> through his blood, shed on the cross. (1:15–20)

Jesus is the perfect human/Adam. "Therefore, just as sin entered the world through one man, and death through sin, in this way death spread to all people, because all sinned. In fact, sin was in the world before the law, but sin is not charged to a person's account when there is no law. Nevertheless, death reigned from Adam to Moses, even over those who did not sin in the likeness of Adam's transgression. He is a type of the Coming One" (Rom. 5:12–14). In these verses, Paul affirms that we are all sinners and that Adam stands at the headwaters of the fall. But Jesus serves as the second Adam who redeems us from sin and institutes a new humanity in which sin no longer controls us and in which we are no longer condemned. In Jesus, God's forgiveness breaks in on those who believe. Or as Paul says elsewhere, "For just as in Adam all die, so also in Christ all will be made alive" (1 Cor. 15:22).

Jesus fulfills the judgment and salvation of Noah. Remember that the flood reveals two powerful realities simultaneously. On the one hand, it shows God's judgment on the world, and on the other hand, it discloses God's patience with and commitment to his creation. Jesus's advent signifies the same two powerful realities simultaneously, God's judgment and his great salvation.

> Then he [Jesus] told the disciples: "The days are coming when you will long to see one of the days of the Son of Man, but you won't see it. They will say to you, 'See there!' or 'See here!' Don't follow or run after them. For as the lightning flashes from horizon to horizon and lights up the sky, so the Son of Man will be in his day. But first it is necessary that he suffer many things and be rejected by this generation.
>
> Just as it was in the days of Noah, so it will be in the days of the Son of Man: People went on eating, drinking, marrying and giving in marriage until the day Noah boarded the ark, and the flood came and destroyed all of them. (Luke 17:22–27)

Jesus fulfills the story of Israel. The Gospel of Matthew tells us not only that Jesus is the "Son of Abraham" (1:1) but also that "out of Egypt I called my Son" (2:15, drawing on Hosea 11:1). Why would Matthew cite Hosea 11:1 in his description of Jesus going down to Egypt? Matthew seems to be highlighting that Jesus is the true Israel, the Israel who never rebelled against God and whose ministry represents a "new exodus" in which Jesus was faithful in a way that Israel had not been.[2]

Moreover, Jesus calls *twelve* disciples as a way of revealing that his life and ministry will fulfill God's law in a way that the twelve tribes of Israel did not. He calls the twelve disciples as a symbolic reconstitution and renewal of the twelve tribes of Israel. He will renew Israel and, indeed, all things.[3]

Jesus fulfills Israel's vocation in the land through baptism. In Matthew 3, we learn that John (Jesus's cousin) is calling people to repentance because the kingdom is very close at hand (v. 2) and is baptizing people in the Jordan River. He even baptizes Jesus. Why is Jesus baptized in the first place, and why does he make a pilgrimage to the desert to be baptized by John in the Jordan River? Probably the most satisfying explanation is that he is fulfilling the story of Israel. Israel crossed the Jordan to be baptized into its missional vocation, but the people continually failed in that vocation and eventually ended up in exile. But Jesus, as the better and more faithful Israel, is baptized in the Jordan before going on to faithfully fulfill his missional vocation. That

2. Clay Alan Ham, "The Minor Prophets in Matthew's Gospel," in *The Minor Prophets in the New Testament*, ed. Maarten J. J. Menken and Steve Moyise, Library of New Testament Studies 377 (Edinburgh: T&T Clark, 2009), 45.

3. Richard Horsley, *The Prophet Jesus and the Renewal of Israel: Moving Beyond a Diversionary Debate* (Grand Rapids: Eerdmans, 2012), 120–22.

is why he is baptized and divinely endorsed as God's "beloved Son" in whom God is "well-pleased" (Matt. 3:17).

Jesus is God. One of the most remarkable, and troubling, affirmations that Jesus makes of himself is his divinity. He claims to be God. The "I am" statements in the Gospel of John indicate this clearly.[4] Drawing on God's self-disclosure formula in Exodus 3, Jesus uses the same terminology to describe himself. In the Greek version of Exodus 3:14, God says that his people should understand his name to be "I am" (*egō eimi*). Jesus picks up on this in the great "I am" statements in John, each time drawing attention to the fact that he is *more* than a prophet, *more* than a sage, *more* than a king, *more* than a priest. Jesus is "I am." Larry Hurtado says that "this absolute use of 'I am' in the Gospels amounts to nothing less than designating Jesus with the same special referential formula that is used in the Greek Old Testament for God's own self-declaration."[5]

Jesus is none other than the God of the Old Testament. So Jesus can say that "the one who has seen me has seen the Father" (John 14:9).[6] It is no wonder that some of the Jews were incensed at Jesus! He was claiming to be God incarnate, the divine Word of God, the Father's final answer to the problem of sin in his world. God answered the problem of the fall by giving himself, in Jesus, on the cross. And in Jesus, God will reign over the earth eternally.

Jesus is the center of Scripture. We have touched on some features, and we could include others: Jesus as the Son of Man, Jesus and Israel's temple worship, and Jesus and Israel's law. Jesus is, in the language of Lesslie Newbigin, the "clue" that opens up the totality of Scripture and the world: he is the clue to all that is. To understand Scripture and the world, we must pursue the clue of Jesus Christ.[7] Moreover, to understand what it means to live *for the King*, we must look to Jesus.

Two fundamental realities from the story of Scripture help us grasp the significance of Jesus: the New Covenant and the kingdom of God. The New Covenant brings God's kingdom to fruition, and the kingdom of God comes in the work of Jesus Christ, who mediates the New Covenant.

4. See John 6:35, 48, 51; 8:12; 9:5; 10:7, 9, 11, 14; 11:25; 14:6; 15:1.
5. Larry W. Hurtado, *Lord Jesus Christ: Devotion to Jesus in Earliest Christianity* (Grand Rapids: Eerdmans, 2005), 371.
6. To be precise, Jesus claims that he and the Father (who is Israel's God, Yahweh) are united, and the disciples will know Jesus as they know the God of the Old Testament. Jesus does the will of the Father who sent him. See discussion in Raymond E. Brown, *The Gospel According to John XIII–XXI*, AYBC (New York: Doubleday, 1970), 631–33.
7. Lesslie Newbigin, *The Light Has Come: An Exposition of the Fourth Gospel* (Grand Rapids: Eerdmans, 1982), 3.

Redemption and the New Covenant

Jesus comes preaching the coming of the kingdom of God. "Jesus went to Galilee, proclaiming the good news [gospel] of God: 'The time is fulfilled, and the kingdom of God has come near. Repent and believe the good news!'" (Mark 1:14–15). Jesus inaugurates the eschatological kingdom. "It is only through this obedient Son [Jesus]—God the Son incarnate—that God's long-awaited kingdom is inaugurated in this world through the new covenant."[8]

Jesus correlates the New Covenant and the coming of the kingdom in his final meal with his disciples, as we will see (Matt. 26:27–29; Mark 14:24–25; Luke 22:15–20). This shows us that the kingdom of God comes in and through the New Covenant, which appears in Jesus. But all this begs the question, What is the New Covenant?

The New Covenant appears most prevalently in the prophetic books of the Old Testament. Although present in other prophetic texts, the exact phrase occurs in only one passage, Jeremiah 31:31–40, which is nested within the broader restoration vision of Jeremiah 30–33. From this section of Jeremiah alone, we see that *all* the covenants find their goal and fulfillment in this New Covenant.

Jeremiah 31:35–37 depicts the New Covenant as a future new creation that is not stained by sin (and thereby reaffirms God's covenant at creation and with Noah). Jeremiah 31:35–37 reveals that all of Abraham's descendants will become productive and find the blessing of God (thus the fulfillment of the Abrahamic covenant). Jeremiah 31:33–34 reveals that in the New Covenant, God changes the hearts of his people so that they love God and obey his law from the heart (hence, a reconfiguration of the Israelite covenant). Jeremiah 33:14–18 portrays the Davidic king on his throne, ruling over God's people and God's land (the fulfillment of the Davidic covenant).[9] These lines of continuity indicate that there are not really *many* covenants but *one* unfolding covenant that leads us to its goal: peace with God in his world in the New Covenant. The New Covenant depicts a future time in which all will be well in the relationship between God and Israel as the people dwell in God's land. Sin will no longer be found in the hearts of God's people, and they will live in perfect peace with their God and in the world.

So what is *new* about the New Covenant? In terms of the structure of the New Covenant, it is not new at all. It is rooted in the one unfolding covenant

8. Peter J. Gentry and Stephen J. Wellum, *Kingdom through Covenant: A Biblical-Theological Understanding of the Covenants*, 2nd ed. (Wheaton: Crossway, 2018), 653.

9. Note that the covenant with David is married with the covenant at creation and with the Abrahamic covenant in Jer. 33:19–22. See also Jer. 33:23–26.

story of redemption that we explored in the last chapter. The New Covenant is rooted in the Abrahamic, Israelite, and Davidic covenants, as we have seen. But there are some distinctive marks of the New Covenant that differentiate it from the others.

Divine forgiveness. Key in the New Covenant is pervasive divine forgiveness. Sin is not *managed* for a time in the New Covenant; sin is forgiven completely and remembered no longer. "'For they will all know me, from the least to the greatest of them'—this is the LORD's declaration. 'For I will forgive their iniquity and never again remember their sin'" (Jer. 31:34). Similarly, "I will purify them from all the iniquity they have committed against me, and I will forgive all the iniquities they have committed against me, rebelling against me" (Jer. 33:8). In the New Covenant, God offers the consummate forgiveness of sin.

Divine transformation of the heart. A major distinctive of the New Covenant is its focus on the internal change of God's people (Jer. 31:31–34). It recalibrates God's law, making it part of the interior life of the believer. In the New Covenant, believers ideally will not need to be told "do not murder" or "do not covet" because the hearts of God's people will be internally imprinted with God's desires. God's law will be written on their hearts and thus will not need to be read from tablets of stone.

Divine presence. Jeremiah 31:33 uses the covenant formula "I will be their God, and they will be my people," highlighting the restoration of the covenant and a reaffirmation of God's presence with his people. God's presence will not be localized for a select few but expanded so that all will know God, from the least to the greatest (Jer. 31:34). Ezekiel 36:22–37, a text that likely builds on the New Covenant concept, carries the idea further by prophesying that God will give a new heart to his people and will breathe the Spirit of God into his people. God's Spirit will be poured out on his people to signify his kingly presence with his people and to enable them to follow the King fully.

Divine promises. In the New Covenant, God will move his people from being landless and shamed to having land and honor. The lost king will reign once again, and lost worship will again ensue in the temple (Jer. 31:38–40; 33:9–26; cf. Ezek. 40–48). The divided kingdom will be united again (Jer. 31:27; 32:36–41). The city of Jerusalem will be restored (31:38–40; 33:9). Vitality will touch the earth, producing a kind of Edenic state in God's land (31:27–28; 33:12–13). God's promises in the New Covenant are grand and wonderful! The kingdom of God, once broken by sin, is restored in full in the New Covenant.

Human repentance and responsiveness to God. God will act to renew his people, and then their hearts will fundamentally change (Jer. 31:18; cf. Lam. 5:21). As God turns to his people in renewal, they return to him (Jer. 30:20;

31:18; Ezek. 36:11).[10] They turn to God as he turns to them, and the resulting relationship is unsullied by sin.[11] They are responsive to their God because God has effectively changed their hearts to love their God (see Jer. 31:33–34; Hosea 2:15).

In summary, the New Covenant is the climactic work of God's redemption of his people. Because of the New Covenant, humanity can rightly live for the King. We can operate with new hearts, filled lives, meaning and purpose, and the ability to know (through the Spirit of God) how to live well in God's world.

The New Covenant is grand and beautiful. It is a complete restoration whereby God offers life, hope, and forgiveness of sin.

> I will certainly gather them from all the lands where I have banished them in my anger, rage and intense wrath, and I will return them to this place and make them live in safety. They will be my people, and I will be their God. I will give them integrity of heart and action so that they will fear me always, for their good and for the good of their descendants after them. I will make a permanent covenant with them: I will never turn away from doing good to them, and I will put fear of me in their hearts so they will never again turn away from me. I will take delight in them to do what is good for them, and with all my heart and mind I will faithfully plant them in this land. (Jer. 32:37–41)

But when will this take place, and how? The remainder of the Old Testament anticipates that it lay in the future, with some partial fulfillment of the New Covenant promises along the way.[12] But the hope of the New Covenant was never fully realized until the advent of Jesus into the world. As we are told in Hebrews 8, Jesus is the mediator of this New Covenant (v. 13). Jesus's coming changes everything. This is extraordinarily good news!

Mediator of the New Covenant

Just prior to his betrayal, torture, and crucifixion, Jesus shares a Passover feast with his followers. The meal was special and ritualized in every detail

10. We should also note how God's people turn to God in exile, and then he "circumcises" their hearts in Deut. 30:1–14. In this, God does his work of renewal, but God's people also turn back to God in repentance of their sin.

11. J. Gordon McConville, *Judgment and Promise: An Interpretation of the Book of Jeremiah* (Winona Lake, IN: Eisenbrauns, 1993), 97: "His [Jeremiah's] 'bring me back that I may be restored' [Jer. 31:18] rests on a play on the verb *šûḇ* which is at the heart of the great solution, and indeed of all theological wrestling with the relationship of divine enabling and adequate human response to God."

12. See, e.g., the partial fulfillment of the New Covenant in Ezra's words in Ezra 7–9. J. G. McConville, "Ezra-Nehemiah and the Fulfilment of Prophecy," *VT* 36, no. 2 (1986): 205–24.

according to the stipulations of Old Testament law (Exod. 12:1–20). The Passover meal, as it was called, celebrated the memory of God's salvation and deliverance of Israel from its servitude in Egypt. The feast gave space and time for God's people to remember how he had rescued them: God had told his people to sacrifice an animal and spatter the blood on the doorposts and lintels of their houses; for those who obeyed, the death angel passed them by (12:21–27). Hence God "passed over" his judgment by looking at the blood, and thereby he spared his people. Food, light, space, smells, and liturgy accompanied the meal, giving a multifaceted experience of remembrance.

Against this backdrop, Jesus infuses the Passover with deeper meaning that centers on his own forthcoming sacrifice for their sins. Jesus tells his disciples that the bread they eat in the meal is his body: "This is my body, which is given for you" (Luke 22:19). It signifies the breaking of his body in death, yet his death will become the nourishment of eternal life for those who consume him. After he breaks the bread, Jesus takes a cup of wine and says to his followers at the meal, "This is my blood of the [new] covenant, which is poured out for many. Truly I tell you, I will no longer drink of the fruit of the vine until that day when I drink it new in the kingdom of God" (Mark 14:24–25). Matthew and Luke record the event similarly, with their own nuances (Matt. 26:26–30; Luke 22:14–20). Thus, Jesus's own body and blood will satisfy God so that he will pass over his judgment.

From Mark 14:22–25, we see that the body and the blood of Jesus are vital elements to the New Covenant. Without the broken body and the shed blood, the New Covenant would not be possible. Jesus perceives that his blood is vital for the "forgiveness of sins" (Matt. 26:28). Jesus's words in that Passover meal go to the heart of what God has done to set right the sin problem that plagued the world since the beginning. To solve the sin problem, God gives Jesus to offer his body and shed his blood for the forgiveness of sins. Once the problem of sin is dealt with, then humanity can live *for the King*.

Jesus sees his impending death on the cross as a *sacrifice*. When we reflect on this point in the context of the covenant story of Scripture, we see that Jesus believes that his sacrifice offers atonement for sin. His blood covers sin and makes it possible for reconciliation with God. His shed blood brings into effect the New Covenant as well.[13] So E. Earle Ellis says, "In an acted parable Jesus interprets the passover 'bread' and 'wine' of his coming death. He thereby

---

13. Luke records Jesus saying, "This cup is the new covenant in my blood, which is poured out for you" (Luke 22:20). Mark identifies it as "my blood of the covenant" (Mark 14:24), with some ancient manuscripts adding the adjective "new."

declares his death to be the means by which the redemptive significance of the passover will be fulfilled. His shed 'blood' brings into being a new covenant and accomplishes a new Exodus, an Exodus from sin and death."[14]

The story of God's redemption in the exodus finds its fulfillment in Jesus's blood poured out at the cross. His broken body and shed blood provide the means of forgiveness, open reconciliation with God, and offer the way to a new future for humanity.

The writer of Hebrews goes on to explore the significance of Jesus's death on the cross as an atoning sacrifice for sin. Hebrews explicitly connects Jesus to the New Covenant in line with the Gospels' portrayal and explains it more fully:

> But Christ has appeared as a high priest of the good things that have come. In the greater and more perfect tabernacle not made with hands (that is, not of this creation), he entered the most holy place once for all time, not by the blood of goats and calves, but by his own blood, having obtained eternal redemption. For if the blood of goats and bulls and the ashes of a young cow, sprinkling those who are defiled, sanctify for the purification of the flesh, how much more will the blood of Christ, who through the eternal Spirit offered himself without blemish to God, cleanse our consciences from dead works so that we can serve the living God? Therefore, he is the mediator of a new covenant, so that those who are called might receive the promise of the eternal inheritance, because a death has taken place for redemption from the transgressions committed under the first covenant. (Heb. 9:11–15)

The point is clear: Jesus *is* the sacrifice by which atonement was made for humanity. If we return to the concept of the New Covenant discussed earlier, we see that the writer of Hebrews saw Jesus's blood as the *means* by which God granted forgiveness.

Hebrews, then, gives a fuller account of the *means* by which the New Covenant takes its shape than what we saw in Jeremiah's prophecy. Jesus is the suffering King who dies on the cross and atones for sin; his death effects forgiveness promised in Jeremiah's New Covenant. This is why Jesus mediates the New Covenant: forgiveness, transformation of the heart, divine presence, divine promises, and human responsiveness come as a result of Jesus's shed blood. In Christ, humans can discover their lives for the King.

The difference between the Old Covenant sacrifices and the New Covenant sacrifice lay in this: while the former sacrifices *managed* sin, Jesus's sacrifice

14. E. Earle Ellis, *The Gospel of Luke*, NCBC (London: Marshall, Morgan and Scott, 1981), 251.

eradicates the blame of sin ultimately. "But now he has appeared one time, at the end of the ages, for the removal of sin by the sacrifice of himself" (Heb. 9:26). In Jesus Christ, sin is dealt a death blow. Jesus absorbs God's wrath for sin, and his blood covers sin once for all.

Because of this fact, it is not entirely correct to say that Christians "do away with" either the Old Testament sacrificial system or the law. In God's redemption story, the sacrificial system finds its redemptive goal in Jesus, who is the once-for-all sacrifice for sin. All who claim his blood as an atoning *covering* for sin, therefore, actively participate in God's Old Testament sacrificial system, albeit in a new and surprising way. Christians embrace the sacrifice of Jesus not to *manage* sin but to do away with it forever.

The guilt of sin was swallowed up by Jesus's blood on the cross. His blood made final atonement for sin. All who claim Jesus's blood for the forgiveness of sin and confess him as Lord find the hope offered in the New Covenant. The divine promises, presence, transformation, and forgiveness are opened to them. In Christ, they can live well in God's kingdom.

Jesus the Messianic King

Perhaps the most significant title for Jesus is that of Christ.[15] The term *Christ* is really a Greek translation of a Hebrew word, *mashiakh*, which, as we saw in the last chapter, means "anointed one." Jesus and his followers unquestionably argue that Jesus is the messiah of Israel, even though not all people share their belief. Jesus declares that the long-anticipated kingdom of God will arrive in and through him. The apostle Paul argues, in fact, that the kingdom of God is none other than the kingdom of Jesus, the Messiah (Eph. 5:5).

Luke, too, presents Jesus the Messiah as the great prophet whom God will raise up like Moses. "As such, he is seen as the last great eschatological and messianic prophet or, to put it the other way around, prophetic Messiah."[16] Luke portrays Jesus in this way in Luke 4:16–22. In this passage, Jesus reads from Isaiah 61:

> He came to Nazareth, where he had been brought up. As usual, he entered the synagogue on the Sabbath day and stood up to read. The scroll of the prophet Isaiah was given to him, and unrolling the scroll, he found the place where it was written:

15. The other significant title for Jesus is the "Son of Man."
16. Ben Witherington III, *Jesus the Seer: The Progress of Prophecy* (Minneapolis: Fortress, 2014), 332.

> The Spirit of the Lord is on me,
> because he has anointed [*mashakh*] me
> to preach good news to the poor.
> He has sent me
> to proclaim release to the captives
> and recovery of sight to the blind,
> to set free the oppressed,
> to proclaim the year of the Lord's favor.

He then rolled up the scroll, gave it back to the attendant, and sat down. And the eyes of everyone in the synagogue were fixed on him. He began by saying to them, "Today as you listen, this Scripture has been fulfilled." They were all speaking well of him and were amazed by the gracious words that came from his mouth.

This sermon highlights for us the center of the biblical story. The passage presents Isaiah's vision of the servant-king, who is "anointed" and imbued with the Spirit of the Lord to deliver the gospel. This figure is God's anointed and appointed messiah-king who will bring God's salvation to all peoples and usher in God's reign.

Can you imagine the power of the message? God's reign is finally here, and it is coming through the messiah! And it is happening now! In his own hometown, Jesus proclaims boldly that he is the messiah-king and that all the eschatological promises Isaiah had looked for are found in him. Jesus claims that, with his advent, Israel's expectation of judgment, peace, and cosmic renewal is crystallized. He comes from Bethlehem (Matt. 2:6), will bring salvation and liberation to the oppressed (Luke 4:18–19), and will reign over the whole of creation (cf. Mark 12:35–37; 13:27; cf. Rev. 21:5).[17] What wonderful news!

It is not surprising that Jesus reads from Isaiah to disclose that he is the messiah. In Isaiah 52:13–53:12, the messiah is also a servant who suffers and dies on behalf of his people, Israel. His suffering brings forgiveness for sins and the renewal of the world (Isa. 53:5–6, 11). This suffering servant–messiah is connected to Israel and the king. Appointed by the Lord, the suffering servant atones for the sins of Israel and the nations as the faithful Israelite king (Isa. 48–53; esp. 53:3–10). His divinely appointed and anointed work will bring about forgiveness of sin (53:10). The anointed King will provide freedom and liberation to God's people and to the land of Israel (Isa. 61; cf.

---

17. L. Schenke, *Das Markusevangelium* (Stuttgart: Kohlhammer, 2005), 264; Cilliers Breytenbach, "The Minor Prophets in Mark's Gospel," in *Minor Prophets in the New Testament*, 33–34.

Luke 4:18–19). However, the messiah's work will ultimately bring renewal to the whole of the created order (Isa. 65).[18]

Despite competing visions of the messiah in Jesus's day, Jesus takes the line that *he* is the (suffering) messiah of Isaiah. He identifies himself as the fulfillment of Isaiah 61, the one who brings forth God's reign into the world.[19] So N. T. Wright rightly says:

> God's plan, to rule his world through obedient humanity [in creation], has come true in the Messiah, Jesus. That which was purposed in Genesis 1 and 2, the wise rule of creation by the obedient human beings, was lost in Genesis 3, when human rebellion jeopardised the divine intention, and the ground brought forth thorns and thistles. The Messiah, however, has now been installed as the one through whom God is doing what he intended to do, first through human-ity and then through Israel. Paul's Adam-christology [in 1 Cor. 15:20–57] is basically an Israel-christology, and is predicated on the identification of Jesus as Messiah, in virtue of his resurrection.[20]

The King of the Cross

But the great scandal of Jesus's day, indeed, *our* day, is that Jesus brought God's kingdom by suffering and dying on a cross. Crucifixion was a great surprise to all, for nowhere did the Scriptures clearly say that the suffering servant, the messiah, must die on a cross. To die on a cross was a great scandal. In fact, an early piece of Roman graffiti pictures an ass on a cross with a man named Alexamenos worshiping the crucified beast. The caption underneath reads, "Alexamenos worships his god."[21] How could the King of the Jews, much less the King of creation, die on a cross? Did this not testify to the *failure* of Jesus's preaching and ministry?

18. For scholarly treatments of the suffering servant, see Darrell Bock and Mitch Glaser, eds., *The Gospel according to Isaiah 53: Encountering the Suffering Servant in Jewish and Christian Theology* (Grand Rapids: Kregel Academic, 2012); Bernd Janowski and Peter Stuhlmacher, eds., *The Suffering Servant: Isaiah 53 in Jewish and Christian Sources*, trans. Daniel P. Bailey (Grand Rapids: Eerdmans, 2004); Adela Yarbro Collins and John J. Collins, eds., *King and Messiah as Son of God: Divine, Human, and Angelic Messianic Figures in Biblical and Related Literature* (Grand Rapids: Eerdmans, 2008).

19. For other messianic conceptions, see Jacob Neusner, William S. Green, and Ernest Frer-ichs, eds., *Judaisms and Their Messiahs at the Turn of the Christian Era* (Cambridge: Cambridge University Press, 1987).

20. N. T. Wright, *The Climax of the Covenant: Christ and the Law in Pauline Theology* (Minneapolis: Fortress, 1993), 29.

21. Everett Ferguson, "Alexamenos," in *Encyclopaedia of Early Christianity*, ed. Everett Ferguson, 2nd ed. (New York: Routledge, 1999), 29.

No. Jesus's death on the cross is the means by which the kingdom of God and the New Covenant become reality. When we look at the cross of Christ, we find the great irony: Jesus is exalted by his humiliation. His humiliation on the cross is for a sinful and broken world. It is through the cross that humanity finds salvation and forgiveness. It is through the cross that all of creation finds renewal. It is through the cross that God exalts Jesus to his highest place of honor. The cross meant Jesus's death, but it meant our life. This was no failure but rather the radical victory of God's redemptive plan through Jesus, the Messiah. On the cross of Christ, Jesus paid the price of redemption.[22]

But the cross testifies to something else as well. The cross testifies that the person on the cross was not a moral fanatic or even the Davidic messiah. "The One who died there was truly the Son of God; he was God incarnate."[23] A human being could not set right the problem of sin. Only God could do that. So God stepped into human form, lived among humanity, and died for our sins on the cross (Phil. 2:6–11). In the cross of Christ, we find the victory of God. Sin and death have been dealt their death blow. This is good news indeed!

The Resurrected King

And yet, the redemption story has one chapter left to be told. The cross is meaningless without what happened after it, for although Jesus died on the cross, he did not stay in the grave. The Scriptures tell us that Jesus rose from the grave, defeating death and securing the promise of what awaits all of creation. Craig Bartholomew and Michael Goheen write, "In the resurrection of Jesus Christ, a new world is dawning. The night of evil has ended. The light of God will fill the whole earth again. The resurrection stands at the centre of the Christian faith."[24] They are right: the resurrection signifies not only that Christ has risen from the grave but also that he will raise us up to newness of life and will one day resurrect the cosmos, purging it of sin and sin's consequences. On that day, we will dwell together with God, in unbroken fellowship with him and one another, under his rule, in his renewed land.

Consider the words Paul wrote in a letter to Christians in the city of Corinth in the first century AD:

22. See the powerful, accurate, and (still) relevant Leon Morris, *The Apostolic Preaching of the Cross* (Grand Rapids: Eerdmans, 1965).

23. W. T. Conner, *The Cross in the New Testament* (Nashville: Broadman, 1954), 158.

24. Craig G. Bartholomew and Michael W. Goheen, *The Drama of Scripture: Finding Our Place in the Biblical Story*, 2nd ed. (Grand Rapids: Baker Academic, 2014), 179.

But as it is, Christ has been raised from the dead, the firstfruits of those who have fallen asleep. For since death came through a man, the resurrection of the dead also comes through a man. For just as in Adam all die, so also in Christ all will be made alive. But each in his own order: Christ, the firstfruits; afterward, at his coming, those who belong to Christ. Then comes the end, when he hands over the kingdom to God the Father, when he abolishes all rule and all authority and power. For he must reign until he puts all his enemies under his feet. The last enemy to be abolished is death. For God has put everything under his feet. Now when it says "everything" is put under him, it is obvious that he who puts everything under him is the exception. When everything is subject to Christ, then the Son himself will also be subject to the one who subjected everything to him, so that God may be all in all. (1 Cor. 15:20–28)

Paul's teaching stands out for its distinctive presentation of the meaning of the resurrection of Jesus. He draws on the biblical story and makes a comparison between Adam and Jesus. Whereas Adam fell into sin and brought death into the world, Jesus, as the new Adam, brought life, which is guaranteed by virtue of the resurrection of his body: "So also in Christ all will be made alive" (1 Cor. 15:22).

Salvation and Judgment of the King

The vision of 1 Corinthians 15 is beautiful and grand, detailing the restoration that comes in the King. But God's restoration in Jesus implies judgment as well. Scripture makes clear that, in the end, God will vindicate those who love him, and he will judge those who reject him. Several Old Testament texts imagine this, particularly when God will judge the nations in an event described with rich imagery and picturesque vision, as one sees in Joel 3:9–16.

The New Testament reveals that the judge on the day of judgment is King Jesus. He is the one with whom humanity must deal. Jesus is the one who will judge the living and the dead (2 Tim. 4:1). As we learned in the second chapter, the first couple's sin kicked open the door for all of humanity to rebel against God. Paul writes, "Therefore, just as sin entered the world through one man, and death through sin, in this way death spread to all people, because all sinned" (Rom. 5:12).

Because of sin, there is death. But death is the doorway to God's judgment. As the writer of Hebrews says, "It is appointed for people to die once—and after this, judgment" (9:27). Similarly, Paul preaches repentance to the Athenians, declaring that God "has set a day when he is going to judge the world in righteousness by the man he has appointed. He has provided proof of this to everyone by raising him from the dead" (Acts 17:31).

In the face of our sin and pending condemnation, God has graciously provided salvation through Christ Jesus. The Gospel of John reads, "For God loved the world in this way: He gave his one and only Son, so that everyone who believes in him will not perish but have eternal life. For God did not send his Son into the world to condemn the world, but to save the world through him" (3:16–17).

Similarly, from the pen of Paul, "All have sinned and fall short of the glory of God," but we can be justified (declared innocent) "through the redemption that is in Christ Jesus" (Rom. 3:23–24). Without receiving this great salvation in which Christ suffers the full wrath of God for our sin, in which Christ Jesus trades places with us, living the holy life we should have lived and dying the death we deserve to die, we will face the wrath of God on our own.

Indeed, Scripture teaches that there will be a final judgment, with Jesus Christ as the supreme Judge. This was Peter's point when he declared, "He [Jesus] commanded us to preach to the people and to testify that he is the one appointed by God to be the Judge of the living and the dead" (Acts 10:42). Christ will judge unbelievers based on their response to general revelation, rendering to them according to what they have done (Rom. 1:18–32; 2:5–7) and meting out judgment in degrees (Matt. 11:22). Hell will involve degrees of suffering (Matt. 11:22–24; Luke 10:12–14), with the worst punishment being reserved for hypocritical teachers of the law (Mark 12:38–40). This is a difficult doctrine but a necessary one, as it is taught clearly in the Scriptures. It is also a great motivator for Christians: if we teach that all humans need to be saved from their sins and simultaneously teach that salvation comes through Christ alone, we should love our fellow humans enough to make known to them the good news that Jesus saves.

The People of the King

God redeems a people for himself so that they might live for the King in every sphere of life. In the Old Testament, this is the people of Israel, who failed to live fully under his lordship. But we have seen how God always draws a people out of the world to become a channel of blessing through which his rule might be revealed. In the New Testament the church becomes a people for the King.

Through the redemption of Jesus, the church is the New Covenant community who lives under Jesus's rule, with Jesus at the head, as King. This community shows the world, in word and deed, that there is a King and calls people to embrace his reign as good news!

This community called the church is made up of those who live for the King. They believe Jesus died and rose again (faith), confess Jesus as Lord and King (confession) and turn away from any other lord in their lives, reject sin (repentance), and live under Jesus's reign (faithfulness). The church was birthed after Jesus was raised from the dead. As recorded in Acts 2, the Spirit of God comes on a crowd of Jewish Christ followers and some non-Jewish converts to King Jesus in the first century AD. The text records that during worship one of Jesus's disciples, Peter, preaches the messianic kingship of Jesus and the forgiveness of sin and calls the people who hear him to repent and believe in Jesus. From this point forward, the early followers of Jesus begin to spread the news of the King to the world. This is the mission of one of the early missionaries—the greatest missionary—the apostle Paul. He wrote much of the New Testament, and his life and ministry are recorded in the book of Acts.

The coming of the Spirit of God at the birth of the church reminds us that the community of the King is a Spirit-filled and Spirit-led community. As we saw in the previous chapter, the Spirit of God is part of the New Covenant, and the people of the King live by the Spirit as they serve Jesus.

There are two primary modes in which the community of the King operates: *gathered* community and *scattered* community. We need to understand both modes if we want to grasp the nature of the church. The gathered community is the people of God gathered for worship: praise, prayer, baptism, communion, preaching of the Word, celebration, and repentance. On Sunday mornings around the world—in grand cathedrals or in simple churches, in ordinary houses or in impoverished huts, under trees in the field or in caves hidden from authorities—the people of the King gather to worship and celebrate Jesus as King. This is the gathered community in worship.

But it is vital to remember that the church also operates as a *scattered* community. That is, the church lives 99.9 percent of its life doing mundane things, participating in ordinary life: work, school, family, sports, leisure, and so on. Jesus is no less King of his people when they are scattered. Rather, his lordship extends into *all* these areas. This means that the scattered community is scattered for multifaceted witness in the totality of human existence: in all things, the people of the King proclaim and promote his rule. We testify in a lost and broken world, through word and deed, that there *is* a King who came in the incarnation and who is coming again to reign eternally in the kingdom of God.

The New Heavens and Earth

And we testify to Jesus's reign until he makes all things new. For those who are redeemed in Christ Jesus, there is a future hope. God the King will renew and restore his good creation. As the apostle Paul writes, "The creation itself will also be set free from the bondage to decay into the glorious freedom of God's children" (Rom. 8:21), indicating that creation will be redeemed as well.[25]

In his sermon "World on Fire," the great Baptist pastor Charles Spurgeon says:

> [Martin] Luther used to say that the world is now in its working clothes and that, by-and-by, it will be arrayed in its Easter garments of joy. One likes to think that the trail of the old serpent will not always remain upon the globe and it is a cheering thought that where sin has abounded God's Glory should yet more abound. I cannot believe in that world being annihilated upon which Jesus was born and lived and died. Surely an earth with a Calvary upon it must last on! Will not the blood of Jesus immortalize it? It has groaned and travailed with mankind, being made subject to vanity for our sake. Surely it is to have its joyful redemption and keep its Sabbaths after the fire has burned out every trace of sin and sorrow.[26]

Spurgeon put it well: God's world will gain its "Easter garments of joy." God the King will restore his good creation. Redemption is God's work that first brings a broken humanity back into a right relationship with him through Jesus and then brings healing to a created order that has been groaning under the weight of human sin.

What will this renewed heavens and earth be like?

- *It will be an environment in which we will leave behind the dark days of the past.* "For I will create a new heaven and a new earth; / the past events will not be remembered or come to mind" (Isa. 65:17).
- *It will be characterized by righteousness instead of sin.* "We wait for new heavens and a new earth, where righteousness dwells" (2 Pet. 3:13).[27]

25. We should point out that the New Testament often uses the language of "salvation" to connote the concept of redemption. But even when the New Testament uses salvation language, it can have overtones of redemption language from the Old Testament. Because of this, salvation certainly means God forgiving the sin of a person so they go to be with him when they die. But salvation, like redemption, also means that God sets things right in time and space.

26. Charles H. Spurgeon, "World on Fire (Sermon 1125)," in *The Metropolitan Tabernacle Pulpit: Containing Sermons Preached and Revised*, vol. 19 (Pasadena, TX: Pilgrim, 1969), 433–45, here 438.

27. The 2 Peter passage also speaks of the present heavens and earth being reserved for a fire on the day of judgment. Although some commentators take Peter to mean that the present

- *It will be a joyful situation in which we never again experience the pain or the consequences of sin.* "Death will be no more; grief, crying, and pain will be no more, because the previous things have passed away" (Rev. 21:4).

This is the doctrine of creation come full circle. The God who gave us the good creation recorded in the Genesis narrative is the God who will give us a renewed creation.

This new heavens and earth will be a renewal and restoration of God's good creation, but it will not be a rewinding of the clock. God's new creation will be more than a return to the original creation. Instead, when God restores his creation, he will renew it in such a way that it will be even better than the original.

- In the new creation, there will be no possibility of sin or rebellion.
- In the new creation, the original creation's garden will be a majestic city.
- In the new creation, the dwelling place of God will be with humanity eternally.

This was God's intention all along. His first commands to Adam and Eve were directives for them to develop his good creation and bring out its hidden potential. And so, the final state will be one that reflects not only God's work but also humanity's work. The Bible's description of the new Jerusalem is one that sees all of the glories and wealth of the earth coming to rest in the renewed city (Isa. 60:5–17). God will be with redeemed humanity continually, even lighting the city by the radiant glory of his Son (Rev. 21:3–4, 23). Together with God, we will reign over the new creation forever (22:5). In the new heavens and new earth, all redeemed humanity will live forever for the King.

The Redemption of the Nations

In light of the new creation, we must include a reality that we will develop more fully in chapter 9. When we live and worship in God's presence in the new heavens and earth, we will do so in the company of countless believers

---

universe will be consumed by fire, we believe that the fire referred to is a purifying fire. Richard Bauckham's interpretation is compelling: he argues that the purpose of the fire in these verses is not the obliteration but the purging of the cosmos. The cosmos will be purged of sin and its consequences, including its ecological consequences. Richard J. Bauckham, *2 Peter and Jude*, WBC 50 (Waco: Word, 1983), 316–22.

who come from every tribe, tongue, people, and nation. God's salvation is so great that it will win a great multitude of incomprehensibly diverse people.

One of the most explicit statements of this reality is found in Matthew 24:14: "This good news of the kingdom will be proclaimed in all the world as a testimony to all nations, and then the end will come." Another striking description is found in Revelation 5:9. There John conveys a vision in which worshipers from all nations are gathered around the throne, singing to our Lord, "You are worthy . . . because you were slaughtered, and you purchased people for God by your blood from every tribe and language and people and nation."

Conclusion

This multinational conclusion is a fitting way to end our exposition of the Bible's grand story. From the very beginning, God manifested his complexity and beauty by making a wonderfully diverse creation. After the fall, the world in all its diversity was marred by sin, but through Christ's redemption, it will be restored to its former beauty. God sent his Son not only to save a people but also to liberate his entire creation, making it the resplendent unity in diversity he always intended it to be.

In Christ's first coming, he launched this great salvation, and in the second coming, he will finalize it. We find ourselves living between those two comings, called to be ambassadors for the God who created us and purchased us with the blood of his Son. In the remaining chapters of this book, we will discuss how we as Christians should live until Christ returns. In a nutshell, the biblical story provides us with a beautiful and powerful message—the good news of Jesus. This good news compels us to be on mission for the King.

But what is the good news—the gospel—really? To answer this question, we need to reflect further on what we introduced in the opening chapter of this volume: we must explore how the biblical story informs the Christian worldview and establishes the Christian mission. It is to this task we now turn.

5

INTERLUDE
Worldview, Gospel, and Mission

*All authority has been given to me in heaven and on earth. Go, therefore,
and make disciples of all nations, baptizing them in the name of the
Father and of the Son and of the Holy Spirit, teaching them to observe
everything I have commanded you. And remember, I am with you always,
to the end of the age.*

Matthew 28:18–20

Introduction

We love to travel. It is in our blood. In fact, we wrote this chapter from
Amsterdam, which is full of wonderful coffee shops that overlook canals
and bustling street life. It is one of Europe's great cities, full of rich history,
extraordinary art, and storied theological vision. Now, we did not just open
the front doors of our houses in America and step into Amsterdam. Rather,
we had to go on a journey from home to there. And on our trip, we made a
stop along the way, a junction that enabled us to turn toward our destination.
If we had neglected to make the stop, we would not have been able to arrive
in this beautiful city.

In a similar way, we have arrived at a significant stop on our journey to
discover what it means to live for the King. Up to this point, we have traveled

together the terrain of the Bible. Its movement from creation to fall to redemption and new creation has helped us understand God, his world and our place in it, and the centrality of Jesus in its story. We have discovered the high mountain peaks of the New Covenant and the kingdom of God. From there, we can understand more of the question we began with: What are people for?

But we need to go further to answer that question. And to move forward, we must pause briefly and reflect on key concepts that we introduced in the opening chapter of this book: worldview, gospel, and mission. As we explained there, worldview, gospel, and mission are understood properly when they are set in relation to and emerge from the biblical story. We could describe their relationship this way:

The Christian worldview emerges from the biblical story.

The biblical story frames the gospel.

The biblical story contextualizes and empowers holistic Christian mission.

To set the stage for the final four chapters of this book, in which we explore the Christian mission in its theological, social, cultural, and global aspects, we will expand on the Christian worldview and gospel that set the stage for mission. So let's begin with worldview.

A Christian Worldview

The English word *worldview* is a translation of the German word *Weltanschauung*, which was first used in the eighteenth century by the philosopher Immanuel Kant. It is sometimes referred to as a "world and life view," or the way humans perceive and act in the world. Since the time of Kant, the term has become part of everyday discourse. But what is a worldview, really? To what are we referring when we use the term?

There are many ways to define the concept, but when we use the word, we do so in line with Michael Goheen and Craig Bartholomew, who write, "Worldview is an articulation of the basic beliefs embedded in a shared grand story that are rooted in a faith commitment and that give shape and direction to the whole of our individual and corporate lives."[1]

A worldview is generally coherent and consistent, and it helps us make sense of life and operate well within the world. A worldview enables us to articulate, a bit more tightly and systematically, basic beliefs from the

---

1. Michael W. Goheen and Craig G. Bartholomew, *Living at the Crossroads: An Introduction to Christian Worldview* (Grand Rapids: Baker Academic, 2008), 23.

biblical story. Because it operates as a kind of map from which we navigate our world, it enables us to answer certain questions about life in a way that is coherent and sensible. What is my perspective on the wrongness or rightness of violence? Is it appropriate to go to movies or listen to music? What kind of jobs are moral, and what kind are immoral? Worldview gives the framework from which one develops responses to these questions. Albert Wolters summarizes: "The decisions you make on these and many other issues are guided by your worldview. Disputes about them often involve a clash of life-perspectives."[2]

The Christian worldview emerges from the biblical story. Notice that a Christian worldview is not the same thing as the biblical story. Why is this so? A worldview is coherent, but it derives from grand stories about life and purpose. To illustrate, cultural anthropologists recognize that the world's civilizations and cultures organize their lives around shared stories and the basic cognitive, affective, and evaluative elements embedded in those stories.[3] These embedded cognitive, affective, and evaluative components compose a worldview. Philosophers sometimes organize those worldviews into broad categories such as theism, deism, naturalism, and pantheism.[4]

Similarly, the biblical narrative is the grand story from which emerges the Christian worldview. For that reason, Christians need to be able to understand and articulate the basic beliefs embedded in the Bible's overarching narrative. These beliefs should shape and give direction to our lives. They should not only describe the world for us but also prescribe for us the right way to live, speak, and act in the world. In addition, as philosopher James K. A. Smith reminds us, they should shape not only our thinking and speaking but also our desires, feelings, and values.[5] Craig Bartholomew rightly presents the relationship between worldview and the biblical story: "A worldview is not yet tightly theoretical [like a systematic philosophy or theology], but it is more systematic than an articulation of the biblical grand story. A worldview attempts to articulate the major elements of the biblical story and their coherence such that it can shape a Christian mind."[6] The major elements of

---

2. Albert M. Wolters, *Creation Regained: Biblical Basics for a Reformational Worldview* (Grand Rapids: Eerdmans, 1985), 5.

3. Paul G. Hiebert, *Cultural Anthropology* (Grand Rapids: Baker, 1983), 363–69.

4. For a concise treatment of worldviews organized according to this type of rubric, see James W. Sire, *The Universe Next Door: A Basic Worldview Catalog*, 5th ed. (Downers Grove, IL: InterVarsity, 2009).

5. James K. A. Smith, *Desiring the Kingdom: Worship, Worldview, and Cultural Formation* (Grand Rapids: Baker Academic, 2009).

6. Craig G. Bartholomew, *Introducing Biblical Hermeneutics* (Grand Rapids: Baker Academic, 2015), 52.

the biblical story that we will explore in this worldview section are the King and his kingdom, rebellion against the King, the redemption of the King, and living for the King.

The King and His Kingdom

The biblical story presents God as the great King over all things. God cannot be reduced to a local deity or an idol who sits on a shelf. The God of the Bible is bigger than our private devotional times and much larger than our church buildings. God, as depicted in Scripture, is the transcendent Creator of the universe. As the Psalms boldly teach and celebrate in song:

> For the LORD, the Most High, is awe-inspiring,
> a great King over the whole earth. (47:2)

> For the LORD is a great God,
> a great King above all gods. (95:3)

These songs celebrate the reign of God, and they reveal that his rule extends over all rivals and over the entirety of the created order: "over the whole earth." The King created the world and structured it in such a way that, if humans would live according to his design, they would flourish. God's creation is good, and the world is the place where humanity was created to appropriately relate to the King, to one another, and to the created order.

As we have seen in the biblical story, God exerts his rule through Jesus, who is heir to the Davidic throne as King of creation. In the prologue to the book of Revelation, John describes the resurrected and glorified Jesus as the "faithful witness," the "firstborn from the dead," and the "ruler of the kings of the earth" (Rev. 1:5). Jesus persevered as the witness to the Father and his plan articulated in the story of Scripture, he rose from the dead as the victor over death and hell, and he is now the King who rules over all things: "John views Jesus as the ideal Davidic king on an escalated eschatological level, whose death and resurrection have resulted in his eternal kingship and in the kingship of his 'beloved' children."[7] If Jesus is King, then no arena of the created world escapes his grand dominion. We like how Abraham Kuyper describes this truth: "There is not a square inch in the whole domain of human existence over which Christ, who is Sovereign over *all*, does not cry: 'Mine!'"[8]

---

7. G. K. Beale, *The Book of Revelation: A Commentary on the Greek Text*, NIGTC (Grand Rapids: Eerdmans, 1999), 191.

8. Abraham Kuyper, "Sphere Sovereignty," in *Abraham Kuyper: A Centennial Reader*, ed. James D. Bratt (Grand Rapids: Eerdmans, 1998), 461, italics original.

The reign of Jesus the King comes in his "eternal kingdom," which extends over the whole of the cosmos (2 Pet. 1:11).

Rebellion against the King

But despite the reign of God in and through his messiah, the biblical story presents the reality of our rebellion against the King. The first couple's sin creates a situation in which all of humanity breaks God's law and lives "against the grain" of his design. All our religious, social, and cultural doings are corrupted and misdirected by our sinful inclinations.

The story of the Bible repeatedly tells of the reality of the fall into sin. God is extraordinarily gracious, calling a wayward world back to live under his reign. But humans, even God's people Israel, whom he had blessed to be a blessing to the whole world, corrupted God's world through their sin.

It is important to remember that, structurally, God's world remained good. Its God-given design is as good as it ever was. But directionally, God's world has become bad. Human beings direct their lives toward wrong ends, toward counterfeit gods and false saviors. This sin and misdirection of our lives is the cause of the world's brokenness and of humanity's experience of evil and suffering. There is no hope of breaking out of the cycle of sin on our own. We need salvation from God. And God answers in his messiah, Jesus.

The Redemption of the King

In the face of human sin, God determined to redeem his creation. And as we have argued, God's redemption is holistic rather than limited. That is to say, the good creation is reconciled by God in Jesus Christ. The King's grace restores and redeems the created order. Through Jesus, God reconciles *all things* to himself. As the apostle Paul says, "For God was pleased to have all his fullness dwell in him [Jesus], and through him to reconcile everything to himself, whether things on earth or things in heaven, by making peace through his blood, shed on the cross" (Col. 1:19–20). Or as Jesus says about the new heavens and new earth, "Look, I am making everything new" (Rev. 21:5). In both of these instances, "everything" is not limited to spiritual things such as souls. Rather the entire creation is refitted and remade to the honor and glory of Jesus, the King.

In the past one hundred years, the world has known Oswald Chambers because of his devotional literature, especially his classic *My Utmost for His Highest*. But some of his other work needs to be explored as well. In a little-known book titled *Conformed to His Image*, Chambers puts an exclamation point on the holistic nature of the King's redemption:

The redemption [of Christ] is not only for humankind, it is for the universe, for the material earth; everything that sin and the devil have touched and marred has been completely redeemed by Jesus Christ. There is a day coming when the redemption will be actually manifested, when there will be a new heaven and a new earth, with a new humanity upon it.[9]

Chambers hits the nail on the head. If the dominion of the King is as wide as creation, then the redemption of the King is as wide as creation. Christ makes *all things* new. This means that we can be saved from our sin and for a life lived rightly under God's reign. Through Jesus, God will set the world aright one day; instead of annihilating the world, he will renew and restore it.

Living for the King

We have explored how the King has a people called the church. As we live as the people of the King, we must recognize some dichotomies that permeate our culture. These dichotomies (sometimes called dualisms) profoundly distort God's holistic redemption of his people, unhelpfully warping the story of Scripture.

The first dualism is that the people of the King operate in two worlds, a sacred world and a secular world. According to this perspective, what we do for God in the gathered church, including pastoral ministry, student ministry, teaching, worship ministry, and so on, counts as sacred, but everything else in the world is secular, including business, art, cinema, books, and the like. Missionary work overseas, evangelism, and maybe nonprofit work in places such as soup kitchens and orphanages get a pass into the sacred world, but everything else is secular.

In this dualism, the most important jobs in life are the sacred jobs, while the secular jobs are second-tier or second-class jobs. Being a pastor is sacred, but being a civil engineer or a businessperson is secular. But the biblical story reminds us that God is redeeming *all things* in Jesus Christ. Business needs redemption just as much as pastoral ministry. Instead of setting the realms against each other, we need to see their appropriate function in creation.

In his foundational work, *Creation Regained*, Albert Wolters provides some visual aids that help us overcome the sacred versus secular dualism. Table 5.1 and figure 5.1 are adapted from his work.

9. Oswald Chambers, *Conformed to His Image / The Servant as His Lord: Lessons on Living Like Jesus* (Grand Rapids: Discovery House, 1996), 13.

Table 5.1: Unbiblical Dichotomy

Secular	Sacred
Business and commerce	Church
Art and music	Pastors and elders
Politics and society	Deacons and ministers
Science and technology	Missionaries and evangelists
Education	Any church-related work

Source: Wolters, *Creation Regained*, 68.

In this dualism, anything not related to the gathered church is secular. Unfortunately, this understanding does not account for the biblical teaching on creation and redemption, as we have explored. If Christ is Lord of *all*, then *all things* are part of God's creation, and all things must be redeemed under his holy rule. Because of this:

- Church work or vocation is not of a *higher* order than any other work in God's world.
- Church work or vocation is *different* from business or art or politics but not better in quality.
- Business, art, politics, science, and education (among other work) are part of God's creation and therefore need to be brought under Christ's lordship. As such, they are not somehow neutral or secular in respect to Jesus.

What the church must discern is how Jesus's lordship extends into the whole of God's creation and human life. We do this by recognizing the antithesis that runs through our world—that is, instead of setting the secular against the sacred, we must realize that the corrupting power of sin runs through the entirety of human culture, tempting humanity away from living under the lordship of Jesus in his kingdom. Figure 5.1 offers a graphic presentation of the divide between the two. As Wolters describes, "The [dividing] line is jagged rather than straight because it represents the battle line between forces of the opposing regimes, and different areas experience varying degrees of liberation or bondage. Moreover, the line *moves*: wherever family life, for example, grows in obedience and conformity to God's creational law, there the kingdom advances and the world is pushed back."[10]

10. Wolters, *Creation Regained*, 67.

Figure 5.1

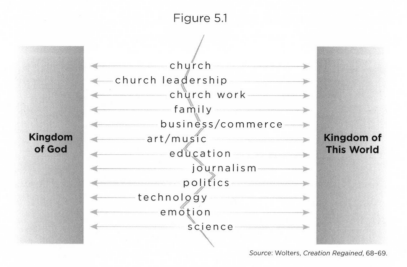

Kingdom of God   church   Kingdom of
                 church leadership   This World
                  church work
                    family
               business/commerce
                  art/music
                  education
                   journalism
                   politics
                technology
                 emotion
                  science

Source: Wolters, *Creation Regained*, 68–69.

The kingdom of this world is corrupted by sin. The kingdom of God rests under the lordship of Jesus Christ. Paul describes how the church has been brought into the kingdom of God and away from the kingdom of this world, which he calls the "domain of darkness." He writes, "He has rescued us from the domain of darkness and transferred us into the kingdom of the Son he loves. In him we have redemption, the forgiveness of sins" (Col. 1:13–14). In his letter to the Christians in Rome, Paul reminds the church not to be conformed to this world but to be transformed by the renewing of the mind, through the power of Jesus Christ (Rom. 12:2).

In every sphere of life, the people of the King must assess how the corrupting power of sin has invaded all aspects of life identified above. Where our world has gone wrong, we seek to bring it under Christ's lordship. Where our world is honoring to Jesus, we celebrate it! Wolters summarizes what it means to live for the King:

> Redemption, then, is the recovery of creational goodness through the annulment of sin [through Jesus's work on the cross] and the effort toward progressive removal of its effects everywhere [through the gospel working itself out in the church]. We return to creation through the cross, because only the atonement deals with sin and evil effectively at their root. Mark's version of the great commission bids us to "preach the good news to *all creation*" (Mark 16:15) because there is need of liberation from sin everywhere.[11]

11. Wolters, *Creation Regained*, 69.

Where our business or church or family has been misdirected by sin, we need the power of the gospel to transform us so that we can redirect the good creation to the glory of Jesus Christ. This redirection comes through the Spirit and through Scripture. The Spirit of God redeems and regenerates his people so they love the Lord and his ways. The Word of God gives us the vision and perspective to see what has gone wrong in the world and how to redirect it to honor Jesus. God's Word, then, becomes the lens through which we see the world and conform it to the demands of the gospel.

The Gospel of the King

This last sentence drives us to reflect on the gospel. We have waited for some time to explore more fully the Christian gospel, which is a powerful proclamation embedded in the biblical narrative. But what is it, and what does the gospel declare?

We get a glimpse of the gospel in Jesus's words presented in Mark 1:14–15. Jesus preaches the gospel of the kingdom and describes it as "good news." The gospel of the kingdom is the good news that God reigns over his people in the world, but to enter into that kingdom people must repent of their sin and believe in the good news! Jesus's proclamation recorded in these verses helps us understand that the word *gospel* is a sort of media term: it is the most significant breaking news of all time. And it is good news!

Ancient extrabiblical literature uses the term *gospel (euangelion)* in similar ways to what we find in the New Testament. In the ancient world, *gospel* was a word that described an announcement of important events that a king had accomplished: the capture of a city, the defeat of an imposing army, the entrance of the king into a town, or other messages about a king's activities.[12] Similarly, when the word *gospel* or "good news" is used in Scripture (as we saw in Mark 1:14–15), it is almost always used as a message or proclamation about something.

What is the content of the breaking news? In a word, Jesus! But to be more precise, it is news about *who Jesus is* and *what he has done*. One of the clearest passages that helps us understand the Christian gospel is 1 Corinthians 15:1–5. This is one of the few passages of Scripture in which the word *gospel* is accompanied by a definition of the word. As historian John Dickson puts it, this passage serves as a helpful "bullet point summary of the gospel."[13] In

12. John P. Dickson, "Gospel as News: *Euangel* from Aristophanes to the Apostle Paul," *NTS* 51, no. 2 (2005): 212–30.

13. John P. Dickson, *The Best Kept Secret of Christian Mission: Promoting the Gospel with More Than Our Lips* (Grand Rapids: Zondervan, 2010), 116.

this passage, the apostle Paul reproduces one of the earliest, if not the earliest, creeds of the Christian church. He writes,

> Now I want to make clear for you, brothers and sisters, the gospel I preached to you, which you received, on which you have taken your stand and by which you are being saved, if you hold to the message I preached to you—unless you believed in vain. For I passed on to you as most important what I also received: that Christ died for our sins according to the Scriptures, that he was buried, that he was raised on the third day according to the Scriptures, and that he appeared to Cephas, then to the Twelve.

According to Paul, therefore, the gospel is an announcement that Paul received and now passes on to others. Significantly, it is an announcement about Jesus. The good news is the following:

1. Jesus is the Christ (the promised messiah).
2. Jesus died a saving death.
3. Jesus died a saving death *for sin*.
4. Jesus died and was buried.
5. Jesus was raised from the dead.
6. Jesus's death and resurrection were in line with the Scriptures' teaching.
7. Jesus's resurrection is a public truth revealed to many witnesses.

Let's break down these points.

Jesus Is the Long-Promised Savior-King

First and foremost, the gospel declares that Jesus of Nazareth is the Christ, the Messiah that God had promised for millennia. In 1–2 Samuel and 1–2 Kings, the messiah is the anointed one, the promised Israelite king who would come from the Davidic line. He is the anointed one who will rule the nations (Ps. 2), the one who will atone for the sins of Israel and the nations (Isa. 53:3–10), and the one who will bring renewal to the whole of the created order (Isa. 65). The resurrected Jesus of Nazareth, the one who was slaughtered publicly on a cross, is, quite literally, the King over all creation!

For Paul, this is not an insignificant point. Before going on to articulate the gospel in full, he must declare Jesus's credentials as the promised messiah. Only in this context does the gospel make sense. The gospel declares that Jesus is the messianic King who was described in Israel's Scriptures and anticipated from long ago.

Practically speaking, this means that one of a Christian's goals in sharing the gospel is to help people understand that Jesus is the Savior that God had promised for millennia. People must see him for who he is in his fullness rather than holding a reductionist view of him (e.g., that Jesus is merely an exemplary moral teacher). People must know who he is before they can truly grasp what he has done on their behalf.

Jesus the King Died a Saving Death for Sin

Paul's bullet-point summary of the gospel reveals more than Jesus's messianic credentials. Taking note of points two and three above, the good news also speaks of Jesus's saving actions. Jesus died a saving death. The cosmic King died on our behalf. He died for sinners like you and me in order to save us from our sin and for a life of good works under his good and wise reign. This is important because it clearly reminds us that we are sinful and in need of a Savior. We cannot save ourselves. The *gospel* is good news because it reveals that salvation from sin belongs to our God!

Any gospel that undercuts or ignores Jesus's saving death is a false gospel. Jesus's saving death stands at the center of the gospel and is like a resplendent jewel with many beautiful facets. Let's look at some of them. In his death, Christ

paid for our sins once and for all (Isa. 53:4–6; Heb. 9:28);

justified us and gave us life (Rom. 5:16–18) so that "therefore there is now no condemnation for those in Christ Jesus" (Rom. 8:1);

bought us out of slavery to sin (1 Cor. 6:19–20) and liberated us from the prison created by our sin (Isa. 61:1–2; Luke 4:18);

appeased God's wrath toward sin (Rom. 3:25) and cleansed us from the defilement caused by sin (Isa. 43:25);

reconciled us to himself (Col. 1:19–20) and to one another (Eph. 2:11–18);

set the world to rights (Rom. 8:21, 23; Eph. 1:10; Col. 1:19–20) so that we can live with him together in a renewed and restored universe.

When we see all the brilliant facets of the great jewel of Christ's saving death, we discover that one of a Christian's goals when sharing the gospel is to help people realize the weight of their sin and the necessity of looking to Christ to save them from it.

The Resurrected Messiah, Seen by Many

Paul's last four points in the list above are important because they proclaim that Jesus the King died and rose again in history, in real space and time, and that his resurrection is public truth. Jesus's death was not an illusion or a figment of someone's imagination. Jesus really died. And he really was buried.

But because Jesus is raised, his death is not the last chapter in his life. Rather, it is the dark moment before the dawn, when new life breaks into our world.

In his resurrection, Jesus the King is given authority and power from God to rule as the sovereign over all creation. The resurrected Jesus says in Revelation 21:5, "Look, I am making everything new." Only a resurrected King can renew the created order! The gospel is not good news without Christ buried *and resurrected from the dead*.

Jesus's appearance to many witnesses (1 Cor. 15:5–8) not only confirms his resurrection to skeptics but also announces the gospel as a public truth. Lesslie Newbigin writes, "When the Church affirms the gospel as public truth it is challenging the whole of society to wake . . . and to accept the calling which is addressed to every human being to seek, acknowledge, and proclaim the truth. For we are that part of God's creation which he has equipped with the power to know the truth and to speak the praise of the whole creation in response to the truthfulness of the Creator."[14] So Paul can say quite clearly in Romans, "Christ died and returned to life for this: that he might be Lord over both the dead and the living" (14:9). The resurrected Christ is Lord over creation, and his resurrection invites us to live under his rule.

In practice, this means that Christians who share the good news of Jesus should help people understand that Christ rose from the dead. In fact, many people saw Jesus after he rose from the dead, and this public truth can be tested and proved. In addition, his resurrection validates his claim to divinity: the one who defeated death is God. His resurrection provides a preview of the way he will raise sinners to new life: we will be raised to eternal life with him. His resurrection reveals the future hope: the resurrected King will one day resurrect the heavens and earth so that they no longer groan under the weight of sin.

What Is the Gospel in Brief?

We have seen how Paul summarizes the gospel in 1 Corinthians 15:1–5. Taking cues from Paul, we might summarize the gospel by saying:

---

14. Lesslie Newbigin, *Truth to Tell: The Gospel as Public Truth* (Grand Rapids: Eerdmans, 1991), 13.

The gospel is a public announcement that God's kingdom arrived in the life, death, and resurrection of Jesus, who is King and Savior, in fulfillment of Old Testament prophecy. The gospel calls for belief, trust, and repentance; in it, God promises that those who heed this call will live with him eternally in the new heavens and new earth.

To put it even more briefly, a Christian could say:

The gospel is the announcement that Jesus the King died to save us from the death caused by sin and rose from the grave to provide new life and purpose today and forever.

Any summary of the gospel is just that—a summary—which means that it will necessarily leave out some of the fullness of the gospel. Gospel summaries ought to drive us more deeply into the Bible to explore its rich exposition of the gospel.

What Is the Christian Mission?

As we reflect on this great gospel—and the biblical storyline from which it emerges—we realize that God's mission involves redeeming his people and restoring his good creation. Or as Jason Allen puts it, "Christianity is not relegated to a couple of 'spiritual' activities a week. . . . The gospel invades our work, our leisure, our errands, and our families. In short, the gospel redeems and transforms all of life."[15]

The good news of Jesus is an invitation to be part of this new transformed community. Through his life, death, and resurrection, he saves sinners from sin and its consequences and for a life under his reign. Based on his death and resurrection, he will one day renew and restore the universe, which is in bondage to sin. When the Son returns, he will resurrect the universe and the bodies of believers so that we can live with him forever in the new heavens and earth.

Both the biblical story and the gospel reveal that the mission of a restored humanity is to glorify God by participating appropriately in his mission.

Because God desires to save sinners from sin and for a life under his reign, we declare to the world his offer of salvation. Because he promises to restore his good creation, we live the creaturely and cultural aspects of our lives in

15. Jason K. Allen, *Being a Christian: How Jesus Redeems All of Life* (Nashville: B&H, 2018), 8.

such a way that the world will know that Christ is our Lord. We do this as a matter of obedience and witness and out of delight for and gratitude to our Lord and Savior. In addition, we live our everyday lives in such a way that we provide a preview of the new heavens and earth, where Christ will establish his reign of justice, peace, and love. In this way, the Christian community provides for the world a seamless tapestry of words and deeds that point to Christ the King and the salvation he provides.

Central to the Christian mission is international mission. After Christ rises from the dead, he appears to his disciples and tells them to make disciples of all the nations. The significance of this command is highlighted and affirmed repeatedly throughout the New Testament (e.g., Matt. 28:18–20) but nowhere more so than in the fifth chapter of the book of Revelation. In this chapter, John receives a vision from God in which a vast multitude from every tribe, tongue, people, and nation gathers around Christ to worship him. This multitude has been redeemed by the blood of the Lamb and now worships him together. In light of God's concern to redeem sinners from among the nations, we as Christians should keep international mission at the center of the church's mission.

Theological, Social, Cultural, Global

In the second half of this book, we will expand on the Christian mission by examining four of its aspects: theological, social, cultural, and global. As you read the next four chapters, you will notice that the four aspects of Christian mission overlap with one another quite a bit. So they are not airtight categories but provisional categories that are helpful for reflecting on the Christian mission.

The Christian mission is *theological* in that it flows out of a person-to-person relationship with the one and only true God. Our love for God fuels our mission in his service. Our mission is also *social* in that it involves interaction with other people made in the image of God. When we speak the gospel to our neighbor, love and serve our fellow church members, or serve in a mercy ministry, we are participating in social aspects of the mission. In addition, our mission is *cultural*. When we honor Christ in our college studies or in our workplaces, we are participating in the cultural aspect of the mission. When we bring our Christian faith to bear on art, science, politics, education, business, or homemaking, we are living missionally in the cultural dimension of our existence. Finally, our mission is *global*. The Bible makes clear that global mission is near to God's heart and central to the Christian mission. We want to preach the gospel and plant churches among every known people group and every known language on earth. When we do so, the churches we plant will be able to live out the Christian mission—theologically, socially, and culturally—among their own people and extend it outward—globally—to other peoples.

A Seamless and Interdependent Whole

These four aspects of the Christian mission are not exclusive of one another. In fact, they go hand in hand. Having a healthy relationship with the one true God (theological) will cause us to seek fellowship with God's people, share the gospel with those who are lost, and engage in mercy ministries to help those in need (social). Further, our relationship with God will inevitably manifest itself in our workplaces and leisure activities (cultural). Similarly, our love for God should naturally lead us to participate in international mission by praying for the lost among the nations, supporting missionaries financially, or going as a missionary to the nations (global).

Just as these four aspects of the Christian mission live in a reciprocal relationship with one another, so do word-based and deed-based ministries. The Christian mission goes forward on the back of both types of ministries. We can compare the relationship between words and deeds to the relationship between a wheel's rim (deeds) and its hub (words). In order for a wheel to move forward, it needs both. Without the hub (gospel words), the wheel will collapse. Without the rim (gospel-centered actions), the hub will have great difficulty moving forward.

Just as a wheel moves forward because its hub and rim are working together, so the Christian mission moves forward through a combination of gospel words and gospel-motivated actions. Without gospel words, the Christian mission collapses. Without deeds, it has difficulty getting traction. Although not every word will be accompanied by a deed, or vice versa, Christians should be looking to witness and obey with words and deeds at all times. So the Christian mission combines theological, social, cultural, and global aspects. And these are mutually reinforcing, each combining words and deeds. Mission, then, is holistic in its scope.

Now, some Christians might resist this idea of a holistic Christian mission. They might understand Christ's redemption as something that transforms a person's private life and personal ethics and that therefore the Christian mission is limited to certain circumscribed activities such as interpersonal evangelism or international evangelism. Under this view of Christianity, social action, cultural engagement, and the like are not, *cannot be*, the realm of mission.

In response, we affirm that interpersonal evangelism and international evangelism are central and vital to the Christian mission. But we also encourage Christians to ask, "How far does Christ's redemption go?" The best answer to that question is that Jesus's lordship is as wide as creation. And if his lordship is as wide as creation, then the Christian mission is as wide as creation—and, by extension, as wide as society and culture. A redeemed humanity who lives under the lordship of Jesus should, therefore, seek to conform to his lordship in every sector of society and sphere of culture. In other words, the redemption and lordship of Christ should cause us to hold a holistic view of mission.

Conclusion

The great Baptist theologian W. T. Conner saw holistic mission not as a problem but as a prerequisite to understanding the nature of the new life found in Jesus Christ. The quotation below is long, but it is a fitting way to conclude this discussion on mission and to frame the final four chapters. In 1945, Conner wrote:

> The Christian mission is to do all the good he can in every realm of life, in every possible way. He is to make regnant the will of God in the whole extent of human life and society. There is no conflict between serving God and helping men. Surely the Christ who healed the bodies of men and performed a miracle to feed the hungry multitude does not represent a God who is displeased with anything that makes this world a better place in which to live. The type of piety that thinks that the only function of religion is to cause a man to withdraw into some monastery and save his own soul and let the world go to the devil—that type of piety belongs to the middle ages, if it belongs anywhere. Nor is the only function of Christianity to save the souls of men from hell in the next life; they need to be made righteous in every relation of life. The regeneration of the individual and the regeneration of society should never be put over against each other as antithetical things; it is not a question of one to the exclusion of the other. They are rather two things that are mutually dependent. The only way to regenerate society is through the regeneration of the individual units of society. And the only power that can regenerate the individual is the gospel of Jesus Christ. Nor has the gospel done its full work in the life of the individual unless he is made right in every relation to life. The gospel makes a man live right in the world, not withdraw from the world.[16]

16. W. T. Conner, *The Gospel of Redemption* (Nashville: Broadman, 1945), 221–22.

6

A THEOLOGICAL MISSION

Radical Monotheism for a Secular Age

*Listen, Israel: The L*ORD *our God, the L*ORD *is one. Love the L*ORD *your God with all your heart, with all your soul, and with all your strength.*

Deuteronomy 6:4–5

Introduction

Russian winters are not known to offer a wide variety of options for how to spend one's evenings. When the temperature remains below zero—sometimes thirty or forty degrees below zero—for months at a time, there is little to do. So when I (Bruce) found myself living in Russia during the winters of 1998 and 1999, I had a great deal of time on my hands. And that is when I first discovered Aleksandr Solzhenitsyn's *The Gulag Archipelago*. Totaling nearly two thousand pages in the English translation, this massive three-volume work kept me busy for more than a few evenings. (I advise readers not to read *The Gulag* in bed, for fear they might fall asleep and be crushed to death midsentence.)

The Gulag is a literary investigation into the Soviet labor camp system known as the Gulag Archipelago, a system in which Solzhenitsyn had been imprisoned and subjected to hard labor and torture for nine years (1945–53). In it, Solzhenitsyn relies on his own experience and the eyewitness testimony of some two hundred survivors to narrate the horrors of the Soviet Union's vast array of prisons, camps, informants, interrogators, spies, and secret police as well as the heroism of ordinary Russian citizens and prisoners. In large part, the literary power of the book arises from Solzhenitsyn's ability to use stories, images, and firsthand encounters to stamp indelibly on the reader's mind the evils of the Soviet era.

No reader of *The Gulag* can forget the introduction to Solzhenitsyn's chapter "Interrogation," in which he reflects on how horrified earlier Russian writers and intellectuals would have been if they had been able to foresee the horrors of the Gulag:

> If the intellectuals in the plays of Chekhov, who spent all their time guessing what would happen in twenty, thirty, or forty years, had been told that in forty years interrogation by torture would be practiced in Russia; that prisoners would have skulls squeezed with iron rings; that a human being would be lowered into an acid bath . . . and that, in the luckiest possible circumstances, prisoners would be tortured by being kept from sleeping for a week, by thirst, and by being beaten to a bloody pulp, not one of Chekhov's plays would have gotten to its end because all of the heroes would have gone off to insane asylums.[1]

Indeed, during the years between the 1917 revolution and the mid-twentieth century, estimates reveal that Soviet authorities killed four to five thousand persons *per week*.

How could so great an evil take root and flourish in the twentieth century? Solzhenitsyn's answer is that, in the Soviet Union's case, many of its most powerful political and cultural influencers were attempting to build a society without reference to God, but such vainglorious intentions led to devastating results. In his famous quip on receiving the Templeton Prize, Solzhenitsyn says the cause of the deaths of sixty million Russians is a result of the Communist revolution: "Men have forgotten God; that's why all this has happened."[2] Similarly, in a chapter of *The Gulag* titled "The Ascent," he explains that the universe possesses a God-given moral law, a divine code of permissions and prohibitions, and for this reason it is always illegitimate for a state to try to redraw the lines between good and evil.[3] For this reason, Solzhenitsyn rejected the Communist Party's attempts to refashion morality in its own image and

---

1. Aleksandr I. Solzhenitsyn, *The Gulag Archipelago 1918–1956: An Experiment in Literary Investigation*, trans. Thomas P. Whitney, 2 vols. (New York: Harper & Row, 1973), 1:93.

2. Aleksandr I. Solzhenitsyn, "Templeton Lecture, London, Guildhall, May 10, 1983," in *The Solzhenitsyn Reader: New and Essential Writings, 1947–2005*, ed. Edward E. Ericson Jr. and Daniel J. Mahoney (Wilmington, DE: Intercollegiate Studies Institute, 2006), 577.

3. Solzhenitsyn, *Gulag Archipelago*, 2:615.

for its own purposes. This atheistic utilitarianism, Solzhenitsyn argues, was no mere "side effect, but the central pivot" of the party's policy.[4]

My years in Russia provided the perfect context for reflecting on the negative consequences of trying to build a society without reference to God—for two reasons.

First, although the Soviet Union dissolved a few years before I moved to Russia, its former member states, including Russia, were still reeling from the coerced secularization of that era. Because I was working as an instructor at several universities in Kazan, Russia, I interacted daily with Russian professors and students as well as their friends and family members. Most of them were deeply skeptical about whether God exists, whether life has any meaning, and whether there are any moral absolutes. Russia's culture—including its art, education, government, businesses, and families—reflected this deep sense of loss.

Second, I was able to compare and contrast the Russian situation with my home context, the United States. I expected to see mostly differences, but other than some rather obvious surface-level variances, I saw many similarities. Although Americans had never experienced a Soviet-style oppression of Christianity, the United States was experiencing its own version of secularization. I had recently graduated from a college in which many of the students harbored the same skepticism about God, meaning, and morality. I saw that our society and cultural institutions, too, were slowly but steadily beginning to reflect the same deep sense of loss.

I found Solzhenitsyn's Templeton Lecture very helpful in making sense of this reality. In this widely acclaimed speech, he explains how the West suffers from the same debilitating godlessness that gave birth to the Soviet Union. Although the West's secularization process has not been as dramatic or as forthright as that of the Soviet Union, it has nonetheless surely but steadily subverted traditional notions of good and evil, replacing them with "political or class considerations of short lived value."[5] The type of secularization Solzhenitsyn is describing, and that which I saw with fresh eyes after my time in Russia, is a radical and idolatrous attempt to re-envision the self and society independently from God. It is a gross reduction of the fabric of reality that neglects the world's Creator, which the biblical story reveals.

In light of such idolatry, we must reintroduce the Bible's radical monotheism, in which the one true and living God offers to set us free from our sin and for a new way of life in which we bring the totality of our personal, social,

---

4. Solzhenitsyn, "Templeton Lecture," 579.
5. Solzhenitsyn, "Templeton Lecture," 581.

and cultural lives into conformity with his good will. And if we are going to reintroduce the Bible's radical monotheism effectively, we need to understand both the nature of idolatry today, especially in the secular Western world, and the Bible's radical monotheism.

Our Secular Age

The unblushing and public nature of Western idolatry today can be explained in three words: our secular age. The contemporary era in Western civilization represents a radical desacralizing of the social order, a move that is unprecedented in human history. Dietrich Bonhoeffer described it as a "world come of age," an era in which we have learned how to manage life without any reference to God.[6] American sociologist Philip Rieff refers to it as the third era in human history, one in which the West's cultural power brokers have attempted to remake its cultural institutions and society without reference to Christianity, leaving Westerners in a world without transcendent meaning or morality.[7]

Bonhoeffer's and Rieff's analyses are helpful, and we will return to Rieff's analysis in chapter 8, but for now we will lean on the work of Canadian philosopher Charles Taylor, who, more than any other, has explored the implications of secularization for the Western psyche.[8] In *A Secular Age*, Taylor describes our era as one in which many people not only disbelieve in God but also consider belief in God implausible and even unimaginable.[9] People view the world based entirely on what they can see or experience and without any reference to a God who exists outside their sight or experience. Taylor describes this situation by saying that Westerners live within an "immanent" frame of reference.

In the immanent frame, belief in God has been displaced from the default position, becoming merely one option among many—and an implausible and unimaginable one at that. The immanent frame brings with it a new "feel" in which believers and unbelievers alike are haunted by doubt. When we reflect on

6. Dietrich Bonhoeffer, "Letter to Eberhard Bethge (June 8, 1944)," in *Letters and Papers from Prison*, Dietrich Bonhoeffer Works 8 (Minneapolis: Fortress, 2010), 425–27.

7. Philip Rieff, *My Life among the Deathworks: Illustrations of the Aesthetics of Authority*, ed. Kenneth S. Piver, Sacred Order / Social Order 1 (Charlottesville: University of Virginia Press, 2006), 1–44.

8. The reflections on Charles Taylor in this section are adapted with permission from Bruce Riley Ashford, "Tayloring Christian Politics in Our Secular Age," *Themelios* 42, no. 3 (2017): 446–51.

9. Charles Taylor, *A Secular Age* (Cambridge, MA: Belknap Press, 2007), 83.

life's meaning, we find a mind-boggling variety of options for how to answer the question. As a result, we become vulnerable and confused, or "fragilized," as Taylor calls it. Surrounded by competing answers to life's biggest questions, we lack confidence in our own beliefs. Thus, we are "cross-pressured," Taylor argues, caught between the secularization of our culture, on the one hand, and the haunting thought that there might be a transcendent God after all, on the other. We find ourselves in perpetual unease.

Notice that Taylor is not saying that most Westerners are atheist or agnostic. He is not saying that religion is disappearing in the West. He does recognize that a great many people, including many of the cultural elite, find it difficult or impossible to believe at all. But more to the point, he argues that religious narratives are contested by so many rival narratives that even religious believers lack deep-level confidence in their own beliefs.

Thus, in a secular age such as ours, Taylor argues, Christians should avoid the error of secular humanists and Christian fundamentalists—namely, presenting our views with a smug condescension.[10] Instead, we should present our faith humbly and sensitively to our cross-pressured and fragilized neighbors, suggesting that Christianity provides the key to human flourishing, ethical living, and the unease caused by realities such as death. In short, we should allow Christian wisdom and virtue to animate our lives and shape our response. And such wisdom emerges from the biblical narrative.

Taylor's account of modernity is richly suggestive and helpful for Christians who recognize that the gospel is a public truth that therefore must be brought into an interface with secularized society and culture.[11] It is helpful for Christians who wish to make Christianity plausible and imaginable again in Western society and culture. As we saw in chapter 5, the gospel is a public truth, and we want it to prevail appropriately on public life. The early church preached the gospel in a way that introduced the God of Jesus Christ to a Roman Empire full of pagan polytheists who considered the incarnation and resurrection implausible and even unimaginable. How can we do the same in our own context? How can we make the Christian gospel once again plausible and imaginable in our fragilized and cross-pressured era?

As Taylor argues, we cannot offer a merely intellectual remedy. If we wish to make the gospel once again imaginable in our liberal society, we

10. Taylor, *Secular Age*, 549–51.

11. The gospel is a public truth in the sense that it announces publicly God's rule as King. The early church proclaimed the gospel in a way that exposed the Roman kingdom as a fraud. It is God through Jesus, not Rome via Caesar, who rules over all. See John P. Dickson, "Gospel as News: *Euangel* from Aristophanes to the Apostle Paul," *NTS* 51, no. 2 (2005): 212–30; Lesslie Newbigin, *Truth to Tell: The Gospel as Public Truth* (Grand Rapids: Eerdmans, 1991).

must not only make an intellectual argument but also offer the world a storied community who embodies its truth.[12] To Taylor's argument, we would add that both the church is this community and the Bible provide its narrative. The church is the community that lives for the King. The church's witness—through words and deeds—can make Christianity plausible and imaginable again.

Monotheism and Mission

Radical Monotheism

From creation all the way through to restoration, the biblical narrative makes vigorously clear not only that God exists but also that there is only one true and living God. The Bible's first assertion is, "In the beginning God created the heavens and the earth" (Gen. 1:1). We may have grown accustomed to this statement, even bored with it, but this is one of the most revolutionary claims in history. This declaration set Genesis apart from other ancient Near Eastern creation accounts, all of which told of multiple male and female gods who were involved in the act of creation and who were themselves created beings.[13] Genesis, by flatly stating that *God* created the heavens and earth, disclosed that there was no other God. This is the oldest codified assertion of what we now call monotheism.

It is difficult to overstate the radical distinctiveness of monotheism. Genesis's opening statement would have seemed as absurd and dramatic in an ancient polytheistic age as it does in our own secular age—though for different reasons. A number of atheist intellectuals, such as Richard Dawkins and Sam Harris, consider it perfectly obvious that God does not exist, arguing that Christian belief is delusional and even evil.[14] Many other people in our secular age do not mock Christianity as Dawkins and Harris do, but they are very skeptical about it. Similarly, ancient Near Eastern audiences would have had great difficulty believing the monotheistic claims of the Genesis account, and some would have even scoffed. In the midst of that polytheistic world, Scripture opened with a thundering statement of God's uniqueness.

12. Taylor, *Secular Age*, 729.
13. See, for example, "Epic of Creation," in *Myths from Mesopotamia: Creation, the Flood, Gilgamesh, and Others,* ed. and trans. Stephanie Dalley, rev. ed. (Oxford: Oxford University Press, 2000), 233–77; Hesiod, "Theogony," in *Theogony Works and Days,* trans. M. L. West (Oxford: Oxford University Press, 1999), 3–33.
14. Among many of their works, see Richard Dawkins, *The God Delusion* (Boston: Mariner Books, 2008); and Sam Harris, *The End of Faith: Religion, Terror, and the Future of Reason* (New York: Norton, 2005).

We can also see the unique identity of Israel's God in Israel's fundamental statement of belief, known as the Shema. It expresses the truth of God's singularity and uniqueness and the implications for life in this world: "Hear, O Israel: The LORD our God, the LORD is one! You shall love the LORD your God with all your heart, with all your soul, and with all your strength" (Deut. 6:4–5 NKJV).

Notice that the Shema does not stop with the affirmation that there is only one God (radical enough) but goes further and identifies this God. He is "our" God, meaning the God of Israel, the God of the Bible. When God called Moses at the burning bush, he identified himself as "the LORD, the God of your fathers, the God of Abraham, the God of Isaac, and the God of Jacob" (Exod. 3:15). Later in the New Testament, Jesus claims to be the same one God who revealed himself to Moses at the burning bush (John 8:58; cf. Exod. 3:14), Paul writes that there is "one Lord, Jesus Christ" (1 Cor. 8:4–6), and the Gospels teach that God is Father, Son, and Spirit (Matt. 3:16–17).

So there is only one God, and he makes himself known as the God of Israel, the God of Jesus Christ, and the God who is a Trinity. Because there is only one true God, it follows that our worship should be directed toward him alone and not toward any other counterfeit god.

In Deuteronomy, God commands, "You shall have no other gods before me" (5:7 NRSV). In its immediate context, this command prohibited Israel from worshiping the gods of the pagan nations, territorial idols representing the religion of each nation. In its broader and more metaphorical application, however, it forbids us from elevating any created being or thing—such as sexual pleasure, wealth accumulation, political power, vocational success, peer approval—to the level of ultimacy that God alone deserves. To elevate a created being or thing to a level of ultimacy is to worship a counterfeit god or idol.

Idolatry is just as alive and well in our secular age as it was when those words were written, which means that our age isn't so "secular" after all. Our idols are rarely golden statues to which we bow down; we usually prefer to pour our souls into metaphorical idols, such as the ones listed above. But our idols are no less real for their intangibility and no less pernicious than the gods surrounding Israel. Only God should be worshiped; only he should be given our ultimate trust, love, and obedience.

God's supreme lordship does not demand simply that we avoid idols. It also demands that we worship him with *all* of who we are. In the Shema, the declaration of God's oneness is followed immediately by a call to love him with the totality of our being. "You shall love the LORD your God with all your heart, with all your soul, and with all your strength" (Deut. 6:5 NKJV). In the

Hebrew language, these words—heart, soul, and strength—indicate a totality of one's being. The word *heart* (*lebab*) denotes the center of a person's inner life, including their intellect, emotions, and will. The word *soul* (*nephesh*) denotes the center of one's religious life, will, passions, and emotions. The word *strength* (*me'od*) denotes the totality of one's physical functions and capacities. In other words, God relates to us as whole persons, calling us into loving relationship with him. He wants us—all of us—for himself alone. And all that we do in life (whether work, friendship, politics, sports, or leisure) should be reflective of our primary love for our God.

God calls us to love him personally with our total being. He calls us to a full-bodied and warmhearted relationship with him. But what does this have to do with our lives as Christians? How does this relate to our mission in the world? The answer is intuitive. If there is only one God, and if he calls all people in all places to worship him with all their being, then we his people are called to point others to him so that they may worship him also.

Relational Monotheism

The Bible's radical monotheism is profoundly relational. We have seen this in the biblical story. Although God is distinct from his creation, he interacts with his created beings, speaking to them, being present with them, loving them.

But even before he relates to his creation, he relates to himself as a Trinity. Father, Son, and Spirit have related to one another for all of eternity. For obvious reasons, this teaching is rejected by atheists, but it is also rejected by followers of other religions. If we were to speak about God's triunity to Buddhists, they might say something like, "There is a one-world soul, but there is no 'personal God' who relates to his creation." If we were to mention it to Muslims, they might say something to the effect of, "God is one, and his oneness cannot include diversity." In response, the Christian message is that God exists (contra atheism) and that he relates not only to himself (contra Islam) but also personally to his creation (contra Buddhism).

Although God's nature as three in one is difficult to comprehend, the concept of unity in diversity is not without analogies in the created world. By way of example, the Bible treats a married couple as two persons in one flesh (Gen. 2:24). It speaks of the human being as one person composed of both body and soul. It describes the church as one organism composed of many believers. Although the Trinity as *sui generis* (one of a kind) cannot be compared exactly with anything in the created order, we can still use these other unities in diversity as examples to help people understand the Bible's teaching.

Scripture never uses the term *Trinity*, but Christians agree that this term best explains the biblical teaching about the one God who is Father, Son, and Spirit. Scripture teaches that God is one in essence and three in persons. Another way to put it is that the one true and living God possesses three centers of consciousness that are capable of communicating, communing with one another, and working together with one another.

God the *Father* is the source, initiator, and fountainhead of divine activity. Scripture illustrates this by comparing a speaker to his Word (John 1:1), by comparing the Father to the Son as the sun is to its brightness (Heb. 1:3), and by other analogies. The *Son* is a word, an expression, and an exhibition. Scripture illustrates this by declaring that the Son is the Word of the Father (John 1:1) and an exact representation of the Father (Heb. 1:3). The *Spirit* is the one who proceeds from the Father (1 Cor. 2:12) and the Son (John 20:21–23), enabling us, his creatures, to understand God and his Word. Scripture illustrates this by describing the Spirit as the one who enables and illumines.

When God acts, all three persons are acting together as one, and yet, each of the three acts with a distinct emphasis. Take, for example, the act of revelation. When God speaks, we understand the Father to be the speaker, the Son to be the Word spoken, and the Spirit to be the one who illumines that Word and enables us to comprehend and believe it. And yet, even though we see each of the persons as performing one aspect of the act of revelation, in reality, all three of them are performing all the aspects together. Theologians refer to this as *perichoresis* (mutual interpenetration).

In summary, God is a triunity, a Trinity. He is one spiritual essence with three persons or centers of consciousness. The three persons of the Trinity have a relationship in which they enjoy mutual fellowship, communication, and activity.

Therefore, because God is inherently relational, he relates also to us, his creatures. Consider the words God gave Moses to declare to Israel: "Now therefore, if you will indeed obey My voice and keep My covenant, then you shall be a special treasure to Me above all people; for all the earth is Mine. And you shall be to Me a kingdom of priests and a holy nation" (Exod. 19:5–6 NKJV).

In effect, God said to Israel the same thing he now says to the church: "I am a God who speaks to you, reveals himself to you, and makes a covenant with you. Yes, I make a promise to you that I treasure you and will make you the type of people who live according to my design for you and who, therefore, will testify to the world that I am the one true and living God." Just as God chose Israel to be a holy nation and a kingdom of priests, so he calls the church to be a holy people who witnesses to the world (1 Pet. 2:9).

God has called us into loving relationship with him. He has allowed us to know and love him and to be known and loved by him. But this relationship is never to be viewed as membership into an elite club or enjoyed merely for our own benefit. God established this relationship with us so that we can be conduits of his love to the world, so that he can work through us to publicly display himself and his salvation to the world. When we trust, love, and obey God, our lives serve as windows through which our friends, family members, coworkers, and neighbors might peer in order to see God's worth and goodness. Our lives are to declare to the world, "There is one God—one majestic and good God—worthy of your all."

But how can we put God's all-surpassing worth and beauty on display through our worship? In what ways does the Bible talk about this personal-theological aspect of the Christian mission? If our lives are windows, what exactly should those around us see through those windows?

In a nutshell, they should see a God determined to set the world aright, to restore it, to bring healing and redirection to the world's corruption and misdirection.

Restorational Monotheism

If not for the brutal Russian winters mentioned at the beginning of this chapter, we might never have discovered that God's salvation is restorative. What does it mean to say that his salvation is restorative? To answer this question, we need to return to the Bible's narrative and explore the meaning of creation, fall, and redemption and the relationship between them.

Think back to God's creation of the world. God called the world into existence, ordered it by means of his word, and stepped back from his work to say, in effect, "This is very good. This is the way things ought to be." Now think about the fall and how humanity's sin has warped and twisted God's good world. One way to talk about the fall's effects on God's world is to speak of God's thesis and sin's antithesis. A thesis is an assertion, and while God's thesis was that the world he had created and ordered was very good, Satan's antithesis (his assertion against God's assertion) is that God's thesis should be questioned and even rejected. In the aftermath of Adam and Eve's sin, the world has continued to be characterized by conflict between God's thesis and Satan's antithesis.

Although the Bible does not use the words *thesis* and *antithesis*, the concepts can be clearly seen throughout. When God created the world, he ordered it so that there would be plants and animals, land and water, men and women, and—as we would later learn—art and science, scholarship and education, politics and economics, business and entrepreneurship, sports and competition. In a word, his good world would be both creational and cultural. That is why God's first commands to humanity (be fruitful and multiply; till the soil; have dominion) directed them to work within creation's order to worship him by engaging in social and cultural activities.

Since that fateful day, however, when Adam and Eve believed and trusted the serpent's word, humanity's words and actions have been warped and twisted by sin. As humans, we find ourselves always living in the tension between God's thesis and Satan's ever-present antithesis. This antithesis takes many forms, but it is any word spoken against God's Word, anything that corrupts or misdirects God's good intentions for his world. To use the terms we introduced in the second chapter, the created world remains structurally good, but our sin consistently corrupts it directionally, twisting it toward wrong ends.

God's response to the antithesis was not to destroy the world and start over again but to renew and restore the world he had already made. The world had become sick, but his saving grace would cure it. Although we, his imagers, had been shot through with the poison of sin, God would send his Son as an antidote to absorb sin's curse and eventually heal our bodies. Similarly, although the physical world has been corrupted and misdirected by humanity's sinful words and deeds, God will send his Son a second time to renew and restore it. Christ's death and resurrection are God's promise that he will provide redemption not only for sinful humanity but also for the cosmos (Rom. 8:19–22; Rev. 21:1).

The Dutch theologian Abraham Kuyper described this renewal especially well when he wrote, "For if grace exclusively concerned atonement for sin and salvation of souls, one could view grace [God's saving works and word] as something located and operating outside of nature [the created world in all its social and cultural dimensions]. . . . But if it is true that Christ our Savior has to do not only with our soul but also with our body . . . then of course everything is different. We see immediately that *grace* is inseparably connected with *nature*, that grace and nature belong together."[15]

This means that for us as believers, we must become conduits of God's saving works and words, not just in one-on-one encounters or religious gatherings but also in the totality of our lives. In other words, whenever we encounter the misdirection that sin causes in any dimension of life—for example, in the realms of education, business, or politics—our Christian interaction in those spheres should help redirect them so that they are pleasing to God.

15. Abraham Kuyper, "Common Grace," in *Abraham Kuyper: A Centennial Reader*, ed. James Bratt (Grand Rapids: Eerdmans, 1998), 173, italics original.

By living "redirective" lives, we become witnesses to the world, previews of Christ's coming kingdom, when all things will be renewed and redirected toward God in Christ.

We are not saying that we should try to force Christianity on our fellow citizens. Neither are we saying that Christian action in the world will cause comprehensive or enduring change socially, culturally, or politically. Instead, we are saying that Christ calls us to be obedient witnesses in the totality of our lives, and for that reason, we should draw on Christian resources to shape our words and actions in all of life. We know that we will not be able to transform society and culture in any comprehensive or enduring manner. Only Christ can do that, and he will do that when he returns. Our ultimate goal is not to win but to witness.

We live in the midst of a cosmic struggle, and although we know that Christ the King will return one day to set the world aright, we also know that he is not universally acknowledged as King today. C. S. Lewis puts it especially well: "There is no neutral ground in the universe. Every square inch, every split second is claimed by God, and counterclaimed by Satan."[16] Thus every act of obedience—in every dimension of Christian life—is part of the Christian mission, a bold declaration that we support God's claim to the throne. And because the assault on his throne comes from every corner of the world, we must aim our redirective efforts at every nook and cranny. We do so aware that one day the struggle will end and our faith will become sight: we will see in all its splendor Christ's kingdom, "a kingdom of all ages, of all spheres, of all creatures."[17]

God among the Idols

But how can we identify, specifically, the ways in which God's world is being corrupted and misdirected in our current era? One especially helpful exercise is to identify some of God's perennial competitors, the counterfeit gods and idols who pose an antithesis to God's thesis. God warns Israel repeatedly about this temptation. Consider the fact that God devotes the first two commandments to this truth, declaring to Israel, "You shall have no other gods before Me" and "You shall not make for yourself a carved image. . . . ; you

16. C. S. Lewis, *Christian Reflections* (London: Geoffrey Bles, 1967), 33.
17. Abraham Kuyper, *E Voto Dordraceno. Toelichting op den Heidelbergschen Catechismus*, vol. 4, 465–66, quoted in Timothy P. Palmer, "The Two-Kingdom Doctrine: A Comparative Study," in *On Kuyper: A Collection of Readings on the Life, Work and Legacy of Abraham Kuyper*, ed. Steve Bishop and John H. Kok (Sioux City, IA: Dordt College Press, 2013), 147–48.

shall not bow down to them nor serve them. For I, the LORD your God, am a jealous God" (Exod. 20:3–5 NKJV). Later, he reiterates his point by rebuking the people of Israel for bowing down to the golden image of a calf (Exod. 32).

Yet, in spite of God's repeated warnings, Israel continues to oscillate between loving God, on the one hand, and loving false gods and handmade images, on the other hand. Ezekiel even goes so far as to speak about the people of Israel setting up idols in their hearts (14:4–5). Israel is told repeatedly to forsake these idols because they are lifeless (Ps. 106:28), powerless (Isa. 45:20), unreal (Jer. 51:17–18), and merely puppets compared to God (Ps. 115; 135). Repeatedly, Israel is told that those who worship false gods and idols are foolish (Jer. 10) and gullible (Isa. 44:20), thieves who rob God of his majesty by worshiping created things instead of worshiping the Creator himself.

In our "enlightened" secular age, we likely dismiss such idolatry as the result of primitive thinking. "How backward these people must have been," we think. "How simpleminded." But our dismissals and condescensions betray the fact that we are essentially the same as those "primitive" and "simpleminded" people.

Many ancient peoples, for instance, worshiped a goddess of sex. The Romans called her Venus; the Greeks called her Aphrodite. They crafted images of her. They held feasts in her honor. They poured out their money to please her and gain her favor. In our modern secular age, have we really advanced beyond this? We have not. We may not have a sex goddess with a particular name, but we still market our products using images of contemporary sex symbols. We may not consume food at banquets held in honor of a sex goddess, but we do consume images of sex goddesses displayed on our computers. We may not visit temple prostitutes, but we pour out the best of our lives to pursue sexual affairs, regardless of the cost to our families. At least the ancients had the insight to recognize when they were worshiping an idol. We follow the same path, all the while congratulating ourselves for our "progress" beyond such primitive superstitions. But idols do not mind if we forget their names, as long as they get our devotion.

The same goes for our worship of money or power or success. Anything that usurps God's rightful place on the throne of our hearts is a false god or an idol. So we can commit the sin of idolatry in a literal sense by bowing down to a statue of a god or in a metaphorical sense by loving and desiring any created thing more than we love and desire God himself. It is this second, metaphorical, sense that proves to be lethal because of its subtlety.

The Bible's teaching about idolatry means that our secular age is really not so secular after all, if secular means nonreligious. The whole world is a playground of the (false) gods, and we humans are worshipers at our core. If we are not worshiping God through Christ, then we are worshiping a false god or a cocktail of false gods nonetheless. This means that our Christian mission in a secular age involves helping people see their fundamentally religious nature and helping them embrace the one true and living God, who alone can save. This also means that if we want to help other people embrace the one true and living God, then we ourselves must continually resist the allure of idols. We must reserve our highest love, trust, and obedience for God through Christ, allowing our love for him to cascade outward as a witness to the world.

Idols and Their Cultural Liturgies

As we learned in the first chapter, God created humans to be lovers, to love him first and foremost but also to love one another and the rest of the created order. After the fall, however, our loves became misdirected and disordered. Instead of loving God first and foremost, and allowing that love to shape our love for one another and the world, we entered the world with a predisposition to love created things more than the Creator himself. This idolatrous predisposition is reinforced by the sinful societies in which we live and whose cultures are corrupted and misdirected by sin; to the extent we are formed by a culture's habits and practices, we are also being formed by its liturgies.

As Christians, we should not forget that we can easily be influenced by cultural idolatry at the same time we are confessing Jesus as Lord. The habits and practices of our secular age influence us to divide our loyalty between God and other gods. This divided allegiance of the heart is accompanied by a divided, or syncretistic, worldview. Theologian Lesslie Newbigin describes his experience on returning to his home country, England, after having served for several decades as a missionary in India: "Since I came to live in England after a lifetime as a foreign missionary, I have had the unhappy feeling that most English theology is falling into . . . syncretism. Ours is an advanced case of syncretism. In other words, instead of confronting our culture with the gospel, we are perpetually trying to fit the gospel into our culture. In our effort to communicate, we interpret the gospel by the categories of our culture."[18]

In light of our own temptation to follow false gods and idolatrous liturgies and our God-given calling to help our neighbors forsake their own false gods and idolatrous liturgies, we must be careful as we approach our cultural context, asking questions such as these:

18. Lesslie Newbigin, *A Word in Season* (Grand Rapids: Eerdmans, 1997), 67.

- What or who is given ultimacy in my culture's habits and practices?
- What vision of the good life is implicit in its habits and practices?
- What type of person will I become if I immerse myself in this particular liturgy?

More than any other contemporary intellectual, philosopher James K. A. Smith has explored this phenomenon of idols and their cultural liturgies. In his book *Desiring the Kingdom*, Smith offers the contemporary mall as an especially helpful example of idol worship at work in our habits and practices.[19] The mall, he suggests, is an intensification of the wider reality of consumerism (the worship of consumption). The mall's halls and stores serve as its sanctuary, and its marketing strategies serve as the mall's evangelism strategy. He writes, "The rituals and practices of the mall and the market . . . capture our imaginations through the sense of sight and sound, touch and taste, even smell. The hip happy people that populate television commercials [and ads at the mall] are the moving icons of the consumer gospel, illustrations of what [consumerism's vision of] the good life looks like: carefree and independent, clean and sexy, perky and perfect."[20] The advertisements at the mall and on TV are icons of the consumer gospel, illustrations of a false vision of human flourishing centering on independence, sexuality, power, and perfection.

To elucidate the mall's false vision of the "kingdom come," Smith offers four basic features for consideration. In paraphrased form, they are as follows:

1. Evil. In the consumerist vision of the kingdom I say, "I'm broken; therefore, I shop." We are depressed because we are unfulfilled. We see a disconnect between ourselves and the people in the advertisements and think we would be fulfilled if we could have what they have.
2. Redemptive Community. Under the consumerist gospel I say, "I shop with others." I am unfulfilled, so I want others to shop with me, to seek fulfillment with me. Ironically, instead of feeling the fulfillment that ought to come as part of a redemptive community, shopping together often fosters envy or other manifestations of dissatisfaction.
3. Redemption. In the consumerist vision I say, "I shop; therefore, I am." Consumption, it is implied, redeems us because it is therapeutic and because it gives us goods and services that promise to make us happy. Ironically, however, the goods and services change from season to season.

19. James K. A. Smith, *Desiring the Kingdom: Worship, Worldview, and Cultural Formation* (Grand Rapids: Baker Academic, 2009), 93–103.
20. Smith, *Desiring the Kingdom*, 95.

What is in (redemptive) one year is out (not redemptive) the next. Consumerists lose their "salvation" several times a year.

4. Mystery. In consumerist religion, there is a "divine" mystery: the puzzle of where all of this "stuff" comes from. What isn't revealed are the evils that often accompany the process of bringing products to market: theft, deception, exploitation. Ironically, whatever fleeting happiness we experience as a result of our consumption might have come at the expense of somebody else's happiness.[21]

In response to our society's false gods and idolatrous liturgies, we as Christians need to resist, not only by exposing them as counterfeit but also by inviting people to worship the true and living God and to experience the authentic liturgy of gospel-shaped habits and practices.

Facilitating a Missionary Encounter with the West

Given the fact that God's good creation has become a playground of the gods, a contested space where false gods and counterfeit liturgies vie for the hearts of humanity, and given that many people in the West have rejected Christianity, having been there and done that, what are God's people to do? How can we participate faithfully in God's mission to redeem humanity from the clutches of these gods and liturgies? How can we minister compellingly to our cross-pressured and fragilized neighbors who know nothing other than the immanent frame?

One Christian theologian who reflected on such questions with exceptional profundity is the Anglican missionary and theologian Lesslie Newbigin. In a story that Newbigin repeated often toward the end of his life, he attended a conference in 1973, where he was seated next to General T. B. Simatupang, an Indonesian general. Simatupang leaned over to Newbigin, as the story goes, and said, "Of course the number one question is, Can the West be converted?" Newbigin writes:

> I knew, of course, that he was right. Among all the cultures which have power in the contemporary world, the culture which originated in western Europe is the most powerful and pervasive. It dominates the cities of most of the world. What is called "modernization" in Asia and Africa is usually co-opted into this way of thinking and behaving. And it is precisely this powerful culture which is most resistant to the Gospel. Christianity is a growing movement in large parts of the Third World, rapidly growing in some places. In the West it

21. Smith, *Desiring the Kingdom*, 96–103.

is on the defensive, if not actually shrinking. Plainly, if one is looking at the global situation of the Christian world mission, the crucial question is: "Can the West be converted?"[22]

Simatupang's question stuck with Newbigin. After returning from several decades of missionary service in India, Newbigin devoted the remainder of his life to answering the question, "How can we bring the West into a missionary encounter with the gospel?" Newbigin answers that, in order to be faithful witnesses, Western Christians need to recover the gospel, indwell the Bible's narrative, and challenge the axioms of Western culture with the axioms of the Bible.[23]

Newbigin is right: not only is Christianity considered implausible and even unimaginable in our Western context, but even the church's understanding of the gospel has been corroded by the acids of Western idols and cultural liturgies. In order for the gospel to gain a hearing, we Christians will need to immerse ourselves in the Bible's narrative so that we can challenge the Western narrative of the world and the basic beliefs embedded in that narrative, many of which are at least partly antithetical to the gospel. We must articulate the gospel in light of the Bible's narrative, challenging the whole of Western society and culture. Newbigin writes:

> When the Church affirms the gospel as public truth it is challenging the whole of society to wake out of the nightmare of subjectivism and relativism, to escape from the captivity of the self turned in upon itself, and to accept the calling which is addressed to every human being to seek, acknowledge, and proclaim the truth. For we are that part of God's creation which he has equipped with the power to know the truth and to speak the praise of the whole creation in response to the truthfulness of the Creator.[24]

All this should be done with the gospel itself, rather than some philosophical argument, as our starting point. The foundation on which Christianity rests is the fact that God through Christ created the world and that God, through Jesus's life, ministry, death, and resurrection, discloses a powerful truth that the human mind cannot grasp on its own.[25]

---

22. Lesslie Newbigin, "Our Missionary Responsibility in the Crisis of Western Culture," DA29.5.2.16, unpublished article, Birmingham, UK, May 1988, p. 1.

23. For an introduction to Newbigin's thought on this topic, see Lesslie Newbigin, *Foolishness to the Greeks: The Gospel and Western Culture* (Grand Rapids: Eerdmans, 1986).

24. Newbigin, *Truth to Tell*, 13.

25. Lesslie Newbigin, *Truth and Authority in Modernity* (Valley Forge, PA: Trinity Press International, 1996), 43.

Significantly, given the strangeness of the story we have to tell—a story of God made flesh, of a crucified Savior, and of a future restoration of the universe—a story that is counterintuitive to a civilization that believes it can satisfactorily manage life without reference to God, the only way we will be able to speak compellingly in our secular age is if we do so together in Christian communities that really believe and embody the story. The only "real hermeneutic of the gospel" is "a congregation which believes it."[26]

Conclusion

Can we really do this? Can the Christian mission go forward in our cross-pressured and fragilized secular age, when society seems immune to the gospel? Can we give effective witness even from a position of social, cultural, and political weakness? The answer is so obvious that we often overlook it. When the just-risen Jesus approached his disciples, he commissioned them to make disciples of all the pagan nations, no matter how implausible or unimaginable the gospel would be to them. And he finished his commission by promising them, "And remember, I am with you always, to the end of the age" (Matt. 28:20). The risen Lord commissions us to be witnesses to pagan societies, and he promises to accompany us on the way so that he can fulfill his mission to redeem all of humanity, even in the most pagan of societies.

More to the point, consider John's version of the Great Commission, in which the risen Jesus says to the apostles, "As the Father has sent me, I also send you" (John 20:21). As Jesus gave the commission, he held out his hands to them, revealing the scars of his crucifixion, not only confirming that he was indeed the crucified One but also prophesying that their public witness would also follow the way of the cross. If our Lord could give powerful witness while hanging from a tree, then we can be his witnesses while relegated to the cultural margins.

Yes, most Christians throughout history have operated from the margins rather than from the centers of power. Operating from the margins, we are given the opportunity to be *prophetic*; just as Jesus declared that he is Lord and Caesar is not, so we must challenge the *cultus publicus* of our Western empires. From the sidelines, we have the opportunity to be *sacrificial*; just as Jesus ministered as a homeless itinerant teacher, we must be willing to serve from a position of weakness rather than of power, and in the face of disapproval instead of applause. With the world considering our gospel implausible

26. Lesslie Newbigin, "Evangelism in the City," *Reformed Review* 41 (1987): 3.

and unimaginable, we are provided the opportunity to be humbly confident; our fallen world will one day be raised to life, made to bow to the King. Since we are privy to this secret, we must remain confident. And since Jesus—rather than we—will secure the victory, we must remain humble. With this humble confidence, we embark on our mission.

7

A SOCIAL MISSION

Relational Monotheism for an Individualistic Age

Let your light shine before others, so that they may see your good works and give glory to your Father in heaven.

Matthew 5:16

Introduction

In a 2015 article, the *Irish Times* invited readers to send in stories of their experiences with loneliness. One reader responded with a brief narrative of her experience with loneliness in marriage. In a moving portion of that narrative, she wrote:

> There is a peculiar type of loneliness that blooms when you are married to someone who doesn't love you.
>
> This is not a periodic loneliness. . . . This is not the type of loneliness that washes over you at night when you're alone and your spouse is overseas on a weeks-long business trip. . . . No. This is a constant loneliness that accompanies your every waking—and sleeping—hour. It is the loneliness that arrests the blood flowing to and from your heart when you share your deepest feelings, only to have them disregarded, disparaged or derided.

It is the loneliness that sees you craving physical contact so much that you scoop up the odd smile sent your direction, and try to turn it into a loving caress. Even if that's only in your mind . . .

Until, one morning, you wake up and realize that you have given away so much that you are a shadow of the shell of the woman you once were.

And then you're lonely for yourself. You want the old you back. You realize that the peculiar type of loneliness that blooms when you are married to someone who doesn't love you has taken root inside you and choked you out of yourself.[1]

This haunting autobiographical reflection on loneliness gives us a peek into a much larger phenomenon—the havoc wreaked on the human soul by our social disconnection. This disconnectedness is something that people of all times and in all places have experienced because of the fall.

In the West, however, the universal experience of social disconnection takes on unique dimensions. Consider the political arrangement of Western nations: liberalism.[2] As we identify it here, liberalism is unique among other political arrangements because it emphasizes individual liberties and rights. An emphasis on liberties and rights is well and good and is something for which we should be profoundly grateful, but because human beings are sinners, this emphasis takes on idolatrous dimensions.

Instead of merely emphasizing personal freedom, we absolutize it, giving ourselves permission to live independently of God. Instead of simply recognizing an individual's worth and value apart from community, we absolutize the individual's worth by viewing communities as nothing more than aggregates of individuals. Instead of merely acknowledging an individual's particularity even in the midst of an enduring relationship, we absolutize that particularity by viewing all relationships, including marriage and family, as contracts that can be broken. It should be no surprise, therefore, when we encounter evidence that our disconnection from God and one another reaps negative consequences.

1. "Lonely People," *Irish Times*, November 17, 2017, https://www.irishtimes.com/life-and -style/people/lonely-people-your-stories-the-kind-of-loneliness-that-makes-my-heart-ache-1 .2343121. See the section beginning with "Other types of loneliness are legitimate, but not this one. How, after all, can you be married and lonely?"

2. We define liberalism according to a broad, historic sense of the term rather than the left/ liberal and right/conservative spectrum we see today. In the popular sense of the word, liberalism is on the left side of the political spectrum, while conservatism is on the right. In the broader and more historic sense of the word, however, most liberals and conservatives are both "liberal" in their shared commitment to democratic rule, free markets, basic human rights, and individual liberty. It is the latter sense we adopt here.

Consider, for example, *Bowling Alone* by political scientist Robert Putnam.[3] In this landmark study of American society, Putnam explores the evidence that more and more Americans are disconnecting from one another and from their communities. Fewer Americans are participating in social activities such as inviting friends over for dinner, visiting their neighbors, or going on picnics. His title plays off research from the early 1990s revealing that even though more Americans than ever were bowling, they were bowling alone rather than in leagues. For Putnam, this research is symbolic of a deeper and broader unraveling of America's social fabric. Putnam points to data from every sector of society, confirming that these unhappy trends are unraveling America's social fabric and causing harm to its individuals, cultural institutions, and communities.

Historian Christopher Lasch approaches our social disconnection from a different angle: self-absorption. In *Culture of Narcissism*, he argues that America's obsession with individual autonomy has fostered a narcissistic culture in which individuals cut ties with families and institutions, living for themselves and their own desires. This culture of narcissism leads to not only a shallow inner life for individuals but also a decadent public life for society at large. According to Lasch, the narcissistic person "seeks . . . to find a meaning in life . . . [and] forfeits the security of group loyalties. . . . He extols cooperation and teamwork while harboring deeply antisocial impulses. He praises respect for rules and regulations in the secret belief that they do not apply to himself. Acquisitive in the sense that his cravings have no limit, . . . he demands immediate gratification and lives in a state of restless, perpetually unsatisfied desire."[4]

According to Lasch, an "ethic of pleasure" has replaced earlier generations' "ethic of achievement," elevating the pursuit of pleasure to the extent that "even the most intimate encounters become a form of mutual exploitation."[5] Ironically, Lasch argues, this focus on independence and self-gratification leads to deep dependence and insecurity.

3. Robert Putnam, *Bowling Alone: The Collapse and Revival of American Community* (New York: Simon & Schuster, 2000).
4. Christopher Lasch, *Culture of Narcissism: American Life in an Age of Diminishing Expectations* (New York: Norton, 1979), xvi. It should be noted that Lasch believed that narcissism is caused by modern corporate capitalism and can be fixed only by a socialist revolution. While he is right that twisted iterations of capitalism foster a narcissistic environment, we think he is badly mistaken to think that a socialist revolution would remedy the situation. For a concise treatment of good and bad forms of capitalism and the flaws of Marxist socialism, see Bruce Riley Ashford, *One Nation under God: A Christian Hope for American Politics* (Nashville: B&H, 2015), 90–93.
5. Lasch, *Culture of Narcissism*, 65.

Finally, consider that the disconnectedness that Putnam and Lasch observed in the late twentieth century has not subsided. Studies reveal that Millennials (the generation born after 1980 and before 1996) are the loneliest and most isolated generation in recent Western history. A 2015 Pew survey reveals that only 25 percent of the teens surveyed spend face-to-face time with friends each day.[6] A 2016 Bank of America market survey shows that 39 percent of Millennials spend more time on their smartphones than they do with family or friends.[7] A 2017 Barna summary reveals that Millennials are the most technologically connected generation (via social media) but, sadly, the most likely to suffer from loneliness.[8] In light of this evidence, it should be no surprise that the American Psychological Association reports that "social isolation may be a greater threat to public health than obesity."[9]

The insights gleaned from Putnam, Lasch, and recent studies of Millennials reveal only a few of the negative effects of social disconnection on individuals, communities, and cultural institutions. As we learned in chapter 2, humanity's broken relationship with God inevitably results in broken relationships with one another. It is no accident that the first four commandments address our relationship with God, while the last six commandments address our relationship with one another. When we are alienated from God, we inevitably alienate ourselves from one another—dishonoring our parents, taking innocent life, breaking our marital commitments, taking what is not ours, making false accusations about others, and coveting others' wealth.

What is the remedy for our social brokenness? As we learned in chapters 1 and 6, God is the ultimate social being, and he created us—humanity—in his image and likeness. Just as God exists eternally as an unbroken fellowship of Father, Son, and Spirit, so he created humanity to live in unbroken fellowship with him, with one another, and with the created order. Even after sin shattered that fellowship, our loving Creator went the second mile, calling us back, through his Son, into unbroken and everlasting fellowship with him. And, as the Bible so often reminds us, an authentic love for God overflows into genuine love for our fellow humans. This is God's design for human flourishing.

6. Amanda Lenhart, "Teens, Technology, and Friendships," Pew Research Center, August 6, 2015, http://www.pewinternet.org/2015/08/06/teens-technology-and-friendships/.

7. Catey Hill, "Millennials Engage with Their Smartphones More than They Do Actual Humans," MarketWatch, June 21, 2016, https://www.marketwatch.com/story/millennials-engage-with-their-smartphones-more-than-they-do-actual-humans-2016-06-21.

8. "Who Are the Lonely in America?," Barna Group, May 15, 2017, https://www.barna.com/research/who-are-the-lonely-in-america.

9. "So Lonely I Could Die," American Psychological Association, August 5, 2017, http://www.apa.org/news/press/releases/2017/08/lonely-die.aspx.

As Christians, therefore, our mission is to introduce the world to God through Christ so that others may experience his love and allow that love to overflow into their relationships with others. Even political scientist Robert Putnam—himself no evangelical—recognizes that the answer to America's social brokenness is deeply theological. "I challenge America's clergy, lay leaders, theologians, and ordinary worshippers," Putnam writes in the conclusion to *Bowling Alone*. "Let us spur a new, pluralistic, socially responsible 'great awakening,' so that by 2010 Americans will be more deeply engaged than we are today in one or another spiritual community of meaning."[10] Going beyond Putnam's limited goal (for Americans to become involved in deeper civic engagement) and his ambiguous means (the formation of generic "spiritual communit[ies] of meaning"), however, our mission is to offer our broken and alienated age a union with Christ and his church that will overflow into a life characterized by gospel words and deeds. As we will see, each aspect of our mission—union with Christ and the church, gospel words, and gospel deeds—is deeply and profoundly social.

Union with Christ and the Church

God's offer of salvation overcomes our alienation from him, reconciling us through the work of his Son. His salvation reconnects us with God through Christ. When God calls us to salvation, his Spirit unites us with Christ (John 14:16–17), and this union with him transforms the way we speak (Rom. 9:1) and act (1 Cor. 15:58). And if we are united with Christ, we are also united with his people, the church. After all, Christ is the head of his body, and if we are connected to the head (Christ), then we will be connected to the body (the church).

It should not be surprising, therefore, that the New Testament emphasizes the significance of the local church. The church is more of a "people who" than a "place where," and the social dynamic of this people is itself a witness to Christ and his gospel. Christ bought the church at the price of his own blood (Eph. 5:23), created the church by the gospel (2:10), and gives it life through the gospel (2:5). The church is by its very nature a witness to the gospel. "Christian proclamation might make the gospel audible," Mark Dever writes, "but Christians living together in local congregations make the gospel visible. . . . The church is the gospel made visible."[11]

This connection between the church's inherently social nature and its mission is made clear in several of the images Scripture uses to describe the

10. Putnam, *Bowling Alone*, 409.
11. Mark Dever, "The Church," in *A Theology for the Church*, ed. Daniel L. Akin, rev. ed. (Nashville: B&H, 2014), 604.

church.[12] These images make clear that the church is a redeemed community rather than merely a collection of individuals, a family whose bonds cannot be dissolved rather than a club whose membership can be broken or revoked.

The first image is *the people of God*. In 1 Peter 2:9–10, Peter writes, "But you are a chosen generation, a royal priesthood, a holy nation, His own special people, that you may proclaim the praises of Him who called you out of darkness into His marvelous light; who once were not a people but are now the people of God, who had not obtained mercy but now have obtained mercy" (NKJV). Notice that Peter calls God's church the "people" of God rather than the "persons" of God. He does so because the church's collective identity is more than the sum of its composite parts. Peter also makes clear that this community has a purpose: to declare God's praises. In verse 9, Peter clearly draws on the identity that God gave Israel in Exodus 19:5–6. Peter proclaims that God's people are "a royal priesthood," "a holy nation," and his "special people." This passage also reworks a portion of Isaiah 43:20–23, which is a passage about Israel's worship. Finally, Peter draws on Hosea 1, saying that the people of God are wayward but have received God's mercy.[13] What does all of this mean? When Peter applies "people of God" language to the church, he is saying that the church is similar to Israel: they are a people whom God has chosen to be a holy community, a people who proclaims God's goodness and praises him publicly for the sake of the nations.[14]

The second image is *the body of Christ*. Paul sometimes uses this image to refer to all believers everywhere (Eph. 4:1–16; Col. 1:18) and sometimes to refer to a particular local church (Rom. 12:4–8; 1 Cor. 12:27). In both uses, this image helps us understand that we are diverse persons who come together to make a unified whole and that each of us belongs to the others in a relationship of mutual love and interdependence. Sadly, this is often the only application that contemporary readers glean from the imagery. But the body of Christ highlights two other crucial truths: we belong to Christ (*Christ's* body), and we are his extension in the world (Christ's *body*). The latter point is so dramatic that we tend to downplay it or ignore it altogether. By calling the church Christ's body, Paul implies that Christ acts in the world through *us*. As Luke points out in the introduction to Acts, his former book (Luke) concerned what Jesus "began to do and teach" (Acts 1:1). This implies that Acts chronicles what Jesus continues to do through his church. Thus, we the church not only are a

12. For our understanding of the missional nature of the images, we are drawing on Michael Goheen, *A Light to the Nations* (Grand Rapids: Baker Academic, 2011), 155–90.

13. John P. Dickson, *The Best Kept Secret of Christian Mission: Promoting the Gospel with More Than Our Lips* (Grand Rapids: Zondervan, 2010), 162.

14. Goheen, *Light to the Nations*, 157–62.

unified redeemed community, diverse in our composition, belonging to Jesus; we also "embody the life of Jesus for the sake of the world."[15]

The third image is *the temple of the Spirit*. Both Peter and Paul describe the church this way. Paul describes the church as the temple of God (1 Cor. 3:16), while Peter writes that we are living stones, being built into a spiritual house (1 Pet. 2:5). Even this image, which is not strictly organic like the first two, shows us the interconnectedness of God's people. We are living stones being built up together. Further, we are being built up together as a holy priesthood, meaning that we, like Israel, are called to mediate God's blessings to the nations. Even though the people of Israel failed to spread God's glory through their temple, God has established a new temple, his people, who have new life and are filled with his Spirit. "Our task as a Church," writes Gregory Beale, "is to be God's temple, so filled with his presence that we expand and fill the earth with that glorious presence until God finally accomplishes this goal completely at the end of time!"[16]

The images Scripture uses to describe the church communicate not only the nature of the church but also, crucially, our mission. Each of the three images mentioned reveals that the church is a community that is missional in its very nature. But what does this mean? Practically speaking, how does the inner sociality of the church connect to its mission? We will list three significant ways in which the church's inner life is missional.

First, the church's public praise is missional. The apostle Peter writes that the church, as a community, is supposed to "proclaim the praises" of the God who called us out of darkness and into the light (1 Pet. 2:9). Paul instructs the church to sing psalms, hymns, and spiritual songs (Eph. 5:19; Col. 3:16). The Psalms tell God's people to sing his praises publicly (Ps. 96) so that the nations will be able to sing his praises also (Pss. 67; 96). The church's worship is a public demonstration of our desire for God and our satisfaction in him.[17] Edmund Clowney calls this "doxological evangelism," and Tim Keller calls it "world-winning worship."[18] God intends for the church's praise to be part of our gospel proclamation. Through our praise, we announce to the world that God is good, that he is worthy of worship. In other words, the church's praise is directed toward God, but it radiates outward to all who will watch and listen.

15. Goheen, *Light to the Nations*, 173.
16. Gregory K. Beale, "Eden, the Temple, and the Church's Mission in the New Creation," *JETS* 48, no. 1 (March 2005): 31. Also see Beale, *The Temple and the Church's Mission: A Biblical Theology of the Dwelling Place of God* (Downers Grove, IL: InterVarsity, 2004), 5–31.
17. John Piper, *God's Passion for His Glory* (Wheaton: Crossway, 1998), 40–41.
18. We owe these two references to Dickson, *Best Kept Secret*, 161.

Second, the church's love for one another is missional. In John's Gospel, Jesus puts it clearly: "I give you a new command: Love one another. Just as I have loved you, you are also to love one another. By this everyone will know that you are my disciples, if you love one another" (13:34–35). Because of God's love for us, we are able to love one another with a divine sort of love. This truth motivated Dietrich Bonhoeffer to write, "When God . . . won our hearts by His love, this was the beginning of our instruction in divine love. . . . Thus God Himself taught us to meet one another as God has met us in Christ."[19] Similarly, it caused Francis Schaeffer to argue that Christian love is the final apologetic.[20] Indeed, when God's people love one another, we proclaim God's love to the world and preview God's future kingdom, in which love will reign supreme.

Third, the church's combined witness in society is missional. In the same passage in which Peter describes the church as the temple of the Spirit and the people of God, he instructs the church to live in such an honorable manner that even the gentiles will notice and glorify God (1 Pet. 2:12). Other passages instruct us to live honorably "in everyone's eyes" (Rom. 12:17), to make known God's wisdom "to the rulers and authorities in the heavens" (Eph. 3:10), to be blameless, living as "stars in the world" (Phil. 2:14–15), and to "behave properly in the presence of outsiders" (1 Thess. 4:10–12). When the church lives in this manner, it serves as a window through which outsiders can view God and his intentions for humanity. When the church does not live in this manner, it obscures and distorts the view.[21]

God has wed himself to a community, the church, whom he has called to be a missional presence in the world, continually proclaiming and pointing to him. We do so by embodying the gospel through public praise, love for one another, and upright lives.

Words of Life

As the Dutch theologian Abraham Kuyper often noted, Sunday morning worship prepares God's people for Monday morning public life.[22] And central

19. Dietrich Bonhoeffer, *Life Together* (New York: Harper & Row, 1954), 24–25.

20. Francis Schaeffer, *The Mark of the Christian* (Downers Grove, IL: InterVarsity, 1970), 26.

21. Christopher J. H. Wright writes of Israel, "The whole history of Israel, we might say, is intended to be the shop window for the knowledge of God in all the earth." C. J. H. Wright, *The Mission of God* (Downers Grove, IL: InterVarsity, 2006), 127. For a fuller exposition of this point, see Bruce Riley Ashford and Danny Akin, "The Missional Implications of Church Membership and Church Discipline," in *Those Who Must Give an Account: A Study of Church Membership and Church Discipline*, ed. John S. Hammett and Benjamin L. Merkle (Nashville: B&H Academic, 2012), 189–204.

22. Abraham Kuyper, *Pro Rege: Living Under Christ's Kingship*, ed. John H. Kok and Nelson D. Kloosterman, trans. Albert Gootjes, vol. 2, *The Kingship of Christ in Its Operation*,

to our public life is an often-overlooked social ministry, that of speaking the gospel. As we learned in chapter 1, God created us as social beings, and part of that is the ability to communicate verbally. After the fall, this verbal aspect of humanity took on added significance. Adam and Eve fell away from God because they failed to heed his words; by means of a redemptive word, God promised to undo the damage caused by our parents' rebellion. A word *spoken* brought us out of nothing into existence. A word *ignored* precipitated our fall. And a word *proclaimed* would bring us back to God.

As God's people, we embrace the gospel, and we pass it along. At the end of his earthly ministry, Jesus charged his disciples with preaching this gospel of the kingdom "in all the world as a testimony to all nations, and then the end will come" (Matt. 24:14). As we learned in chapter 5, Christians speak the gospel in its most focused form as an announcement about the salvation provided by Christ, but we also speak the gospel in its fuller form by telling the story of Jesus's life, death, and resurrection and by doing so in the broader context of the whole biblical story.

When we speak the gospel, we are engaged in what the Bible calls evangelism, or telling people about Jesus in the hope that they will trust in him for salvation and serve him as their King. We present Christ in the power of the Spirit, knowing that we cannot compel a person to embrace Christ and that Christ alone can save the person to whom we are talking. "The way to tell whether in fact you are evangelizing," writes J. I. Packer, "is not to ask whether conversions are known to have resulted from your witness. It is to ask whether you are faithfully making known the gospel message."[23] We evangelize because we love Christ and we love our neighbors. And we leave the results to him.

Gifted Evangelists

When Christ rose from the dead, he gave spiritual gifts to his people so that, together, we can minister effectively. Several lists of these gifts are given in Scripture: Romans 12:6–8; 1 Corinthians 12:4–11; and Ephesians 4:11–16. None of the lists are identical, and each contains gifts unique to that list. This indicates that the gifts outlined aren't comprehensive but are manifestations

Collected Works in Public Theology (Bellingham, WA: Lexham, 2017), 113–28; Abraham Kuyper, "Rooted and Grounded: The Church as Organism and Institution," in *On the Church*, ed. John Halsey Wood Jr. and Andrew M. McGinnis, trans. Harry Van Dyke et al., Collected Works in Public Theology (Bellingham, WA: Lexham, 2016), 55.

23. J. I. Packer, *Evangelism and the Sovereignty of God* (Downers Grove, IL: InterVarsity, 1961), 41.

of the Spirit's activity in the church. As Paul says, "A manifestation of the Spirit is given to each person for the common good" (1 Cor. 12:7).

One of those gifts is the gift of the evangelist. "[Christ] himself gave some to be . . . evangelists . . . equipping the saints for the work of ministry, to build up the body of Christ" (Eph. 4:11–12). But what is an evangelist, and how would a person know if they have the gift of the evangelist? And if a person does not have the gift of the evangelist, does that mean they are off the hook when it comes to the difficult, often awkward, and sometimes offensive task of sharing the gospel with people who are not Christians?

An evangelist (*euangelistēs*) is a person who is uniquely gifted in their ability to present the gospel (*euangelion*). Although the New Testament does not tell us much about day-to-day ministries of these evangelists, we know enough to say confidently that some of them were traveling evangelists and others worked within the context of a settled congregation.[24] So evangelists might operate within the context of one local church, or they might work regionally or globally. Timothy is an example of an evangelist who served in both manners. For many years, he traveled and spoke the gospel alongside Paul (Phil. 2:22; 1 Thess. 3:2), but in later years, he settled down in Ephesus, where Paul encouraged him not only to teach believers but also to continue doing the work of an evangelist (2 Tim. 4:5).

How do we identify contemporary evangelists? As with all the spiritual gifts, the gift of evangelism isn't described in full in Scripture. John Dickson's approach, however, seems to faithfully reflect the biblical picture. He offers four criteria.[25] First, evangelists are those who can present the gospel clearly, taking biblical truth and making it accessible for the listener. Second, evangelists relate well to unbelievers. They may not necessarily be extroverts or overly gregarious, but they enjoy befriending those who do not yet believe and are able to understand them well enough to speak the gospel to them in a compelling manner. Third, evangelists have a strong desire to present the gospel. They are not just good at it; they also love doing it. Spending time with unbelievers energizes them. Fourth, evangelists are those whose lives are marked by godliness. Their speech about Christ is matched by their love for Christ. Their lives are visible demonstrations of the gospel that they claim to love. Although ordinary Christians may—and should—exhibit some of these characteristics, evangelists will exhibit all of them in strong measure.

24. Peter T. O'Brien, *The Letter to the Ephesians*, PNTC (Grand Rapids: Eerdmans, 1999), 299.
25. Dickson, *Best Kept Secret*, 150–53.

Just as God gifts some Christians as evangelists, he gifts others as pastors. Both evangelists and pastors are necessary if we are to speak the gospel faithfully. Evangelists focus more on bringing nonbelievers to faith; and while pastors do evangelize, they focus more on equipping believers to live out that faith. But both ground their message in the finished work of Christ—that is, the gospel. The difference is found most manifestly in audience and emphasis: speaking either with Christians or non-Christians and encouraging them either to look to Christ for the first time or to keep their eyes trained on him.

Everyday Christians

Although God has specially equipped certain Christians as evangelists, he in no way limits the Christian mission to those persons. As mentioned above, the gift of the evangelist is meant to spur the rest of us on to share Christ. The evangelist's special gift does not preclude the rest of us from embracing our responsibility to share the gospel. In fact, most of the time, the gospel goes forward on the backs of ordinary Christians, not exceptional evangelists.

This is why Peter instructs the church to "be ready at any time to give a defense to anyone who asks you for a reason for the hope that is in you" (1 Pet. 3:15). Most evangelistic opportunities arise in the course of our everyday lives and, in Peter's telling, as a result of a specific question: Why so hopeful? As Lesslie Newbigin points out, the sermons in the book of Acts are all occasioned by some unexpected event, prompting people to ask, "What is going on here?" The answer to their question is, "What is going on here, and the reason for our confident hope, is that God's kingdom has arrived in the life, ministry, death, and resurrection of Jesus Christ, and is affirmed by the presence of the Spirit."[26] In the midst of a society trapped within the immanent frame, disappointed by the fallen world around them, and unsure if their lives have any transcendent meaning, our confident and joyful hope forms a stark contrast.

In 1 Peter 3:15, Peter does not instruct us to preach to every person we meet. Neither does he say that he expects us to successfully persuade every person with whom we share the gospel. But he does expect us to be ready. And if Christ is our hope, then the Spirit will enable us to articulate *why* we have that hope. Neither our naturally introverted personalities, nor our fears and insecurities, nor our lack of theological training should keep us from engaging in spiritual conversation. It is no burden to speak about what we love. Just as we might speak in a relaxed and natural manner about our families or friends,

---

26. Lesslie Newbigin, *The Gospel in a Pluralist Society* (Grand Rapids: Eerdmans, 1989), 117.

we can engage in conversation about the one we love the most—the Lord Jesus Christ. As C. S. Lewis noted, "All enjoyment spontaneously overflows into praise. . . . We delight to praise what we enjoy because the praise not merely expresses but completes the enjoyment; it is its appointed consummation."[27]

Colossians 4:5 says, "Be wise in the way you act toward outsiders; make the most of every opportunity" (NIV). Every encounter with another person is a unique opportunity, a chance to present the truth, the goodness, and the beauty of God to someone made in God's image. Because these opportunities are so precious, we must be wise enough to recognize their value and embrace them accordingly.

Later in the same passage, Paul reminds us that our speech should be "always full of grace, seasoned with salt" (Col. 4:6 NIV). In other words, our tone and demeanor matter. I (Bruce) learned this lesson the hard way when I was in college. During my childhood years, I had been cowed by peer pressure and was very hesitant to share the gospel. When I was not at church or home, I tended to hide the fact that I came from a Christian family. So during my college years, as I began to express my faith publicly, I found doing so both challenging and liberating. Unfortunately, I did not always express it appropriately. I remember having placed a bumper sticker on my car that said, "Get a life. Be a Christian." One day as I walked out of the Barnes and Noble to return to my car, I noticed that somebody had taken a crowbar or a tire iron and had bashed in the bumper of my car at just the place where I had placed my sticker. As I drove home that day, I realized my bumper sticker had in fact conveyed the wrong tone, one of mockery and condescension rather than grace and humility.

The Gospels portray Jesus as a friend of sinners who spent much of his time with the unbelievers of his day. In fact, Matthew tells us that Jesus socialized with sinners so regularly that people assumed he was a big-time sinner himself (11:19). However, his friendship with sinners was not a sign that he was like them (in their sinfulness); rather, it was a sign that he loved them. Similarly, Paul socialized with pagans and even scolded Peter for not being gospel-minded on this issue (Gal. 2:14). The Jews and even many Christians continued to criticize Paul for being so familiar with unbelievers, but Paul refused to change course. Like Paul, we can spend time with those who do not yet know Christ, because the gospel compels us to cross social boundaries we would never have dreamed of crossing. Like Jesus, we can be friends of sinners by socializing with them and wisely taking every opportunity to present Christ and the gospel.

27. C. S. Lewis, *Reflections on the Psalms* (New York: Harcourt, 1958), 94–95.

Many Christians find it intimidating to share the gospel with people, either because they are not specially equipped as evangelists or because of the negative responses people often make to their overtures. But the good news is that God has equipped every Christian to be a witness in a way that fits their basic personality, education, and communication abilities. God does not need you to be someone else to use you. But he does need you to yield yourself to Someone Else.

When I (Bruce) was in college, struggling to find my feet as a Christian witness, I found a book that explored the Bible's portrayal of different evangelistic approaches Christians might take. I was encouraged as I read the six approaches outlined by the authors, because I realized I did not have to fit into any one mold but could allow the Lord to guide me based on context, personality, or other factors. The six approaches are as follows:

1. Peter's *confrontational* approach. From Acts 2:14–40 and other passages, it is clear that Peter was a preacher who did not mince words. He was convinced of the gospel's truth, and he communicated his gospel convictions boldly and directly.

2. Paul's *intellectual* approach. In Acts 17:16–34, Paul gives a reasoned and culturally informed presentation of the gospel. Maybe we could imagine his approach being similar to that of a professor.

3. The blind man's *testimonial* approach. In John 9:1–34, the blind man shares his faith by giving his testimony. Particularly encouraging in his story is the simplicity of his message. When challenged theologically, he admits his ignorance. "I don't know about all your theological categories," he says, "but I do know this: Yesterday I couldn't see. Today I can."

4. Matthew's *interpersonal* approach. In Luke 5:27–31, we read the story of Matthew the tax collector. Immediately after he begins following Jesus, Matthew throws a big party at his house, to which he invites all his tax collector and "sinner" friends. We might not immediately recognize this as evangelism, but sometimes simply getting people "in the vicinity" is a huge step.

5. The Samaritan woman's *invitational* approach. John 4:1–42 contains the story of the Samaritan woman coming to believe in Jesus as Messiah. Immediately after her conversion, she gathers a group of people and brings them back to Jesus so they can encounter him for themselves.

6. Dorcas's *service* approach. From Acts 9:36–42, we learn that Dorcas's life was marked by good works, especially helping the poor. She dies prematurely, but Jesus raises her from the dead in order to put her back

on the job embodying Christ's love for the world. When loving Christian service is combined with loving gospel words, the result is a compelling witness.[28]

Speaking the gospel is a social ministry that is incumbent on every Christian and vital to the Christian mission. Not every Christian has a charismatic personality or is a gifted speaker, but every Christian can and should share the gospel. God spoke a word that brought humanity into existence. Via the serpent, Satan spoke a word against God's word, and the first couple ignored God's word and embraced the serpent's, thus precipitating humanity's fall. And, significantly, God through the Son proclaimed a word—the gospel—that would reconcile humanity back to God.

Gospel Deeds

One of the more remarkable ways that we point to Christ is through showing mercy to those who have need. When I (Bruce) lived in Russia, I spent some time over lunch one day reading the book of James, reflecting on his insight that pure and undefiled religion involves helping the helpless, such as orphans and widows (1:27). I remember feeling convicted that I rarely served financially disadvantaged or socially marginalized persons and praying that the Lord would provide an opportunity.

I left the café to return to my apartment and walked out into the cold winter air. As I walked down a short alley toward my flat, I heard a noise and looked up. There in the dumpster just a few feet away from me was a woman staring at me. She was just as startled by my presence as I was by hers. She was wearing the tattered clothes of a homeless person and was eating a portion of food she had found.

I stood there face-to-face with this woman, the October sunlight failing to warm her but succeeding in spotlighting her destitution. And at that moment, I sensed the presence of Christ and imagined him saying to me, "If you have done it to one of the least of these, you have done it unto me." I had arrived in Russia only a few weeks earlier; my language abilities were so poor that I could not even construct basic sentences. I had little idea how to help her, so I offered the only thing I had at the moment.

I approached her, offered a financial gift that would secure a few meals, looked her in the eye, and tried to articulate John 3:16–18 in my broken

28. Bill Hybels and Mark Mittelberg, *Becoming a Contagious Christian* (Grand Rapids: Zondervan, 1996), 119–33.

Russian, using the few words I knew to try to tell her that my gift to her ultimately came from God. In response, she motioned for me to come closer, and when I did, she bent down and embraced me. She kissed me on the cheek repeatedly and thanked me. The smell of alcohol mixed with other unpleasant odors nearly overpowered me. But as she embraced me, I sensed the Lord laying hold of me also, addressing me from James 1:27 and affirming that, although this woman was worthless in the world's eyes, she was of the greatest value and worth in his. If I showed love to her, I was showing love to him. If I showed contempt to her, I was showing contempt to him.

Unable to communicate in her language, I eventually walked away from the dumpster, down the alley, and to my flat. I had not done anything heroic—I had given this woman a few rubles and spoken gospel words to her in deficient Russian. It is difficult to imagine how my actions might have affected her in any significant way. However, the encounter did serve as a clear marker in my life, one reminding me that a genuinely Christian life involves loving and serving those who need help—physically, psychologically, and economically. The salvation God provides—the kingdom he brings—is one in which all facets of human life are renewed and restored. As previews of his kingdom, therefore, we want to minister to God's imagers in the wholeness of their being.

Love Knows No Bounds

The Bible's teaching about Christian deeds in service to our neighbor is crystalized in a story Jesus told about a Samaritan who showed mercy to a wounded stranger (Luke 10:25–37). This story makes clear the connection between genuine faith and loving action in the world. Like James 1:27, this passage teaches that the person who loves God will also love their neighbor in tangible ways, even if the person who needs love is their enemy.

The story opens with a lawyer stepping up to test Jesus. "How can I get eternal life?" he asks. Jesus, as he often does, responds with a question. "What does the Jewish law say?" Unsurprisingly, the lawyer rattles off two verses from the Torah—Deuteronomy 6:5 and Leviticus 19:18. Love God and love others. Not a bad answer. But Jesus does not accept the lawyer's textbook response as the end of the exchange; instead, he exhorts the lawyer to practice what he preaches. If we love God, we will also love our neighbor (cf. 1 John 4:20).

The lawyer, however, cannot take the subtle rebuke. Instead, he presses the issue of whom he is obligated to love. Like many Jews of his day, he appears to have been occupied by drawing lines in the sand, identifying those persons or groups to whom he had no obligations—such as the despised Samaritans, who differed from him ethnically and religiously. Jesus responds with a story about a (presumably Jewish) man who is assaulted as he travels on the road to Jericho and whose medical needs are ignored by Jewish religious leaders but attended to by a Samaritan layperson.

People in Jesus's audience would have known the treachery of the road to Jericho, a seventeen-mile stretch of road that winds and descends through a rocky desert populated by highway robbers.[29] In this dark alley of a road, the man falls into the hands of robbers who strip him, beat him, and leave him half dead.

Jesus tells of three passersby as the man lies on the side of this desolate road. The first passerby is a priest who sees the man and passes by on the other side. He may have passed by out of fear of robbers or perhaps because he was unwilling to defile himself by touching a man who might die. The second passerby is a Levite. Like the priest, when he sees the bloodied man, he crosses to the other side and keeps going. In those days, the Levites were religious officials, inferior to the priests but nonetheless culturally elite people who were responsible for the temple's worship and for enforcing temple restrictions. They were the religious police of Jesus's day. But neither he nor the priest is willing even to approach the dying man, much less help him.

At this point in the story, modern and ancient audiences alike know what to expect. The third passerby . . . that one will be the hero! But who will it be? Jesus's first hearers, of course, would have expected a Jewish man to enter the story. But instead, Jesus says, "A certain Samaritan . . ." In making a Samaritan the hero, Jesus deals a devastating blow to the religious ego of the lawyer and to many persons in his audience. The Jews despised the Samaritans, and some Samaritans returned the vitriol by attacking Jewish pilgrims on their way to Jerusalem. Yet in Jesus's story, the Samaritan traveler takes the time to bandage the man's wounds and transport him to an inn. He even makes an advance payment to the innkeeper, ensuring that the wounded man will be taken care of until he is better. "This compassion," Tim Keller writes, "was full-bodied, leading him to meet a variety of needs. This compassion provided friendship and advocacy, emergency medical treatment, transportation, a hefty financial subsidy, and even a follow-up visit."[30] All this from the representative of a despised ethnic and religious minority.

After concluding the story, Jesus heightens the offense by exhorting the lawyer to emulate the Samaritan. In other words, the Christian mission necessarily involves decentering ourselves in order to prioritize and love other people, even—and especially—if they differ from us ethnically, religiously,

29. I. Howard Marshall, *The Gospel of Luke*, NIGTC (Grand Rapids: Eerdmans, 1998), 447.
30. Tim Keller, *Ministries of Mercy*, 2nd ed. (Phillipsburg, NJ: P&R, 1997), 11.

or in some other significant manner. The Christian mission calls us to get involved in risky, dirty, inconvenient, challenging, and often thankless ministry for the benefit of our fellow humans. This type of ministry is especially powerful as it unsettles the social, cultural, and political status quo, crossing over the false boundaries our society has imposed. It is motivated by Christian love and serves as a preview of Christ's coming kingdom, which will be characterized by unbroken and eternal love.

Justice and Mercy

Jesus's story of the good Samaritan crystallizes two major threads of biblical teaching: that God saves his people not only *from* their sin but also *for* a life characterized by justice and mercy, and that he calls his people not only to *speak* the gospel with their lips but also to *show* it with their lives. Just and merciful actions are central to the Christian mission because they are central to God's mission. For proof, one need look no further than the opening chapters of Scripture. When God created the first couple to lovingly manage his good creation, his design was for them to do so in an unbroken relationship with him and with each other. After the fall, however, when they found themselves alienated from God and from each other, God promised to send a Redeemer who would restore their relationship with him and—ultimately—with each other.

Thus, when the legal expert asked Jesus how he could be sure of eternal life, Jesus responded by making clear that anybody who truly loves God will also love their neighbor. How can we say we love God, the apostle John asks, unless we also love our brothers and sisters (1 John 4:20–21)? This is why Scripture is littered with references to justice and mercy. Old Testament law was given to govern all of Israel's communal life, including not only its religious rituals but also the entire fabric of its social and cultural life. Israel was to embody God's disposition of mercy toward the poor and the debtor (Deut. 15:1–18). It was commanded to do justice and love mercy while walking humbly with its God (Mic. 6:8). Similarly, in the New Testament, Jesus ministered to those who were sick, outcast, and disenfranchised (Matt. 11:4–5). He told the rich young ruler to give all that he had to the poor (Mark 10:17–21), told the questioning lawyer to love his neighbor like the good Samaritan (Luke 10:25–37), and in both instances made the point that true love for God necessarily flows over into love for others. He even went so far as to say that if we neglect the hungry, sick, naked, and homeless, we are neglecting Jesus himself (Matt. 25:31–46). The early church took hold of this clear biblical teaching in such a manner that there was not "a needy person among them" (Acts 4:32–37).

In other words, the vertical (Godward) dimension of the Christian life should never displace the horizontal (social) dimension. Instead, God intends for the vertical dimension to enhance and shape the horizontal, such that we are willing to minister to other people in the everyday realities of their lives. "It comes more natural to us to shout the gospel at people from a distance," John Stott writes, "than to involve ourselves deeply in their lives, to think ourselves into their culture and their problems, and to feel with them in their pains."[31] Rather than merely shouting from a distance, we should come near and get involved. "A Christianity," writes W. A. Visser 't Hooft, "which has lost its vertical dimension has lost its salt and is not only insipid in itself, but useless for the world. But a Christianity that would use the vertical preoccupation as a means to escape from its responsibility for and in the common life of man is a denial of the incarnation, of God's love for the world manifested in Christ."[32] Jesus's love for God the Father issued forth in a love that came near to us; likewise, our love for God should issue forth in a love that goes to others.

Our embodiment of the gospel through social justice and mercy ministries should never replace intentional verbal evangelism. Likewise, our verbal evangelism should never displace Christian action. As Lesslie Newbigin puts it, "Words without deeds are empty, but deeds without words are dumb."[33] At times, the gospel word will be easy while the deed is costly; at other times, the deed will be easy and the word costly.[34] We must have the courage to cling to both.

Conclusion

The social aspect of the Christian mission—as it manifests itself through interpersonal evangelism, the church's inner life, and mercy ministries—is especially significant in our individualistic and secular age. Yet in our experience, Western churches seem infected to some extent with the same fragmentation and disconnection experienced by society at large. Thus, we must immerse ourselves in the biblical vision for the church, praying that the Lord of the church will enable us to conform more closely to his vision for the church.

Fortunately, the Western church can learn much from Christians in Africa, Asia, and Latin America, many of whose churches do not suffer from

31. John Stott, *Christian Mission in the Modern World* (Downers Grove, IL: InterVarsity, 2008), 40.

32. Norman Goodall, ed., *The Uppsala 68 Report* (Geneva: WCC, 1968), 317–18. We owe this reference to Stott, *Christian Mission*, 34.

33. Lesslie Newbigin, *Mission in Christ's Way* (Geneva: WCC, 1987), 11.

34. Newbigin, *Mission in Christ's Way*, 14.

the same social maladies as Western churches do. In fact, historians such as Philip Jenkins have foregrounded the explosive growth of Christianity in these regions, along with the subsequent influence these churches are beginning to have on Western Christianity.

Jenkins offers an example from the recent history of the Anglican Communion. In 1998, the Lambeth Conference was convened as a gathering of Anglican church leaders from around the world. At the conference, the African bishops took the lead in rebuking Western churches and leaders for succumbing to the dictates of the sexual revolution by discarding biblical views of sexuality. "The unscriptural innovations of North American and some western provinces on issues of human sexuality undermine the basic message of redemption and the power of the Cross to transform lives. These departures are a symptom of a deeper problem, which is the diminution of the authority of Holy Scripture."[35] Indeed, the Western church has struggled to conform to God's vision for it, sexual and otherwise, because of its belittling of biblical authority.

If Western Christians will model themselves after African, Asian, and Latin American churches whose strong inner life is cultivated by an embrace of one another and of God's Word, they will stand a better chance of being less individualistic, less isolated, and less disconnected.

Thus, together with the global church, let us offer our broken and alienated age a union with Christ and his church that will heal people's broken relationship with God and with one another.

35. Philip Jenkins, "Believing in the Global South," *First Things* 168 (December 2006): 13–14.

8

A CULTURAL MISSION

Restorational Monotheism
for a Decadent Age

Then God said, "Let us make man in our image, according to our likeness." . . . God blessed them, and God said to them, "Be fruitful, multiply, fill the earth, and subdue it."

Genesis 1:26, 28

Introduction

In his classic work *Christ and Culture*, H. Richard Niebuhr identifies five historic ways Christians have understood the relationship between the Christian faith and a person's cultural context.[1] In the book, Niebuhr examines two strong biblical themes, each prominent but apparently contradictory. On the one hand, we are encouraged to love the world, just as God himself so loved the world (John 3:16). On the other hand, we are told not to love the world because love for the world proves that we do not love God (1 John 2:15–17). Although Niebuhr was content simply to leave these two statements at odds,

1. H. Richard Niebuhr, *Christ and Culture* (New York: Harper & Row, 1951). For contemporary critique of Niebuhr, see Craig A. Carter, *Rethinking Christ and Culture: A Post-Christendom Perspective* (Grand Rapids: Brazos, 2006).

our belief in the unity of Scripture means that we must reconcile the two. In other words, we must come to a biblically shaped understanding of how Christians should relate to the world with regard to culture.

In our experience, most Christians understand intuitively that cultural engagement should not be characterized by uniform approval or categorical dismissal. After all, Jesus instructs us to be *in* the world but not *of* it (John 17:14–18). So how do we accomplish being in the world but not of it? In addition, how much do cultural institutions and products matter to God, and how much should they matter to us?

In this chapter, we will argue that culture matters to God and that it should matter to us. Indeed, every aspect of the Christian mission is unavoidably cultural because God created humans as fundamentally cultural beings. We build houses, drive cars, listen to music, and eat meals. We engage in conversation and make judgments about religion, business, education, politics, and sports. We have worldviews that influence the way we think and feel about these cultural experiences. Indeed, the world God created is profoundly and inescapably cultural. We can no more escape culture than we can live outside our own skin. Everything that makes us human—rather than, say, primate— also makes us cultural.

A Cultural Sickness unto Death

An additional challenging factor is that every culture is to some extent antithetical to Christianity. No culture conforms perfectly to God's ideal. Every culture is a mixed bag, lying somewhere between the biblical ideal and the worst-case scenario. The West is no exception. As we mentioned earlier, Western nations have been experiencing a radical desacralizing or disenchantment of their social and cultural orders. In other words, many Western societies are gradually remaking their social arrangements and cultural institutions, purging them of Christian influence and disconnecting them from transcendent meaning and morality.

In chapter 6, we drew on Charles Taylor's *A Secular Age* to help us understand our secular age and its effect on Western people's psyches. Remember that the secular nature of our age does not imply that most people in Western nations are atheist or agnostic. It does not imply that religion will disappear in the West. Religion in general, and Christianity in particular, is here to stay. However, when we describe our context as *secular*, we are saying at least three things. We are saying that a great many people consider Christianity implausible and even unimaginable. More to the point, we are saying that

Christianity is contested by so many other ideologies that even committed Christians tend to lack deep-level confidence in their own beliefs. Finally, we are saying that the very people who consider Christianity implausible—such as atheists and agnostics—are haunted by transcendence and thus lack deep-level confidence in their own beliefs.

In this chapter, we will complement Taylor's insights by drawing on the writings of sociologist Philip Rieff to explore the effects of secularization on Western cultural institutions and products.[2] Rieff was one of the twentieth century's most influential sociologists and cultural commentators. Although he was not a Christian, his work is especially helpful for Christians living in a secular age. In the Sacred Order / Social Order trilogy published just before his death, he offers a perceptive diagnosis of the theological sickness of Western culture.[3]

In the first volume of the trilogy, *My Life among the Deathworks*, Rieff explores the way many powerful people in the West have collaborated to reorganize society without reference to God. He organizes Western history into three cultural eras. During the first era, Western cultures tended to be pagan and polytheistic, organizing their societies around a pantheon of fickle and volatile gods. First-era societies maintained social order through a system of taboos and they expected their leaders—the cultural elite—to be able to manipulate the gods and change the course of history.

During the second era, Western cultures tended to be monotheistic. People believed in one God, a Trinity, who reveals himself to his creatures and endows life with meaning and significance. Although Western nations were deeply flawed and fell short of Christian ideals, Christian monotheism nonetheless shaped their societies and cultural institutions in very real ways. These second-era societies taught virtue didactically but also reinforced virtue through cultural institutions (such as schools, businesses, or courts), which themselves were influenced by Christianity. Thus the West's culture shaped the habits and desires of successive generations, albeit imperfectly, promoting virtue and opposing social and cultural decadence.

---

2. For a more extensive exploration, see Bruce Riley Ashford, "A Theological Sickness unto Death: Philip Rieff's Prophetic Analysis of Our Secular Age," *Themelios* 43, no. 1 (2018): 34–44; Bob Goudzwaard and Craig G. Bartholomew, *Beyond the Modern Age: An Archaeology of Contemporary Culture* (Downers Grove, IL: InterVarsity, 2017), 126–44.

3. Philip Rieff, *My Life among the Deathworks: Illustrations of the Aesthetics of Authority*, ed. Kenneth S. Piver, Sacred Order / Social Order 1 (Charlottesville: University of Virginia Press, 2006); *The Crisis of the Officer Class: The Decline of the Tragic Sensibility*, ed. Kenneth S. Piver and Alan Woolfolk, Sacred Order / Social Order 2 (Charlottesville: University of Virginia Press, 2007); *The Jew of Culture: Freud, Moses, and Modernity*, ed. Kenneth S. Piver, Arnold Eisen, and Gideon Lewis-Kraus, Sacred Order / Social Order 3 (Charlottesville: University of Virginia Press, 2008).

So the first and second eras recognized the sacred underpinnings of society and culture, the divine authority that endows the world with meaning and instructs individuals in the way of life. Third-era cultures, however, wish to detach society and culture from their sacred origins, limiting the real world to what science can study and locating moral authority in the self. Whereas each of the first two eras recognized that human identity is construed *vertically* via one's relationship to God or gods, the third era rejects the vertical so that it can construe human identity *horizontally* without reference to deity. Without the positive influence of sacred order, Western culture has become a culture of deathworks; its products and institutions, devoid of sacred influence, have increasingly brought social and cultural decay.

Rieff argues that this patently irreligious view of society is not only foolish and destructive but also, ultimately, vain. We can no more live without a religious orientation than we can communicate without a linguistic system or breathe without a pulmonary system. "Culture and sacred order are inseparable. . . . No culture has ever preserved itself where there is not a registration of sacred order."[4] Human beings are deeply and inescapably religious; the more we deny it, the sicker and more twisted our social and cultural institutions become.

Western Christians who agree with Rieff's assessment may be tempted to withdraw from culture as much as possible or to rewind the clock by attempting to retrieve the Christian social order of the second era. But such responses are futile. We cannot withdraw from culture because God created us as cultural beings, and we cannot return to an earlier age. Instead of withdrawing or yearning for an earlier era, Rieff argues, we must push onward toward a fourth era in which sacred order will once again undergird society and culture. We must build communities and institutions that recover the notions of divine revelation and authority and of transcendent meaning and morality. A fourth world era will not enact itself, so it awaits a people who will speak and act responsibly.

Rieff's work is prophetic in the way it cuts to the heart of the West's social and cultural illness. Indeed, many of the West's power brokers are in the middle of an unprecedented attempt to rip the sacred foundations from underneath social order, unmooring our society to float on its own, slowly but surely to its demise. Thus, the West's malady is theological in nature, and it is a sickness leading to social and cultural death. And yet, Rieff's work leaves us without a sufficiently formed prognosis and prescription. Although he calls for a religiously and morally responsible people to speak and act responsibly, he does not sufficiently describe that people or enumerate what it means to

4. Rieff, *My Life among the Deathworks*, 12.

speak and act responsibly. Thus, in this chapter, we will explore ways in which God's people can speak and act responsibly in our cultural contexts.

Culture as a Work and a World

The word *culture* is nowhere found in the Bible, but the concept is everywhere present in its pages. But before we approach the biblical narrative for clues concerning a faithfully Christian view of culture, we need to get a handle on its etymology. The word *culture* comes from the Latin term *cultura*, which literally means "cultivation." It was a farming term, referring to the process of taking the raw materials of the earth and creating fruitful order. Tilling the soil and tending the garden were cultural activities in that literal sense of the word. And it reminds us of our calling as human beings at creation: we are culture makers.

We have Cicero to thank for the more metaphorical use of the word: "*Cultura animi philosophia est*," he wrote. "Philosophy is the cultivation of the soul."[5] Applying the farming analogy to the human condition, Cicero argued that philosophy achieved for the soul what farming did for the earth—namely, it served to develop, create, and draw out latent potential. Later, in the early days of modernity, Westerners employed the word *culture* to refer to the sophisticated artistic, musical, architectural, and intellectual accomplishments of society's elite persons. From this perspective, a select people understood true culture, but the masses did not. And an even smaller circle of people actually contributed to culture.

Still later, the word *culture* was used to refer to the best things a society had to offer. And since some societies had more to offer than others, societies could be placed on a spectrum from primitive to cultured, from barbaric to civilized. Unsurprisingly, Western intellectuals who developed the idea considered their own societies rich with culture while labeling the rest of the world uncultured or less cultured.

But the concept of culture would broaden yet again in the nineteenth century, moving closer to contemporary usage. Instead of referring merely to good societal products, the word *culture* was increasingly employed more comprehensively as the way in which any society conceptualized the world—as a *worldview*.[6] By this rubric, culture was not confined to certain societies and lacking in others. It was inherent in *every* society.

5. Marcus Tullis Cicero, *Tusculanae Disputationes* 2.5.13.
6. Wilhelm von Humboldt was the first to talk about culture as a *Weltanschauung* or a *Weltansicht* (i.e., worldview). See James W. Underhill, *Humboldt, Worldview, and Language* (Edinburgh: University of Edinburgh Press, 2009), 16–19.

This nineteenth-century conception of culture has many merits but is insufficient. For a more apt understanding of culture, we suggest a definition provided by the Christian anthropologist Paul Hiebert. Culture, he asserts, is the "more or less integrated systems of ideas, feelings, and values and their associated patterns of behavior and products shared by a group of people who organize and regulate what they feel, think, and do."[7] Culture, therefore, covers quite a bit of ground.

First, culture has to do with a society's ideas, feelings, and values. Human communities share a certain number of core ideas, and they hold these ideas inflexibly. These basic beliefs are so ingrained that most people recognize them only when they are challenged or violated. These ideas provide the categories with which we experience life. They color what we perceive as plausible or implausible, reasonable or ridiculous. For instance, in contemporary American society, it is generally assumed that time is linear (and not cyclical). Such an idea, though assumed and unarguably true for the average American, is just as unarguably false to the average Indian person.

Human communities also share certain feelings. The range of these emotions, of course, is uniform; regardless of social and cultural context, all humans experience grief and joy, disappointment and wonder. But we interpret and express these emotions in different ways. What enrages people in one society may warm the hearts of people in another, and what people in one society find gorgeous may turn the stomachs of people in another. Our tastes in music, clothing, food, and film represent differing cultural feelings toward these products.

In addition, societies share certain values. Some actions are good, while others are bad. Certain habits are right, and others are wrong. Most societies exhibit flexibility regarding many value judgments, but no society exists with completely relativistic values. Something stands unquestioned in the center.

Second, cultures are more or less integrated systems. Because the various aspects or components of a culture are integrated, divorcing an idea from a value or a value from a feeling becomes difficult. Each bleeds over into the other. Consider the example of human equality. The core idea is that all people are equal, and this idea leads us to value humans over, say, chickens (we may eat the latter but not the former). It is also an idea that leads to emotions: we are enraged when certain people are treated in subhuman ways or encouraged when we see segments of humanity flourishing. As the system that unifies our

7. Paul G. Hiebert, *Anthropological Insights for Missionaries* (Grand Rapids: Baker, 1985), 30.

ideas, feelings, and values, culture is the comprehensive fabric holding these potentially disparate threads together.

Yet, as Hiebert's "more or less" reminds us, the cultural system is messy. Consider several examples. Fringe groups may challenge a society's status quo. A society may experience gross incongruities between ideas and feelings. A new technological advancement might inadvertently begin to shift a long-standing cultural value. One society may encounter another, resulting in both cultures changing in unpredictable ways. Cultures are integrated, but the reality of ongoing cultural change makes this integration perennially tentative.

Third, cultures have patterns of behavior and products associated with their way of living. Culture, then, is something that we make and something that we do. Human communities have unique forms of clothing, housing, transportation, and myriad other cultural products. We rarely stop to think about our cars or our undergarments as cultural items, but societies offer various products to address the same issues. Our behaviors, too, contribute to culture. Americans react to criticism quite differently than Koreans do, and the composite patterns of behavior of many people create a cultural identity.

Hiebert's definition points out the most intriguing element of culture: on the one hand, culture appears to be something that we make, while on the other hand, culture appears to be something that makes us. Both are true. On the one hand, we make culture. We create music. We write poetry. We invent televisions and computers and smartphones. We design strip malls and town houses, skyscrapers and cathedrals. But, on the other hand, even as we are making these things, they are in turn shaping us. We are influenced by the very products we make. This is captured succinctly in—of all places—a recent Jeep commercial: "The things we make, make us."[8] Thus, as Kevin Vanhoozer puts it so aptly, culture is both a "work" and a "world." Culture "is a *work* because it is the result of what humans do freely, not as a result of what they do by nature," and it is a world because culture creates "a meaningful environment in which humans dwell both physically and imaginatively."[9]

8. Jeff Zwart, *Jeep—The Things We Make, Make Us*, Wieden+Kennedy, 2010, https://ben hughes.com/jeep/. The full text of the commercial is rather insightful considering the banality of most contemporary advertisements: "The things that make us Americans are the things we make. This has always been a nation of builders, craftsmen, men and women for whom straight stitches and clean welds were matters of personal pride. They made the skyscrapers and the cotton gins, Colt revolvers, Jeep 4x4s. These things make us who we are. As a people, we do well when we make good things, and not so well when we don't. . . . The things we make, make us."

9. Kevin J. Vanhoozer, "What Is Everyday Theology? How and Why Christians Should Read Culture," in *Everyday Theology: How to Read Cultural Texts and Interpret Trends*, ed. Kevin J. Vanhoozer, Charles A. Anderson, and Michael J. Sleasman (Grand Rapids: Baker Academic, 2007), 26.

Christianity and Culture

Now that we have an initial grasp on the concept of culture, we can go back to the Scriptures to inquire about the role of culture in the Christian mission. Indeed, even though the biblical writers never employed a Hebrew or Greek word that could be translated as "culture," we would be committing a colossal error by believing that the concept of culture does not pervade the pages of Scripture. Similar to other theological terms—such as *monotheism* or *Trinity* or even *theology*—the word may be absent but the concept is present. From Genesis's opening chapters through to Revelation's final paragraphs, the Bible makes clear that God created men and women as profoundly cultural beings.

To explore the Bible's teaching about culture, we must once again return to the biblical narrative, looking at culture through the lens of creation, fall, and redemption. Each plot movement is significant; if we ignore, minimize, or obscure any of the three, we do so at the expense of corrupting and misdirecting the Christian mission.[10]

God's Creational Design for Culture

As we learned in chapter 1, God created the world from nothing (Gen. 1:1), and that which he created he considered "good" and "very good" (1:4, 10, 12, 18, 21, 25, 31). In a discussion of Christianity and culture, this point should not be lost. If God created the world good, and if culture is created from materials furnished by God, then culture cannot be bad in and of itself. Even though many people historically have considered the physical world evil or inferior, Scripture does not and Christians must not.

In addition, we learned that God created human beings in his *tselem* and *demut*, or his image and likeness (Gen. 1:26–28). The Hebrew word for image (*tselem*) signifies representation, while the word for likeness (*demut*) signifies resemblance. The two words are used in a mutually reinforcing manner to point to a single reality. As human beings, we resemble and represent the One who made us.[11] Unlike the animals, we are uniquely fitted to act on God's behalf.

So how did God expect humans to go about representing and resembling him? He gives us clues by surrounding his statement about human nature

10. D. A. Carson makes a similar point in his *Christ and Culture Revisited* (Grand Rapids: Eerdmans, 2008), 44–45.

11. For a fuller exploration of how humans represent God as discussed in Genesis, see the fantastic work of Catherine L. McDowell, *The Image of God in the Garden of Eden: The Creation of Humankind in Genesis 2:5–3:24 in Light of the* mīs pî pīt pî *and* wpt-r *Rituals of Mesopotamia and Ancient Egypt*, Siphrut 15 (Winona Lake, IN: Eisenbrauns, 2015).

with various instructions about how humans should live. In the first chapter of Genesis, just as we are told that God created us in his image, we are also told that he instructed the first couple to lovingly manage the physical environment in which they lived, to fill the earth with their descendants, to name the animals, and to till the soil of the garden. These commands are deeply social and cultural.

Consider God's command to till the soil. This imperative is agricultural in that God expected Adam to produce food by working the garden. But the command is also cultural in the broader sense of the word in that he was saying something like, "Here is my good creation. It is yours to work with. Do something with it. Bring out its hidden potential. This is what makes you different from the animals. This pleases me."

History reveals many ways human beings have brought out the hidden potential of God's creation. We have not only cultivated the earth to produce food and categorized earth's animals by giving them names but also cultivated relationships to produce flourishing families, legal systems to create order and peace, educational institutions to develop hearts and minds, and works of art to explore the aesthetic dimension of life. Whenever we do these types of things, we are fulfilling God's design for us as cultural beings. Cultural activity is ordained by God.

Historically, Christians have sometimes found it difficult to embrace, or have even ignored, this biblical teaching because they have unintentionally embraced cosmic dualism, a perverted and unbiblical view of the physical world. Dualism divides the world into two realms—the visible (physical) and the invisible (spiritual)—praising the invisible realm as good while denigrating the visible realm as inferior or even evil. But Christians must reject this kind of dualism. God the King created the whole world—including its visible and invisible aspects—and thus the created order in its totality is God's good creation.

Albert Wolters summarizes this well: "God does not make junk, and we dishonor the Creator if we take a negative view of the work of his hands when he himself takes such a positive view. In fact, so positive a view did God take of what he had created that he refused to scrap it when mankind spoiled it, but determined instead, at the cost of his Son's life, to make it new and good again. God does not make junk, and he does not junk what he has made."[12] Thus, we must never assume that certain spiritual practices, such as meditation and prayer, are inherently good while other (more material) endeavors,

---

12. Albert M. Wolters, *Creation Regained: Biblical Basics for a Reformational Worldview*, 2nd ed. (Grand Rapids: Eerdmans, 2005), 48–49.

such as engaging in politics, having sex, or playing sports, are inherently bad. Prayer and meditation can be done in ways that displease God, while politics, sex, and sports can be done in ways that please God.

Humanity's Sinful Misdirection of Culture

As we learned in chapter 2, the biblical narrative took a dark turn when the first couple tried to usurp God's throne. But the throne wasn't within reach, and their failed attempt brought serious repercussions. Humans would no longer live in a paradise marked by universal flourishing and delight. Instead, they would live in a world shot through with sin and its effects. The fall "was not just an isolated act of disobedience but an event of catastrophic significance for creation as a whole."[13] Adam and Eve's rebellion marked a turning point in history, as the entire created order would be affected.

After the fall, Adam and Eve continued to be cultural beings, but their cultural doings were now corrupted by sin. Scripture teaches that the heart is the central organizer of a person's life and that religion is embraced in the heart. In other words, if we can identify the object of a person's worship, then we can identify the central organizer of that person's life. Now consider a directional metaphor. To the extent that a person's heart is pointed toward God in Christ, that person's heart will organize that person's words and actions to point toward Christ. Alternatively, to the extent that a person's heart ascribes ultimacy to sex or money or power, that person's heart will organize their words and actions toward that idol. Thus, a person's cultural activities are either directed toward God in Christ or misdirected toward another god or an idol.

Moving to a macrolevel, something similar can be said about entire societies. As Bob Goudzwaard notes, three biblical principles should undergird our understanding of sin in relation to individuals, societies, and cultures.[14] First, each person serves a god of some sort. Second, each person's god transforms her into its own image. Third, people structure society and culture in their own image. In other words, people's religious impulses impact society and culture at large.

So even after the fall, the cultural aspect of God's world remains structurally good. In other words, it is good that there is such a thing as culture and that humans are cultural beings. The created world is still God's world, and it is still structured in such a way that we can bring out its hidden potential, whether in art, science, politics, economics, sports, business, or entrepreneurship. And

13. Wolters, *Creation Regained*, 53.
14. Bob Goudzwaard, *Aid for the Overdeveloped West* (Toronto: Wedge, 1975), 14–15.

yet, because of the fall, culture is misdirected. Although the raw materials of creation remain good, and although we remain cultural beings, sin corrupts the way we make culture and experience culture. Wolters writes, "Anything in creation can be directed either toward or away from God. This double direction applies not only to individual human beings but also to such cultural phenomena as technology, art, and scholarship, to such societal institutions as labor unions, schools, and corporations and to such human functions as emotionality, sexuality, and rationality."[15]

What, then, does the fall teach us about the role of culture in the Christian mission? It teaches us that cultural activity is marked by a great antithesis. We live in a world at war. The battle rages all around us, between the kingdom of light and the kingdom of darkness, between Christ and Satan, and between truth and error. This great struggle between light and darkness cuts across the entire creation and every human culture. No arena of life is off-limits.

This invisible war, represented in Paul's writings by principalities and powers, always manifests in visible, tangible cultural realities. It is not merely or exclusively an ethereal battle between angels and demons, happening somewhere high above our heads. It is rather a gritty struggle in the everyday spheres of human existence. We are on the front lines of a cosmic civil war.

So when the New Atheism, for instance, promotes a story of science devoid of any divine referent, this is not merely a scientific approach. It is one manifestation of rebellion against Christ's lordship, a tangible expression of demonic revolt. Or when a philosopher promotes moral relativism, this is not merely an attempt to liberate humanity from oppressive norms. Instead, it is an assault against the kingdom of light, with the assault taking place in the cultural sphere of philosophy. Similarly, when a man cheats on his spouse for the sake of "love" or indulges in endless video games or television shows instead of spending time with his family, something larger than personal sin is involved. Indeed, this is an instance of the evil one's struggle for control, with the struggle taking place in the cultural sphere of the family.

Christ the King's Redemptive Restoration of Culture

If God had not revealed himself in Scripture, we would have little reason to think that history is headed in the right direction. As we write this chapter, it is Christmastime, a season of promise in the midst of darkness. But for many people, Christmas is a false hope. As Henry Wadsworth Longfellow writes in his well-known carol "Christmas Bells":

15. Wolters, *Creation Regained*, 59.

In despair I bowed my head;
"There is no peace on earth," I said;
"For hate is strong,
And mocks the song,
Of peace on earth, good-will to men!"

What promise is there that the good will ultimately win? The answer, as Longfellow well knew, was in the Christmas story itself:

God is not dead, nor doth He sleep;
The Wrong shall fail
The Right prevail,
With peace on earth, good-will to men.

While the world's cultures are right now corrupted and misdirected by the antithesis, the celebration of Christmas reminds us that God is on the move, fulfilling his promise to destroy the serpent and undo the curse of sin (Gen. 3:15; Gal. 3:16). He will not allow his good creation to languish in darkness and chaos but will return to redeem and restore. Although the evil one and his minions mock our hope of redemption, God will not rest until he sees his purposes through. Christ's incarnation proves the lengths he will go to recover what was lost. His sacrificial death—for us and for the world—and his triumphant resurrection should forever settle the question of which kingdom will prevail.

And his kingdom will prevail from the inside out. God's salvation is not one that discards the created order. Nor is it one, ultimately, that will rescue us up and away from it. Instead, he will bring heaven to earth. He will renew and restore the created order, from top to bottom. Just as God in the beginning created "the heavens and the earth" (Gen. 1:1), he will one day provide for us "a new heaven and a new earth" (Isa. 65:17; Rev. 21:1). In other words, Jesus Christ's salvation extends to God's *people* but also beyond them to God's *cosmos*, so that in the end "creation itself will also be set free from the bondage to decay" (Rom. 8:21). This world will be one "where righteousness dwells" (2 Pet. 3:13) and one filled with cultural products such as art and architecture (Rev. 21), thus fulfilling God's good purposes for his world.[16]

This final restoration will not only undo the curse of sin but also usher us into a new era of cultural activity. When Christ returns, he will not eradicate

---

16. For further reflection on the new earth and its implications, see Russell D. Moore, "Personal and Cosmic Eschatology," in *A Theology for the Church*, ed. Daniel L. Akin, Bruce Riley Ashford, and Kenneth Keathley, rev. ed. (Nashville: B&H Academic, 2014), 711–14.

the cultural aspect of our existence but instead bring healing and redirection to it. He will not send us back to a garden but forward to a glorious and flourishing city, the new Jerusalem, which will be characterized by art, architecture, song, and more.

In light of Christ's redemption, what role should culture play in the Christian mission? It should play a vital and undeniable role. God created us as cultural beings, and we should leverage the cultural aspects of our existence to glorify God and witness to the world. We should allow God's saving works and Word to shape our culture making, our cultural analysis, and our experience of culture and, in so doing, pray that the Lord will cause our efforts to serve as a preview of God's coming kingdom.

Different Kinds of Culture

As we have noted, God created humans as cultural beings, and the cultural aspect of our lives is quite diverse. In reflecting on this reality, the great theologian Abraham Kuyper imagined the realm of culture as a complex and multifaceted relationship between various spheres. We think this spatial analogy is helpful, so we will take a few moments to explore Kuyper's framework of thought.[17]

In understanding Kuyper's thought, it is helpful to remember a phrase employed in the opening chapter of Genesis: "according to their kinds" (vv. 11–12, 21, 24–25). Indeed, we are told that God created the animals according to their kinds, with each kind being unique from the others. Each species follows God's pattern for it, an ordered pattern of unity in diversity. Similarly, Kuyper reasoned, we have good reason to believe that this pattern extended to culture also. When we look at the patterns unfolding in Scripture and in history, it makes sense to say that God created different "kinds" of culture, such as art, science, politics, and business. Although the Bible does not mention these kinds of culture in the first chapter of the book of Genesis, it does explore those realities in other biblical books and in the pages of history. Richard Mouw addresses a criticism that is sometimes made—namely, that if the Bible does not explicitly mention a concept, then we should not teach it. He responds that Kuyper and his colleagues, such as Herman Bavinck, were going

> beyond the explicit statements of Scripture to explore larger patterns of coherence that can shed light on the patterns and implications of what the Bible

17. Abraham Kuyper outlined his views for an American audience in his Stone Lectures, delivered at Princeton Theological Seminary in 1898 and published as *Lectures on Calvinism* (Grand Rapids: Eerdmans, 1943).

explicitly says. That's precisely the kind of thing that happens when theologians write treatises on the Trinity. . . . There is a "fit" of sorts between the actual biblical passages Kuyper and Bavinck allude to and the more speculative claims they make. The Bible does address in very specific terms how God shapes and governs the creation. What Kuyper and Bavinck are trying to do is to catch the spirit of those specific references in order to talk in more general terms and categories about how God structures and orders created life.[18]

Kuyper argued that each sphere of culture has its own center, or reason for being. Art explores the aesthetic dimension of life. Science advances knowledge of the world. Government achieves justice for the various individuals and communities under its purview. And so forth. Similarly, each sphere has its own circumference, or boundaries, limiting its jurisdiction. If government exists to achieve justice, then what business does it have meddling in a local church's ordination? Conversely, what business does a Christian denomination have trying to take control of the government? Thus, Kuyper described this cultural reality as "sphere sovereignty."[19] Under God's kingship, each sphere has sovereignty, or integrity, over its unique territory. God is sovereign over every sphere, but no sphere is sovereign over the others.

If God created the spheres and gave them reasons for existence, then it follows that when they function according to his design, they glorify God and cause humans to flourish. Thus, the spheres of culture are rife with potential for Christian witness. In order to discern the best way to bear witness in a given sphere of culture, we should ask three interrelated questions, each relating to one of the acts of the biblical narrative: What is God's creational design for a given cultural reality? How has human sin and idolatry corrupted and misdirected this cultural reality? And finally, how can we as Christians bring redirection to this sphere of culture by shaping our cultural engagement in light of God's saving works and Word?

Each sphere of culture was created by God, each was poisoned by the fall, and each will be restored in the last day. But between the fall and God's final restoration, Christians have a tremendous opportunity to enter into these spheres to shape them toward God's purposes for them. Because of the antithesis between the prince of darkness and the God who is Light, the cultural aspect of our existence will be a constant struggle. But we must not shrug our shoulders in apathy, slouch into withdrawal, or lash out in anger. In the

18. Richard Mouw, *Abraham Kuyper: A Short and Personal Introduction* (Grand Rapids: Eerdmans, 2011), 48.

19. For more on this, see Abraham Kuyper, "Sphere Sovereignty," in *Abraham Kuyper: A Centennial Reader*, ed. James D. Bratt (Grand Rapids: Eerdmans, 1998), 463–90.

end, Christ will prevail. And until then, our cultural witness should serve as a preview of what the world might be like when God rules in a renewed and restored creation.

In summary, cultural activity takes place under the absolute lordship of Christ. God through Christ is the Creator of all, and as such, he is the King over all. He is not merely the Lord over our hearts or our quiet times; he is the Lord over our work, our leisure, and our civil lives. He is not merely sovereign over local church gatherings; he is the Lord over political and military endeavors, entrepreneurial and scholarly achievements. No piece of our ("secular") life is to be sealed off from Christ's lordship. Every square inch of it belongs to Christ and ought to be made to honor him.

Conversely, because cultural activity takes place under Christ's lordship, it must happen in Christ's time and according to his pattern. Throughout history, Christians have been tempted to take the realms of culture by force as if they could usher in God's kingdom through human action. But this is a perversion of God's agenda; it undermines God's purposes rather than advancing them. Our role is not to establish God's kingdom. Christ will do that. Our role is to walk in obedience to him, working out the gospel's implications in every sphere of culture and allowing God to use our humble efforts to bring renewal and redirection to our corners of culture. Thus, our cultural activity should be characterized by humility rather than pride, persuasion rather than coercion, and a willingness to sacrifice and even suffer. In so doing, we honor God's design for cultural life and provide a preview of his coming kingdom.

Government and Politics

Of the many dimensions of culture—art and science, politics and economics, family and church, scholarship and education, business and entrepreneurship, sports and competition, and more—we will explore two dimensions briefly to illustrate what faithful Christian witness might look like in our modern age. The first dimension we will explore is politics.

When asked how to engage in politics faithfully, a Christian might be tempted to jump directly to specific policy issues or to immediately articulate the platform of a particular political party. Yet, without first setting up a broader Christian framework for understanding government and politics, we will inevitably have a fragmented and distorted view of these realities. Thus, we must return once again, briefly, to the biblical narrative to gather clues about God's design for government and politics.

From the doctrine of creation, we learn that God is the King of the world and that he has chosen to govern the world through us, his representatives. He has given us a mandate to lovingly manage the world (Gen. 1:26–28), including its cultural spheres. One of those God-given spheres encompasses the realm of government and politics. Indeed, God commanded the first couple to be fruitful and multiply, and as the human race multiplied, there would need to be some sort of collective ordering of human communities— determining when the holidays would be held, on which side of the road to drive, and who would do the upkeep for common areas such as parks or theaters. Thus politics, as the art and science of persuading fellow citizens on matters of public significance, would necessarily have been part of life before the fall.

After the fall, human rebellion led to the corruption and misdirection of every aspect of human life (Gen. 4–11), with the sphere of politics being no exception. In the aftermath of the first couple's sin, the political sphere remained structurally good (good in the fact of its existence), although throughout history, it has always and everywhere been misdirected (twisted toward idolatrous ends) to one degree or another. Thus, governments never achieve justice in an enduringly perfect manner; often, they perpetrate great injustices. Likewise, citizens engage in politics (attempts to persuade other people about public matters) in unjust, unloving, and disordered manners. But politics is not the problem. Politics is not dirty in and of itself. It is a good aspect of our world created by God. It is creationally good, but it has been misdirected in disastrous and self-serving ways. The problem is not politics but sin.

In the immediate aftermath of the fall, God promised redemption, and as Scripture unfolds, we learn that his redemption through Christ is deeply and inescapably political. It is a mistake to view Christianity as apolitical (as if Christianity does not get bogged down in something as terrible as politics). But we must clarify. Christianity, as we know it from Scripture, is not apolitical, but we must remember that Christ's redemption does not cohere with the sinful ways associated with politics today.

Christ's redemption, and thereby Christianity, is profoundly political in the sense that the gospel announces that Jesus is Lord, with the implication that Caesar and worldly authorities are not (Mark 12:17). The governments and political leaders of our world have legitimate authority and power, but they have it only because the Lord allows, and one day they will not have it at all. So we give to the authorities their due (Rom. 13:1–7), but we should never give them what is due Christ alone—our ultimate allegiance. The gospel is also political in the sense that Christ's lordship has real implications for the way Christians should think about public matters and the way we should carry ourselves in public. And finally, the gospel is political in that Christ will return one day to consummate his kingdom, in which justice will roll down like the waters (Amos 5:24; Rev. 21–22).

Unmasking Political Idols

If Christ's lordship has real implications for the way Christians should think about public matters, how can we get a handle on a Christian way of approaching the political sphere? One significant way is to unmask false gods and idols that pervert our politics and public life. We might start by identifying perennial idols—such as sex, money, and power—and their negative effects on politics and public life, all the while considering how to undermine these idols through our Christian witness. Or we might start by cataloguing the specific political ideologies of our modern age, such as liberalism and conservatism, subjecting them to an idol analysis so that we can carve out a more faithful path of Christian witness.

This second path of evaluating modern political ideologies is the one taken by Christian political scientist David Koyzis. His work is exemplary in its attempt to carve out a consistently faithful approach to politics in our secular age. In his award-winning book, *Political Visions and Illusions*, Koyzis argues that each of the West's political ideologies ascribes ultimacy to some aspect of the created world and promises to "save" our society by fighting the "evils" that threaten its chosen idol.[20]

Prominent Western political ideologies include liberalism, libertarianism, conservatism, progressivism, socialism, and nationalism.[21] Classical political liberalism and contemporary libertarianism ascribe ultimacy to an individual's right to be free from external restraints such as social, cultural, and moral norms. Conservatism tends to absolutize the conservation of a nation's social norms and cultural heritage, usually seeking to conserve the social and cultural conditions of a particular era in that nation's heritage. Progressivism is the opposite of conservatism, as it tends to ascribe ultimacy to progress, seeking to enact grand social reform agendas that purge the nation of various evils. Nationalism tends to ascribe ultimacy to a nation and usually identifies a particular criterion—such as race or culture or homeland—as the unifying feature of the nation; those persons who do not fit the criterion are treated as inferior or evil. Finally, socialism idolizes material equality and/or communal

---

20. David T. Koyzis, *Political Visions and Illusions: A Survey and Christian Critique of Contemporary Ideologies* (Downers Grove, IL: IVP Academic, 2003), 13–41.

21. For a briefer treatment than Koyzis's, see Bruce Riley Ashford, *Letters to an American Christian* (Nashville: B&H, 2018), 46–54.

ownership and goes to extraordinary lengths to redistribute society's wealth and force economic equality.

In response to modern political ideologies, Koyzis encourages Christians to embrace a nonideological alternative shaped around Christian principles. In response to classical liberalism and modern libertarianism, this alternative would accord a legitimate place for human rights and individual liberties. But it would refuse to treat the individual as sovereign, and it would define our rights and liberties not only in terms of freedom *from* certain restraints but also in terms of freedom *for* a virtuous way of life.

In response to conservatism, it would accord a proper place for tradition but would recognize that traditions, like all human works, are corrupted and misdirected by sin. In response to progressivism, it would recognize the value of social reform but would refuse to put its hopes in, or ascribe messianic status to, grand social reform agendas. In response to nationalism, it would accord a legitimate place for human community, however defined, but would reject any effort to make that community the object of our ultimate allegiance to which all other allegiances must submit. Finally, in response to socialism, it would ascribe to government a limited legitimacy to norm the nation's economic life but would reject socialist expectations that the government can save society through forced material equality and communal ownership.

Distinguishing between Church and State

Another angle from which to address Christianity and politics is to evaluate political platforms in light of God's intentions for the various cultural spheres.[22] If each sphere has its own God-given purpose for existence, and if each sphere has divinely instituted jurisdictional limits, then the ideal political arrangement is one that respects those purposes and jurisdictions. In particular, political arrangement shaped by Christian principles would reject the twin political pitfalls of statism, in which the state oversteps its boundaries by inappropriately interfering with the healthy development of the other spheres, and ecclesiasticism, in which the institutional church oversteps its boundaries by attempting to control political leaders, dictate public policy, or otherwise operate outside its God-given mandate.

22. A number of contemporary political scientists and public theologians have set forth proposals based on the sort of societal pluriformity Kuyper articulated. In addition to Koyzis, see James W. Skillen, *The Good of Politics* (Grand Rapids: Baker Books, 2014); and Richard J. Mouw and Sander Griffioen, *Pluralisms and Horizons* (Grand Rapids: Eerdmans, 1993). In a different way, James K. A. Smith also draws on Kuyper's public philosophy. See Smith, *Awaiting the King: Reforming Public Theology*, Cultural Liturgies 3 (Grand Rapids: Baker Academic, 2017).

This is not to say that the government should never exercise its authority in relation to another cultural sphere. If, as we believe, government exists to achieve justice for the various individuals and communities under its purview, then it will need to exercise such authority from time to time. As Abraham Kuyper notes, government has the right and duty to intervene in three instances:

1. Inter-spherical conflicts. The government may adjudicate disputes between two or more spheres. For example, it may resolve a conflict between the spheres of business and education by restricting a brothel or a strip club from operating close to a middle school.

2. Intra-spherical conflicts. The government may adjudicate a conflict within a given sphere by, for example, protecting the strong from harming or oppressing the weak or intervening in a childcare business to prevent a caretaker from abusing a child. Similarly, it may interfere with the hazardous working conditions at a biochemical facility.

3. Trans-spherical conflicts. The government has the right and responsibility to address needs and challenges that affect several spheres and that cannot be addressed adequately by any one sphere. For example, the government is justified in taxing its citizens to provide libraries, parks, and highways or in creating safety standards that protect citizens' interactions in various spheres.[23]

Similarly, even though the institutional church has neither the divine calling nor the practical competence to run the government or dictate public policy, it can and should influence the political sphere in two specific ways. On Sunday morning, as the church gathers to declare that Jesus is Lord, it should make clear that Caesar and other worldly powers are not. In doing so, the church nourishes its true political identity in Christ and foreshadows the day when Christ will return to install a one-party system and reconstitute the world under a reign of justice and peace. Any church that gathers its people under Christ's lordship and inculcates them into a Christian way of life will, secondly, affect its people's approach to politics and public life. Any Christian who is serious about Christ's lordship will be keen to unmask the idolatrous pretensions of modern political ideologies. Any Christians who are committed to love of neighbor will be better prepared to seek the common good in their political party involvement, political conversations, and voting practices.

23. Kuyper, *Lectures on Calvinism*, 97.

. Thus, a recognition of sphere sovereignty serves as a system of checks and balances, not at the surface level by dispersing governmental power but at a deeper level by dispersing cultural power. Each sphere has a God-given reason for being and a divinely instituted delimitation of its jurisdiction, and Christians who wish to serve their nation can do so by using their energies and expertise to help conform these spheres to their divine design.

Being Christian in Public

In addition to unmasking political idols and making appropriate distinctions between church and state, there are myriad other ways our Christian faith should inform our politics and public life. Among the many principles or imperatives that could be enumerated, we will address a view of the ones relevant to our Christian witness in public.

One of the most important things Christians can do is to seek the common good of their nation rather than merely looking out for their own. Similar to the way God instructed captive Israel to "seek the welfare of the city" in which they were exiled (Jer. 29:7), so we as Christians should love our neighbors enough to seek the good of our nation rather than merely the interests of our own political, economic, or racial tribe. If we cannot cultivate this sort of gospel-centered love for neighbor, then we will be nothing more than a clanging cymbal.

A second imperative for Christians is to be civil in our public demeanor. Amid the West's toxic public square, Christians' political interactions should stand out from the fray. Our public speech and political actions should reveal the difference Christ makes when he takes lordship of our lives. As representatives of Christ the King, we must combine grace and truth by being convictional and civil. Without conviction, we will be public wimps. Without grace-fueled civility, we will be yet another political loudmouth or bully.

Third, we should pray for wisdom in how to articulate our views in the public squares of our secular age. Sometimes putting all our cards on the table, giving explicitly Christian reasons for our views, will be best. Other times giving a more general rationale or giving sociological, legal, or commonsense reasons for our views will be best. Either way, the goal is to glorify God by conforming the political aspect of our lives to his design.

A fourth imperative is to be realistic in what we expect from politics. Politics is neither a savior nor a nothing. As I (Bruce) have written elsewhere, "Ironically, these two perspectives tend to feed off each other. Those who imbue politics with messianic and salvific expectations are most liable to conclude—even if it takes years to get there—that politics is not worth it after all and must be abandoned [as an activity unworthy of our time]."[24] Instead of being a savior or a nothing, politics is a real but limited way of embodying our Christian faith in a fallen world.

Finally, we should determine to play the long game and take the broad view. Instead of putting all our eggs in the basket of short-term political activism, thus limiting our effectiveness and opening ourselves to the temptation of sacrificing our witness on the altar of immediate results, we should consider how to best maintain our witness politically over the long haul. And because politics is only one—very limited—dimension of our cultural witness, we should expend our energies in every sphere of culture, including business, education, art, science, and sports. When we do so, the cumulative effect of our combined cultural witness will be all the greater.

William Wilberforce

Many Christians have served faithfully in the political realm, and many stories can be told of God's blessings on their efforts. But for now, we must be content to highlight one brief story, that of an English politician, William Wilberforce.

Wilberforce was born in 1759 in Yorkshire, England. As a young man, he was quite popular and gained a reputation for being a worldly individual. As he was confronted with the claims of the gospel, he hesitated to embrace Christ seriously because he worried that he would be excluded from social circles. Soon, however, he experienced what he called a "deep conversion" to Christ.

Wilberforce had been elected a member of Parliament in 1780, at the age of twenty-one, and had served for five years. After his conversion, he wondered whether he should resign from Parliament to become a pastor. On the advice of several Christians, including the famous hymn writer John Newton, Wilberforce realized that God was calling him to a mission in the political sphere—to bring an end to slavery in England. Over the course of the next four decades, he worked to abolish the slave trade, with his parliamentary motions failing to gain a sufficient number of votes. In the midst of these failures, Wilberforce refused to back down. In one of his memorable speeches, he exhorted Parliament:

> Let us not despair; it is a blessed cause, and success, ere long, will crown our exertions. Already we have gained one victory; we have obtained, for these poor

---

24. Bruce Ashford and Chris Pappalardo, *One Nation under God: A Christian Hope for American Politics* (Nashville: B&H Academic, 2015), 1.

creatures, the recognition of their human nature, which, for a while was most shamefully denied. This is the first fruits of our efforts; let us persevere and our triumph will be complete. Never, never will we desist till we have wiped away this scandal from the Christian name, released ourselves from the load of guilt, under which we at present labour, and extinguished every trace of this bloody traffic, of which our posterity, looking back to the history of these enlightened times, will scarce believe that it has been suffered to exist so long a disgrace and dishonour to this country.[25]

Seeking to gain victory, he helped form the Anti-Slavery Society in 1822. But soon thereafter poor health caused him to resign from Parliament. By God's grace, two days before Wilberforce died, he received word that Parliament had voted to abolish slavery throughout the majority of the British Empire.

Wilberforce's story illustrates well our cultural mission. He recognized that the idols of wealth accumulation and national pride underlay the British Empire's slave trade. He operated in two cultural spheres, challenging British churches to disciple their people concerning human dignity and challenging the British government to intervene in other spheres (family, commerce) where the weak (slaves) were being abused by the strong (owners). He carried himself like a Christian in public and drew on the immense resources of the Christian faith to guide him and strengthen him in his mission to abolish slavery.

Higher Education

Like politics, higher education is a significant dimension of our cultural world, rife with potential for furthering the Christian mission. The founders of Harvard University certainly thought so. Consider that in 1643 they published a brief pamphlet outlining their mission statement: "Let every Student be plainly instructed, and earnestly pressed, to consider well [that] the maine end of his life and studies is *to know God and Jesus Christ which is eternall life*, John 17:3, and therefore to lay *Christ* in the bottome, as the only foundation of all sound knowledge and Learning."[26] Like Harvard's founders, we believe that Jesus Christ is the foundation of all learning, the clue to understanding the world as a whole.

An exploration of the biblical narrative reveals that God through Christ created the universe. Because Christ created the world, he provides the source,

25. Speech before the House of Commons, April 18, 1791, in *The Parliamentary History of England, from the Earliest Period to the Year 1803*, Vol. 4 (London: Forgotten Books, 2018), 278.

26. "New England's First Fruits," quoted in Perry Miller and Thomas H. Johnson, *The Puritans* (New York: American Book, 1938), 702, italics added.

unity, and motivation for the educational task. He is its source not only because he endowed us with the rational, creative, relational, and physical capacities we employ as we study but also because without his creative work, there would be no world to study. Similarly, Christ provides the unity of the educational task. Because the many diverse aspects of creation have a common source, this diversity of created things is actually a unity in Christ (Eph. 1:10; Col. 1:15–22). A central aim of teaching and learning is to understand this unity. Finally, Christ provides the motivation for our study. If we love Christ, we will want to know him and his work as well as possible.

The Decentering of Christianity and the Disintegration of Higher Education

Rightly directed, higher education is a well-paved road on which we can travel deeper into the knowledge of God. But wrongly directed, it disorients us and leads us down deceptive roads and toward dead ends. Just as any given cultural context is flawed and deficient, so any given system of higher education is flawed and deficient in its own ways.

Consider American universities. In spite of the many merits of the American system, its significant flaws have increasingly come to light in the past few decades. Allan Bloom famously argued that the American university has become a superficial self-esteem factory, specializing in self-affirmation rather than self-examination.[27] More recently, James Piereson has pointed out that education is now a "bottom-line" industry in which many colleges and universities "have come to resemble Fortune 500 companies with their layers of highly paid executives."[28] Richard Arum and Josipa Roksa reveal how our colleges are producing graduates unable to capably read, write, or learn.[29] David Dockery warns that special interest groups threaten to hijack education, operating as they do in service of spurious ideologies.[30] In sum, America's culminating educational institution, the university, is characterized by the disappearance of serious dialogue about the meaning of life, a diminishing of essential skills such as reading and writing, and a capitulation to special interest groups and financial interests.

27. Allan Bloom, *The Closing of the American Mind: How Higher Education Has Failed Democracy and Impoverished the Souls of Today's Students* (New York: Simon & Schuster, 1987).
28. James Piereson, "What's Wrong with Our Universities?" *New Criterion* 30, no. 1 (September 2011): 17.
29. Richard Arum and Josipa Roksa, *Academically Adrift: Limited Learning on College Campuses* (Chicago: University of Chicago Press, 2011).
30. David S. Dockery, *Renewing Minds: Serving Church and Society through Christian Higher Education*, rev. ed. (Nashville: B&H Academic, 2008), 2.

Perhaps most importantly, many American universities have been corrupted and misdirected by their firm rejection of the Christian worldview on which they were founded. Historian George Marsden has shown how the once-pervasive influence of Christian theology on college campuses has virtually disappeared.[31] Whereas Christ had originally been understood as the source, catalyst, and unifying head of the university curriculum, he has not only been decentered but also made unwelcome on many campuses. At best, the Christian worldview is considered irrelevant. At worst, it is viewed as a dangerous impediment to serious scholarship.

Christianity's exit has not been without consequences. Where the Christian worldview once served to integrate seemingly disparate fields of knowledge, that center has been removed. Without a center for the curriculum, students are presented with a fragmented and distorted worldview, a hodgepodge of knowledge.[32] In some classrooms, this disintegration has created a lush environment for the emergence of a sort of garden-variety relativism. In other classrooms, it has created a vacuum, and the empty center has often been filled by materialistic scientism, the belief (discussed earlier) that science is the only sure form of knowledge. Regardless, we can be sure that the removal of Christ from the center creates an environment in which college students are indoctrinated in educational rituals that instill non-Christian visions of the good life, causing them to form dispositions and affections antithetical to the Christian faith.[33] Thus, the decentering of Christianity negatively affects college students' hearts and minds.

Recentering and Reintegration

In light of the university's misdirection, how can Christians enter into this significant arena to bring renewal by redirecting it toward its true end in Christ? There is no easy answer. But we must encourage Christian young people to embrace higher education as a high calling in Christ. We must encourage those who are gifted to earn the highest degrees in their fields of study so that they can enter our public and private universities with the

31. George Marsden, *The Soul of the American University: From Protestant Establishment to Established Nonbelief* (Oxford: Oxford University Press, 1994).

32. Craig G. Bartholomew, *Contours of the Kuyperian Tradition: A Systematic Introduction* (Downers Grove, IL: IVP Academic, 2017), 291–94.

33. James K. A. Smith, *Desiring the Kingdom: Worship, Worldview, and Cultural Formation* (Grand Rapids: Baker Academic, 2009), 215–30. In this significant book, Smith argues that a truly Christian education is one that not only inculcates a Christian worldview but also provides a set of habits, patterns, and rituals that help the student learn to properly love and live in the world.

intention of honoring the Lord in their classrooms. We must put in the hard work to build universities that teach from within a Christian worldview and embody a Christian way of life.

I (Heath) am extraordinarily grateful to be part of a distinctively Christian university at Oklahoma Baptist University, and I (Bruce) am part of a distinctively Christian college at The College at Southeastern. The goal is to integrate the Christian faith—that is, the supreme lordship of Jesus in all spheres of life and all academic disciplines—so that Christ's authority might be seen and experienced in education. We so appreciate the image that Lesslie Newbigin provides for Jesus: he is the clue of all that is.[34] If his insight is true, and we believe that it is, then in education, we must pursue the clue of Jesus to discover how his lordship might be revealed in his good world. Christ, the center and the clue of all that is, must be pursued so that we can discover his authority and our place in his good world.

Only by recovering our lost center in Christ can we reintegrate the learning process so that the diverse disciplines once again form a unity—the original vision behind the "uni-versity." As Craig Bartholomew has argued, we must pay careful attention to how the Bible should shape our teaching and learning, avoiding the twin temptations to use the Bible in ways it was not intended, on the one hand, and to treat the Bible as irrelevant, on the other hand.[35] If college administrators will join the effort, together with professors they can initiate students into a "constellation of practices, rituals, and routines that inculcates a particular vision of the good life by inscribing or infusing that vision into the heart (the gut) by means of material, embodied practices."[36] Thus our universities will be places of information (via the Christian worldview) and formation (via Christian practices). They will enrich the mind and shape the desires of the heart.

In order to build universities marked by the Christian worldview and way of life, administrators, teachers, and scholars will need to fulfill their vocations with both faithfulness and excellence. In regard to faithfulness, we must follow a model of "faith seeking understanding," allowing the Christian view of the world to frame our teaching and learning and to provide fruitful avenues for research. "The purpose of Christian education," writes T. S. Eliot, "would not be merely to make men and women pious Christians. . . . A Christian education must primarily teach people to be able to think in

---

34. Lesslie Newbigin, *The Finality of Christ* (London: SCM, 1969), 65–87.

35. Bartholomew, *Contours of the Kuyperian Tradition*, 308. See also Bruce Riley Ashford, "What Hath Nature to Do with Grace? A Theological Vision for Higher Education," *Southeastern Theological Review* 7, no. 1 (Summer 2016): 3–22.

36. Smith, *Desiring the Kingdom*, 26.

Christian categories." [37] We also must follow a model of "faith seeking right practice," allowing the Christian faith to shape the rhythms of a university's curricular and cocurricular activities.

Christians must also strive for excellence in scholarship. Over the past fifty years, very few evangelicals have risen to the highest posts at prominent research universities. In fact, many of the most crucial and influential fields at elite universities—such as religious studies, physics, biology, literary criticism, and political science—are characterized by the conspicuous paucity of evangelical minds. The net effect is not surprising. A behemoth culture-shaping institution has been left largely to those who find Christian belief implausible and detrimental to education. As the universities go, so goes our culture.

Thus, our desire for faithfulness and excellence will cause us to follow the threefold pattern of discerning God's creational design for higher education, evaluating the ways it has been corrupted and misdirected, and then finding ways to bring healing and redirection.

Swimming against the Current

There are many Christian administrators and professors working faithfully within Western universities, and there are many stories of God's blessings on attempts to bring renewal to academic disciplines and college campuses. Among the stories that could be told, Alvin Plantinga's is one of the most instructive. As an undergraduate student, Plantinga majored in philosophy at a small Christian college, Calvin College, in the mid-twentieth century, a time when very few philosophers were committed Christians. He distinguished himself in his philosophy courses at Calvin and eventually went on to receive a PhD in philosophy from Yale. Over the next five decades, he taught philosophy at several universities, published hundreds of articles and books, and served as president of the American Philosophical Association.

Plantinga's example is instructive because his research and writing were undertaken with the view that Christ is the clue to the universe. He considered his Christian belief a boost, rather than a hindrance, to his scholarship. In fact, he and a small group of Christian philosophers, including William Alston, Nicholas Wolterstorff, and Ronald Nash, were so influential that they were the catalysts for a reformation in American philosophy departments. In fact, atheist philosopher Quentin Smith bemoans Plantinga's enormous influence when he writes:

37. T. S. Eliot, *Christianity and Culture* (New York: Harcourt, Brace, 1940), 22.

By the second half of the twentieth century, universities and colleges had become in the main secularized. . . . This is not to say that none of the scholars
in the various academic fields were realist theists in their "private lives"; but
realist theists, for the most part, excluded their theism from their publications
and teaching, in large part because theism . . . was mainly considered to have
such a low epistemic status that it did not meet the standards of an "academically respectable" position to hold. The secularization of mainstream academia
began to quickly unravel upon the publication of Plantinga's influential book
on realist theism, *God and Other Minds*, in 1967. It became apparent to the
philosophical profession that this book displayed that realist theists were not
outmatched by naturalists in terms of the most valued standards of analytic
philosophy: conceptual precision, rigor of argumentation, technical erudition,
and an in-depth defense of an original world-view. . . .

Realist versions of theism, most influenced by Plantinga's writings, began to
sweep through the philosophical community, until today perhaps one-quarter
or one-third of philosophy professors are theists, with most being orthodox
Christians. Although many theists do not work in the area of the philosophy
of religion, so many of them do work in this area that there are now over five
philosophy journals devoted to theism or the philosophy of religion, such as
Faith and Philosophy, *Religious Studies*, *International Journal of the Philosophy of Religion*, *Sophia*, [and] *Philosophia Christi*. . . .

Quickly, naturalists found themselves a mere bare majority, with many of
the leading thinkers in the various disciplines of philosophy, ranging from philosophy of science (e.g., Van Fraassen) to epistemology (e.g., Moser), being
theists. The predicament of naturalist philosophers is not just due to the in-
flux of talented theists, but is due to the lack of counter-activity of naturalist
philosophers themselves. God is not "dead" in academia; he returned to life
in the late 1960s and is now alive and well in his last academic stronghold,
philosophy departments.[38]

As Smith laments, Plantinga's scholarship was a major catalyst for the
resurgence of Christian theism within American philosophy departments.
What he fails to note sufficiently is the small cadre of Christian philosophers
who worked together with Plantinga to foster this movement. In fact, this
movement was birthed at a lunch in a German restaurant in Chicago at which
Plantinga, Nicholas Wolterstorff, Ronald Nash, William Alston, and a few
others determined to start an organization of Christian philosophers. They
were concerned about the marginalization of Christianity in philosophical
circles and worked together to bring about a renaissance of Christian theism

38. Quentin Smith, "The Metaphilosophy of Naturalism," *Philo: A Journal of Philosophy* 4,
no. 2 (2001): 3–4.

in the field of philosophy. Out of this meeting the Society of Christian Philosophers (SCP) was born, which eventually gave birth to the scholarly journal
Faith and Philosophy. The SCP now boasts a membership of approximately
one thousand, while *Faith and Philosophy* is one of the most respected journals of philosophy in the English-speaking world.

The story of Alvin Plantinga and the rise of Christian theism in American
philosophy departments reminds us that Christianity is neither irrelevant nor
antithetical to scholarship. Quite the contrary: it is a catalyst for excellence.
And when faithful Christian scholars work together in community, the results
can be astonishing.

Conclusion

We began this chapter with a brief exploration of the decentering of Christianity in Western cultures. Drawing on Philip Rieff, we noted that many of
the West's power brokers are in the midst of a historically unprecedented
attempt to build a society and culture without reference to God. Rieff's argument reminded us of Charles Taylor's argument (summarized in chapter 6)
that our secular age is characterized by the view that Christian monotheism is implausible and even unimaginable. Another way of putting it is that
the West's reigning "plausibility structures" (the cultural frameworks within
which things make sense) call into question historic Christianity.

In response, we have argued that the cultural dimension of life provides
Christians an especially significant way to further the Christian mission.
Through our faithfulness in the realm of culture, we can turn the tables on
our secular age by calling into question *its* plausibility structures. As we allow
ourselves to be shaped culturally by God's saving works and words, as we
seek to be faithful in the cultural dimensions of our lives, we will challenge
the reigning secular framework of thought.

A culture's plausibility structures are not normally part of a person's con-
scious thought processes. Instead, plausibility structures are like the air we
breathe. We do not notice them because they are so thoroughly a part of
our culture. Thus, questioning them does not occur to us. If we wish to be
faithful to Christ, however, we must identify these frameworks and challenge
them with the gospel.[39]

As Lesslie Newbigin argued, a community that believes and embodies the
story is the best way to speak compellingly to the West's plausibility structures.

39. Lesslie Newbigin, *A Word in Season* (Grand Rapids: Eerdmans, 1997), 67.

When the church gathers on Sunday mornings to worship Christ the King, it shapes the identity of God's people and sends them back into the culture as Christ's representatives. Sunday morning worship is vital for a Christian's Monday morning cultural calling.

And if the church is to prepare God's people to challenge the West's plausibility structures, it must do so with Scripture as its authority. As Christians, we are a people whose way of thinking is shaped by the Bible's narrative. We "indwell" the Bible's story so that it provides the framework within which we approach everything in life and so that we will be alert to rival Western stories that find the clue to the universe in sexual freedom, scientific knowledge, or Western political institutions. No matter what the West's power brokers say, the biblical narrative provides a better (more plausible!) framework within which to live and think in this world. Thus, as Newbigin argues, we must immerse ourselves in this story:

> We have to soak ourselves in this story, so that we more and more understand that it is the real story and that the story that we are listening to on the radio and in our newspapers is to a very large extent phoney. The real issues are the ones that we recognise when we let this story shape our thinking. Then it is in this context that we have to think about the various decisions we have to make, small or great. We have to do the best thinking we can, we have to consult wise friends, we have to ask for God's guidance, and we have to act. There is no way in which we can settle the matter for us. God does not relieve us of personal responsibility. We can be wrong, but we can also know that if our trust is in Jesus, God can cope with our mistakes. Having done all we can, we must be prepared to take our stand even if we are in a small minority.[40]

The Bible, and not its rival secular narratives, is the true story of the whole world. And if we are to fulfill our mission, we must give it primacy in the cultural dimension of our lives.

---

40. Lesslie Newbigin, "Biblical Authority," DA29.3.17.1, unpublished article, Birmingham, UK, n.d., p. 6.

9

A GLOBAL MISSION

*Realized Monotheism
for an International Age*

> And they sang a new song:
>
> > You are worthy to take the scroll
> > and to open its seals,
> > because you were slaughtered,
> > and you purchased people
> > for God by your blood
> > from every tribe and language
> > and people and nation.
> > You made them a kingdom
> > and priests to our God,
> > and they will reign on the earth.
>
> Revelation 5:9–10

Introduction

Toward the end of the twentieth century, Western intellectuals poured forth streams of books interpreting and analyzing the international order and often prognosticating about the future. In one of the more famous volumes, *The End of History and the Last Man*, political scientist Francis Fukuyama argued that the end of the Cold War would give rise to a global situation in which the historic struggle between ideologies would end, Western values would triumph, and democracy would become the final form of government. Though Fukuyama has since modified his view, *The End of History*'s utopian and Westerncentric view of history still seems to represent the ultimate hopes and dreams of many people.[1]

A few years later, Samuel Huntingdon's *The Clash of Civilizations and the Remaking of World Order* appeared as a thinly veiled attack on Fukuyama's theory. In it, Huntingdon argued that there would be no global embrace of liberal democracy and Western values. Instead, the globe would experience deep-seated conflict, and the West would be at a disadvantage. For Huntingdon, religion and culture would form the focal point of international politics, and this would make many of modernity's previous controversies look like minor kerfuffles. The world's most basic units of order are civilizations, Huntingdon argued, and these civilizations would increasingly come apart instead of coming together. Critics have pointed out many deficiencies with Huntingdon's book, but his thesis seems to give voice to the view of many people.[2]

During the same time, scores of historians and cultural commentators evaluated the emerging reality of globalization. In *Preparing for the Twenty-First Century*, one of the more significant volumes, historian Paul Kennedy traced the emergence and development of mass communication, global finance, international travel, and multinational corporations, combining them with explosive demographic growth and concluding that the global community was surpassing the nation-state in importance. In another more popular book, *The World Is Flat*, journalist Thomas Friedman stated famously that the world is now (almost) flat. Since the turn of the century, a series of economic, technological, and political factors have coalesced to produce a massive change in global culture in which the world is now hyperconnected, and we are ever aware of its hyperconnectedness. Although a number of forms of resistance to this hyperconnectedness are now emerging, globalization represents the great hope of many people in the West.[3]

But more important than any of those books or theses is an overlooked development that gives the world a peek into God's plan for the culmination of history: the explosive growth of Christianity among people groups

---

1. Francis Fukuyama, *The End of History and the Last Man* (New York: Free Press, 1992).
2. Samuel Huntingdon, *The Clash of Civilizations and the Remaking of World Order* (New York: Simon & Schuster, 1998).
3. Paul Kennedy, *Preparing for the Twenty-First Century* (New York: Vintage, 1994); Thomas L. Friedman, *The World Is Flat: A Brief History of the Twenty-First Century* (New York: Picador, 2005).

around the globe. In one of the most significant explorations of this reality, *The Next Christendom*, historian Philip Jenkins showed how Christianity's center of gravity is shifting to the South and the East or from Europe and North America to Asia, Africa, and South America. In a series of other articles and books, Jenkins traced the doctrinal implications of this shift: the new churches of the South and the East identify with the biblical world and have a high view of biblical authority, and thus their forms of Christianity are more conservative than those of many Western denominations.[4]

For Christians who have paid careful attention to the biblical narrative and the Christian mission, Christianity's explosive growth will come as no surprise. Christianity's unique ability to transcend national and cultural barriers stems from God's determination to woo the nations to himself.[5] As God spoke to Habakkuk, so he speaks to us today.

> Look among the nations, and see;
>   wonder and be astounded.
> For I am doing a work in your days
>   that you would not believe if told. (Hab. 1:5 ESV)

For Habakkuk, that wonder was a response to judgment. But for us, that wonder is a response to grace.

God is on the move among the nations, drawing people from every corner of the earth to come under his sovereign rule and loving embrace (Rev. 5:9–10). This thread of the biblical narrative—God's mission to the nations—runs through the entire narrative and, with each twist and turn in the plot, calls God's people to join him in his mission. As we will see, this international thread is on colorful display in the nation of Israel, the life and ministry of Jesus, and the nature of Christ's church.

Israel's Mission to the Nations

In our experience, Christians often hear "international mission" and immediately fast-forward through the Old Testament to the New. Yet, as we

4. Philip Jenkins, *The Next Christendom: The Coming of Global Christianity* (Oxford: Oxford University Press, 2002); Jenkins, "After the Next Christendom," *IBMR* 28, no. 1 (January 2004): 20–22; Jenkins, *The New Faces of Christianity: Believing the Bible in the Global South* (Oxford: Oxford University Press, 2005).

5. Yale professor Lamin Sanneh, Gambian native and Christian convert from Islam, argues that Christianity is unique among world religions in its ability to transcend social, cultural, and national barriers. Lamin Sanneh, *Whose Religion Is Christianity? The Gospel beyond the West* (Grand Rapids: Eerdmans, 2003).

noted in chapter 3, God promises to make Abraham's name great and to make his family into a great nation so that Abraham's offspring can be a blessing to the nations. God always intended for his people to be a light to the nations. J. H. Bavinck writes, "If we investigate the OT . . . thoroughly, it becomes clear that the future of the nations is a point of the greatest concern. It is in itself striking how often the OT discusses the future of these peoples and interests itself in the salvation that will one day be their lot."[6] International mission, therefore, does not find its genesis in the New Testament but in Genesis.

Consider how the Bible's opening chapters declare God's creatorship and lordship over all things and all people (Gen. 1–2) and the way the nations of the earth are listed as a kind of backdrop for Genesis, the Pentateuch, and, ultimately, the whole Bible (Gen. 10).[7] Consider also the heightened tension created by the nations' attempts to unify themselves by building a tower apart from God (Gen. 11). "Let us make a name for ourselves," they agree, "otherwise, we will be scattered throughout the earth" (11:4). God looks down from heaven on their project and responds by confusing their languages so that they cannot again unify themselves apart from him.

In the midst of this incident of international rebellion, God acts to catalyze his mission to the nations. Calling Abraham, God promises to bless him, make him a great nation, and make his name great, all so that he can be a blessing to all the families of the earth (Gen. 12:1–3). As time passes, Abraham and his family become a great nation—the nation of Israel. In the book of Exodus, we learn that God delivers Israel from slavery in Egypt so that the people can mediate his deliverance to the nations (Exod. 19:4–6). In a striking divine utterance later in Israel's life, God, through Moses, reaffirms his international intentions:

> Look, I have taught you statutes and ordinances as the LORD my God has commanded me, so that you may follow them in the land you are entering to possess. Carefully follow them, for this will show your wisdom and understanding in the eyes of the peoples. When they hear about all these statutes, they will say, "This great nation is indeed a wise and understanding people." For what great nation is there that has a god near to it as the LORD our God is to us whenever we call to him? And what great nation has righteous statutes and ordinances like this entire law I set before you today? (Deut. 4:5–8)

6. J. H. Bavinck, *An Introduction to the Science of Missions*, trans. David H. Freeman (Phillipsburg, NJ: P&R, 1960), 11.

7. John H. Sailhamer, *The Pentateuch as Narrative: A Biblical-Theological Commentary* (Grand Rapids: Zondervan, 1992), 130–34; John H. Sailhamer, *NIV Compact Bible Commentary* (Grand Rapids: Zondervan, 1994), 23.

Indeed, God placed the people of Israel on the international stage and gave them his law so that their corporate holiness would cause the nations to notice the matchlessness of their God.

Christopher J. H. Wright describes God's intentions for Israel in terms of gravitational draw. God intends for Israel to serve as a sort of "missional magnet."[8] Israel's obedience to God attracts pagan seekers (1 Kings 8:41–43), incites admiration (Jer. 13:1–11), compels worship (Isa. 60), and attracts approval (49:6). This is why Israel sings songs requesting God's blessing so that the nations will be saved and join in that blessing (Ps. 67). This is why Isaiah speaks of Israel as a light to the nations (Isa. 49:1–6). God chooses Israel from among all the nations of the earth, but he does so for the sake of all the other nations.

The Law as a Light to the Nations

When God calls the people of Israel to bless the nations, he does not leave them on their own to try to figure out how. He gives them the law not only for their own good but also for the good of the nations. In *A Light to the Nations*, Michael Goheen writes, "This is why the law's instruction to Israel covers the whole scope of human life. The people of Israel now serve a new covenant Lord, the God of creation. They owe him their undivided loyalty and must consecrate their social, economic, familial, and political structures—indeed the whole of their personal, social, and cultural lives—to him. The Torah creates a community and a people whose life is to be a light to the world."[9]

To understand God's intention for the law, we must remember that the first couple—and, indeed, all of us thereafter—used their freedom to rebel against God. This rebellion and its consequences were systemic, corrupting the entirety of every aspect of the world. And because every aspect—personal, social, and cultural—is now corrupted and misdirected, what we need is not unbridled freedom but directions. This is what the law provided: it was a way for God's people to consecrate the whole of their personal, social, and cultural lives to God.

God gave the law, therefore, so that Israel could be a "contrast community." As the people conformed to God's design for their lives, they would stand out

8. Christopher J. H. Wright, *The Mission of God's People: A Biblical Theology of the Church's Mission*, ed. Jonathan Lunde, Biblical Theology for Life (Grand Rapids: Zondervan Academic, 2010), 131.

9. Michael W. Goheen, *A Light to the Nations: The Missional Church and the Biblical Story* (Grand Rapids: Baker Academic, 2011), 40.

as a contrast to the nations. As their corporate obedience cast light backward on God's original design for creation and forward to his future salvation, it would also shine outward toward the nations.[10] God called the people of Israel to live comprehensively righteous lives in front of the nations. And, although God's law applies differently today than it did to ancient Near Eastern Israel, God still calls us to apply his saving works and Word to every aspect of our personal, social, and cultural lives. No aspect of our existence lies outside his jurisdiction.

Three Successive Eras of Mission to the Nations

There are times when Israel lives up to its remarkable calling. Yet, on the whole, Israel's story is characterized by its failures. Instead of confronting the pagan nations' idols, they often worship them. Instead of conforming to God's law, they often rebel against it. As a result, God's ideal plan is never realized. But even as God judges Israel, he still works out his plan to bless the nations by blessing Israel. As Goheen shows, God reaffirms Israel's missional calling throughout three successive eras of missional failure—tribal confederation, monarchy, and diaspora.

During Israel's early years, the nation is a tribal confederation.[11] Because Israel is a mere confederation of tribes rather than a monarchy under a powerful human king, the people have a unique opportunity to demonstrate that God is sufficient as their divine King. Instead of capitalizing on the opportunity, the people rebel against God and demand that he give them an earthly king (1 Sam. 8:5). God relents and gives them a king.

Oscar Wilde once noted that there are two tragedies in life: one is not getting what you want; the other is getting it. The second tragedy happens when God gives Israel an earthly king. He allows the nation to reduce itself to being merely one monarchy among many.[12] It is not the panacea Israel had hoped for. Human kingship quickly loses its luster as the people learn—painfully—that emulating their neighbors is not a blueprint for success. But God is not finished with Israel. He renews their mission, calling Israel's human kings to help Israel submit to God's divine kingship. As Israel's kings obey God, his greatness will be displayed to the nations. However, more often than not, Israel's kings lead the way in idolatry and corruption, eventually causing God to judge them by sending them into exile under pagan rule.

10. Goheen, *Light to the Nations*, 39–42.
11. Goheen, *Light to the Nations*, 51–54.
12. Goheen, *Light to the Nations*, 54–60.

Thus begins Israel's identity as a *diaspora* (a scattered people). Yet even as an exiled people living under God's judgment, their missional calling remains.[13] Living as a minority people in the midst of the nations makes their obedience exceedingly complicated, causing them great suffering at the same time that it offers enormous opportunity. The biblical stories of Daniel, Shadrach, Meshach, and Abednego are exemplary, as these faithful Israelites carve out paths of faithful witness, including nonviolent protest, imprisonment, and attempted execution. But if the cost they pay is great, God's faithfulness is greater, as the world's most powerful leaders respond by declaring to their empire the greatness of the Israelite's God (Dan. 3:28–30; 6:25–28). Indeed, when Israel is faithful, even in exile, God works in and through the people's obedience to shine his light on the nations.

Jesus's Mission to the Nations

The Old Testament concludes with Israel scattered across the face of the earth—adrift, helpless, broken. The significance of Israel's failure cannot be overstated. The people's disobedience not only leads to severe discipline from the hand of God but also muffles God's saving voice to the world. Yet, despite Israel's failure, hope remains. Goheen writes,

> The Old Testament story ends with both failure and hope. Israel has failed in its calling to be a light to the nations; it has been overcome by the darkness of the nations around it. God had judged the people of Israel and sent them into exile. Nevertheless, the prophets have ignited in the hearts of the scattered people a small flame of hope. In the last days God will act again in power through the Messiah and by his Spirit to restore his rule over all nations, all creation. God will gather and purify Israel, the temple will be rebuilt, the land will be cleansed, and the Torah will be obeyed. God will be King again—over the whole earth.[14]

Just as he did in Abraham's day, God chooses one for the sake of the many. Far from abandoning his plan with Israel, he narrows the focus. Now, not Israel but Israel's coming *messiah* will usher in God's kingdom. God promises a fresh start, and as has so often happened in the past, it will all hinge on one person.

13. Goheen, *Light to the Nations*, 60–66.
14. Goheen, *Light to the Nations*, 68.

Jesus's Missional Life

The New Testament opens with the birth of the long-awaited Messiah, Jesus, who comes proclaiming that, with his birth, the kingdom of God has arrived (Mark 1:15; Luke 4:21). The kingdom of God—the power that defeats all God's enemies, saves humanity from sin, and renews God's creation—has at last been inaugurated. But it has not yet been realized. The rightful King of the earth has entered the world to set it aright. And yet, things did not look quite like anyone had expected. In fact, the kingdom of God will not be fully consummated until a later time. So the King has come, not as a conquering hero but as a suffering servant, the secret vanguard of God's international mission.

Even though the Messiah's arrival is less triumphant than people expect, it is nonetheless powerful. In his life and ministry, the curse of sin and death begin to unravel. To borrow one of J. R. R. Tolkien's famous sayings, everything sad is coming untrue.[15] In Jesus, the life-giving power of gospel words and gospel deeds unite. Jesus's miracles, for instance, highlight how words and deeds corroborate each other. Jesus often demonstrates power over nature, sickness, demons, even death. These are never merely displays of raw power, magic tricks to impress the crowd. We have no record of Jesus levitating or catching flaming arrows in his bare hand. Instead, Jesus performs miracles that demonstrate his lordship while also illustrating his saviorship. His miracles not only prove that he is the rightful King but also give us a glimpse of what his restored kingdom will one day look like.

Consider, for example, Jesus's calming of the stormy Sea of Galilee (Matt. 8:23–27). In making a raging storm quietly submit to his spoken word, Jesus shows that he is Lord over the same waters he spoke into existence. He is no mere man, as the disciples immediately recognize: "What kind of man is this? Even the winds and the sea obey him!" (Matt. 8:27). The answer: this man is God, the Lord. But Jesus does not conquer the winds and the waves simply to prove his lordship. He also does it to give the world a preview of the restored kingdom. A day is coming when there will be no threatening storms, no tears, no suffering, no fear, no death.

Jesus's Missional Death and Resurrection

Jesus will set the world to rights, but he will not do it all at once, and in his first coming, he will not come in force. Rather than coming with military might and political power, he comes as a suffering servant. The Gospel writers all compose

15. Those are the words of Tolkien's fictional character Samwise Gamgee to Gandalf. J. R. R. Tolkien, *The Return of the King* (New York: Random House, 1955), 246.

their books with a focus on the events of one crucial week, when Jesus sacrifices his life on behalf of the world. And the early church declares his crucifixion and resurrection an announcement of good news for the world. As noted in chapter 5, 1 Corinthians 15:1–5 provides an instructive summary of this gospel:

> Now I want to make clear for you, brothers and sisters, the gospel I preached to you, which you received, on which you have taken your stand and by which you are being saved, if you hold to the message I preached to you—unless you believed in vain. For I passed on to you as most important what I also received: that Christ died for our sins according to the Scriptures, that he was buried, that he was raised on the third day according to the Scriptures, and that he appeared to Cephas, then to the Twelve.

Indeed, Jesus's death and resurrection display God's thesis for the world: that his kingdom has arrived in the life, death, and resurrection of Jesus, who is King and Savior, in fulfillment of Old Testament prophecy. The gospel calls for belief, trust, and repentance; in it, God promises that those who heed this call will live with him eternally in the new heavens and earth. Or to put it more briefly, in Jesus, God declares that Jesus the King died and rose again in order to save us from our sins and set the world to rights.

This is what Jesus has been trying to tell his disciples even though they have difficulty comprehending. Jesus's death may have looked like a defeat to those without eyes to see or ears to hear, but through the eyes of faith, it is actually a moment of profound victory. Jesus is nailed to the cross, but it is the evil one who truly suffers defeat that day. In Jesus's death, God the King takes on himself the sins of the world—the ultimate act of the one for the many—so that we might be saved from sin and for life under his reign. Buried in the ground, Jesus is separated from the Father, but raised on the third day, he joins the Father in making a public promise concerning the raising of sinners to new life, the raising of our bodies when he returns, and, ultimately, the resurrection of the heavens and earth themselves. These events take place publicly because the gospel is a public truth. As Paul says before King Agrippa, "This was not done in a corner" (Acts 26:26).

The Church's Mission to the Nations

Jesus's Missional Commission

After Jesus's resurrection, he gives his disciples a clear and compelling mission. In Matthew's telling of this Great Commission, Jesus speaks to them, saying, "All authority has been given to me in heaven and on earth. Go, therefore, and make disciples of all nations, baptizing them in the name of the Father and of the Son and of the Holy Spirit, teaching them to observe everything I have commanded you. And remember, I am with you always, to the end of the age" (28:18–20).

This great missional imperative is not some sort of ad hoc directive ("Oh, wait! One more thing. I almost forgot . . .") but the fulfillment of God's mission for Israel and his mission through Jesus. Indeed, as Leon Morris demonstrates, Matthew wrote his Gospel account in order to show that Christianity is the fulfillment of Old Testament faith, the flowering of God's seminal work through Israel.[16] Matthew's Gospel begins by showing Jesus's connection to Israel's King David, continues by showing the reality of the kingdom through Jesus's teaching and miracles, and promises a future consummation of that kingdom, a consummation in which the gentiles finally have a place. In Matthew, the first people to meet Jesus are gentiles, and the last people in focus are gentiles too.

This is the context of the Great Commission. It is not an afterthought but a concise summary of the whole Christian mission, a compact rendering of the gospel's implications for the Christian life. This passage, Matthew 28:18–20, describes the Christian mission as one that unfolds under Jesus's authority, according to his Word, and with his presence. It is a passage about lordship, discipleship, and presence. Jesus Christ is the supreme Lord of the universe, and on that basis he commands us to invite all people everywhere to receive his salvation and submit to his lordship, remembering all the while that our mission is undergirded by his presence and power.

Consider the first declarative: "All authority has been given to me in heaven and on earth" (Matt. 28:18). In these few words, Jesus's audience understood that he was declaring his own authority as supreme Lord of the entire universe. In saying that he has all authority "in heaven and on earth," Jesus makes a deliberate reference to the opening chapters of Genesis and prophesying his second coming. Jesus is the one who created "the heavens and the earth" (Gen. 1:1), and he is the one who will usher in a renewed heavens and earth (Rev. 21:1). In one little phrase, Jesus points backward to creation and forward to a renewed creation, establishing that he is both Creator and Redeemer, both Lord and Savior.

Based on his kingly authority, Jesus instructs his disciples to "make disciples of all nations" (Matt. 28:19). By telling them to *make disciples* of the nations, he is asking them to live out the apprenticeship they had served under

16. Leon Morris, *The Gospel according to Matthew*, ed. D. A. Carson, PNTC (Grand Rapids: Eerdmans, 1992), 2–4.

him. "Just as I lived my entire life in submission to God the Father (for your sake), so I want you to live your entire life in submission to me (for the sake of others)." And by telling them to make disciples of *all nations*, he makes clear his intent to work though his people to broadcast the gospel to every corner of the created order. As the Father has sent Jesus as a light to the nations, so Jesus sends them as a light to the nations (John 20:21).

In making disciples, we are "baptizing them in the name of the Father and of the Son and of the Holy Spirit" (Matt. 28:19). When a person comes to faith in Christ and is baptized, baptism serves as a picture of the gospel and a preview of the future. As believers are immersed in water and then raised from it, they receive not only a picture of Christ's death and resurrection for the forgiveness of sins but also a preview of the day when he will return to set the world aright. And as believers are baptized, they also make a public proclamation that they are now the treasured possession of the Triune God. They take on his name and become part of his family.

In making disciples, we are also "teaching them to observe everything I have commanded you" (Matt. 28:20). As we mark these new disciples out as God's own, we impart to them all of Christ's teachings, and since Jesus affirmed every jot and tittle of Scripture (5:17), he wants us to impart to them all that Scripture teaches. This is not merely an arbitrary requirement, as if Jesus simply thought Bible trivia was important. No, Jesus Christ himself is the towering actor in all of Scripture (Luke 24:25–27). When we teach disciples Scripture, we teach them about Christ. He is the clue to history, the key that unlocks the meaning of the whole.

Finally, as we make disciples, we should remember that Jesus is "with [us] always, to the end of the age" (Matt. 28:20). Given the formidable nature of the commission—making disciples of all nations, including secular nations, pantheist nations, polytheist nations, and Islamic nations—Christ the King walks alongside us and empowers us. And he will be with us until the end. In other words, Jesus is saying to his ancient Near Eastern disciples and to us, "When the world's history is over, I will be there. When the dust has settled and every empire is a distant memory, I will be standing. And because I will be standing, so will you. Because of my death and resurrection, world history has a deeply joyful ending. So follow me and have no fear; the darkness is drawing short, and a new dawn is coming."

The Church's International Mission

The book of Acts reveals what actually transpired in response to Jesus's commission. While the Gospels were written about what Jesus taught and did during his earthly ministry, Acts is about what Jesus *continues* to do and teach (Acts 1:1). At the very beginning of Acts, Jesus instructs his disciples, "But you [the disciples] will receive power when the Holy Spirit has come on you, and you will be my witnesses in Jerusalem, in all Judea and Samaria, and to the end of the earth" (1:8). This promise is both a reaffirmation of the Great Commission and an implicit structure for the entire book as Acts proceeds by recording the spread of Christianity from Jerusalem (1:12–5:42) to Judea and Samaria (6:1–12:25) and to the ends of the known world (13:1–28:31).

The gospel begins its spread in Jerusalem, in the heartland of the Jews. Peter preaches his Pentecost sermon in Jerusalem, and Jews from around the world believe in Christ (Acts 2). In the following chapters, the apostles follow Peter's example, evangelizing Jews in Jerusalem and thus causing significant social, cultural, and political upheaval. They proclaim the gospel with gravity and a sense of urgency, since they believe, as Peter says, that "there is no other name under heaven given to people by which we must be saved" (4:12).

Soon, the explosively growing church experiences an intense persecution that causes Christians to be scattered across the empire. In Acts 6–8, we read about the ministry of some of these ordinary Christians in Judea and Samaria. Philip, an early church deacon, preaches cross-culturally (and miraculously) in Samaria and sees Samaritans come to faith in Christ. Stephen, another deacon, sees similar ministry success until his faithfulness leads to an untimely end. But even as Stephen is martyred for the sake of Christ, he follows the example of Jesus, praying for his attackers' forgiveness.

Stephen's God-given courage could have gone unnoticed by a man named Saul, who stood by approving of Stephen's death. The believers of that day certainly do not expect Saul—who is known for threatening them with persecution and death—to cause anything but continued trouble. And yet, in God's irony, Saul soon becomes a Christian and the most fervent missionary of his (or any) day. The remainder of Acts focuses on the spread of Christianity to the ends of the earth, largely through the travels of this murderer turned missionary.

Empowering the church's mission is the Spirit of God. Jesus instructs his disciples to wait until they receive the Spirit (Luke 24:49; Acts 1:8). Only with the Spirit will they be encouraged and empowered to take the gospel to the ends of the earth. The outpouring of the Spirit in Acts 2 proves that Jesus has his priorities straight. God's Spirit is able to accomplish in a few minutes what the disciples could not have manufactured in a lifetime without him. Those who were full of fear during Jesus's trial and crucifixion now preach the gospel with courage and power. "Repent and be baptized," Peter cries out, and thousands respond (Acts 2:38–41).

Accompanying the church's preaching was the planting of new churches. The book of Acts emphasizes the church's centrality by recording that, as soon as the Spirit arrived, he forms a church (Acts 2:40–47). This pattern of Spirit-led gospel proclamation followed by Spirit-led church formation continues not only through the end of Acts but also in the pages of history since. Then and now, local churches serve as the nerve center of Christian teaching and learning, fellowship and worship, witness in word and witness in deed. Local churches provide the nourishing environment in which believers can grow strong in Christ and learn to love God, one another, and a broken and wayward world.

The Church's International Future

The book of Revelation provides a glimpse of the fruit of the church's international mission. In a vision to the apostle John, we are made privy to a future day when vast multitudes of humanity will worship Christ and praise him for his great salvation (Rev. 5). The vision is worth tracing in some detail, given the insight it provides into the Christian mission.

In this vision, it is revealed to John that Jesus is both the "Lamb who was slain" and the "Lion of the tribe of Judah." In other words, the vision confirms to John that the Jesus who shed his blood on a cross is indeed the King of the world. Although he suffered in his first coming, he will set the world to rights in his second coming. In response to the lamblike lion, the multitudes break forth into praise, singing of the Lamb,

> You are worthy to take the scroll
> and to open its seals,
> because you were slaughtered,
> and you purchased people
> for God by your blood
> from every tribe and language
> and people and nation.
> You made them a kingdom
> and priests to our God,
> and they will reign on the earth. (5:9–10)

And,

> Worthy is the Lamb who was slaughtered
> to receive power and riches
> and wisdom and strength
> and honor and glory and blessing! (5:12)

A few chapters later, we are made privy to God's vision of the eternal state, one in which the redeemed multitudes dwell in the presence of God in a cosmos purged from sin and its effects, never again to experience death or suffering or sadness:

> Then I saw a new heaven and a new earth; for the first heaven and the first earth had passed away, and the sea was no more. I also saw the holy city, the new Jerusalem, coming down out of heaven from God, prepared like a bride adorned for her husband. Then I heard a loud voice from the throne: Look, God's dwelling is with humanity, and he will live with them. They will be his peoples, and God himself will be with them and will be their God. He will wipe away every tear from their eyes. Death will be no more; grief, crying, and pain will be no more, because the previous things have passed away. (Rev. 21:1–4)

The entirety of the Christian mission moves toward this final reality. "All of Christian theology," writes Russell Moore, "points toward an end—an end where Jesus overcomes the satanic reign of death and restores God's original creation order. . . . In Scripture the eschaton is not simply tacked on to the gospel at the end. It is instead the vision toward which all of Scripture is pointing—and the vision that grounds the hope of the gathered church and the individual believer."[17] The book of Revelation, then, informs the Christian mission by providing a glimpse of its consummation. Because when we have been made privy to the end of the script, the middle of it will never look the same again.

The Church's Mission from the Middle of the Script

A Witness to the Nations

From the beginning of time, God's intention has been to fill the earth with the knowledge of his glory, to be known and worshiped throughout the entirety of his good creation. This was his purpose in creating our world, saving Noah, choosing Abraham, commissioning Israel, and taking on human flesh. More specifically, God's purpose is to shine the light of salvation on the nations. In that sense, Jesus's Great Commission is nothing new. But in another sense, his parting words do offer something new—an outward trajectory. Jesus

---

17. Russell D. Moore, "Personal and Cosmic Eschatology," in *A Theology for the Church*, ed. Daniel L. Akin, Bruce Riley Ashford, and Kenneth Keathley, rev. ed. (Nashville: B&H Academic, 2014), 671.

takes the centripetal commission given to Israel—devote yourselves to God so that the nations will be drawn to you—and adds the centrifugal element— devote yourselves to God by going to the nations.

Therefore, the Great Commission should cause us, as Christians living in the modern West, to reflect critically on what it means to be witnesses to the West. As we discussed in chapter 6, Lesslie Newbigin is known for calling the church to bring the West into a missionary encounter with the gospel. Newbigin was right, and we should heed his call. After all, Western nations are included in the gentile nations of whom Jesus told his disciples to make disciples. Furthermore, the West is the most powerful cultural force in the world today, both for good and for bad. Thus this book has addressed Western Christians as its primary audience and has urged Western Christians to take seriously the multiple dimensions of their witness in our secular age.

But Jesus's command is inescapably centrifugal. We are also propelled forward into cross-cultural ministry in international contexts, especially to people groups among whom there is little or no gospel awareness. And this mission is necessarily Christ centered. Consider the Christ-centered mission encapsulated in John's vision, as the multitudes sing, "You were slaughtered, and you purchased people for God by your blood from every tribe and language and people and nation" (Rev. 5:9). Similarly, consider Peter's declaration that "there is no other name under heaven given to people by which we must be saved" (Acts 4:12) and Paul's words to the Athenians, "The One whom you worship without knowing, Him I proclaim to you. . . . [God] has appointed a day on which He will judge the world in righteousness by the Man whom He has ordained" (Acts 17:23, 31 NKJV). Since the incarnation of Jesus, God has ordained that the mission is to proclaim the name of Christ.

Such a Christocentric focus has never been easy for people to swallow. The Sanhedrin found Peter's exclusive claim offensive and threatened him to keep quiet about it. The Athenians scoffed at Paul's insistence that one man could mediate salvation and that this salvation could involve resurrection. And in contemporary Western society, the idea that one religious tradition leads to God while others do not is seen as regressive, backward, and hateful. One prominent author counsels that we should shift from the unfounded dogma that Christ is at the center to the realization that God is at the center, with Christ as simply one body orbiting God.[18] This view, known as pluralism and embraced by many mainstream Western Christians, is counter to biblical teaching.

18. John Hick, *God and the Universe of Faiths* (London: Macmillan, 1973).

A Witness Centering on Local Churches

In the book of Acts, Jesus's disciples approach him to ask about a timetable for his return. Instead of answering their question, Jesus instructs them to wait until they receive the Spirit. They do wait, and when they receive the Spirit, the first things they are moved to do are to speak the gospel and gather as churches.

In fact, as missiologist David Hesselgrave notes, the early church's international mission strategy centers on local churches, a strategy that Paul's ministry pattern exemplifies.[19] Paul is discipled by a church that sends him out as a witness to surrounding nations (Acts 13:1–4). This pattern continues as the early church regularly sends missionaries to other cities and nations. As the missionaries preach the gospel (13:14–41), they gather newly converted Christians into churches (13:43).

These new churches then become the God-given context in which the new believers are built up in the faith through teaching, worship, fellowship, and witness (Acts 14:21–22; 15:41). The churches soon develop their own leadership (14:23) and no longer need the missionary's presence, so the missionary commends them and leaves to work in other areas (14:23; 16:40). Missionaries keep a close relationship with the churches they start, communicating with them by mail and sometimes by returning to minister in person (15:36; 18:23). Missionaries also communicate back to their home churches, relaying the good news to the churches that had sent them as missionaries in the first place (14:26; 15:6–21).

The centrality of local churches should come as no surprise. Just as God called Israel to be a light to the nations by shaping its corporate life around his revealed Word, so he calls the church to be "the light of the world," "a city on a hill," and "the salt of the earth" (Matt. 5:13–16). The point in each of these metaphors is that the church is supposed to live in such a distinct way that the world, seeing its way of life, might glorify God. As Christians, we are told to live honorably "in everyone's eyes" (Rom. 12:17) and to make known God's wisdom "to the rulers and authorities in the heavens" (Eph. 3:10). We are instructed to be blameless (Phil. 2:14–15) and to live quietly and reputably in the home and in the workplace so that we may "behave properly in the presence of outsiders and not be dependent on anyone" (1 Thess. 4:10–12). In sum, we are instructed to conduct ourselves honorably so that the world will see our lives and glorify God (1 Pet. 2:12).

Thus our international mission should involve established churches sending from their midst missionaries who will preach the gospel and plant churches,

19. David Hesselgrave, *Planting Churches Cross-Culturally: North America and Beyond*, 2nd ed. (Grand Rapids: Baker Books, 2000), 93–321.

especially in nations where there is little or no gospel witness. And it will involve newly formed churches whose members are empowered to be gospel witnesses to their own nations and people groups.

A Witness Combining Words and Deeds

In the Gospel of John, Jesus articulates his missional commission by saying, "As the Father has sent me, I also send you" (20:21). *Mission* literally means "sending," and Jesus says that our sent-ness will reflect his own. One of the most significant ways the Christian mission should reflect Christ's mission is in its potent combination of words and deeds. Jesus gives discourses, and he feeds hungry people. He prophesies, and he heals lepers. He preaches the gospel of the kingdom, and he does miracles that give a preview of the kingdom's future consummation.

In our own day, we must speak the name of Christ and declare his gospel. Gospel proclamation must never be displaced as the center of our mission. No amount of gospel-inspired deeds can do what gospel words can do: articulate the saving story of Christ crucified, buried, and resurrected and invite sinners to be saved. We must name Christ and speak his gospel to the nations, especially in contexts where Christ is not known.

Yet at the same time we must engage in actions that show God's love for the world and provide a preview of his coming kingdom. If we speak the gospel with our lips but refuse to show its shaping power in our lives, our words will most likely fall on deaf ears. Just as Jesus's miraculous deeds complement his life-giving words, so our gospel words should be matched by gospel-shaped deeds. Through our deeds, we provide the world a picture of Jesus's love and a preview of his coming kingdom.

Thus, when the gospel is preached and churches are formed in new contexts, those churches continue the mission. They gather on the Lord's Day to proclaim that Jesus is Lord, and they disperse throughout the week, giving comprehensive witness to Christ through word and deed in the totality of their personal, social, and cultural contexts.

A Witness with Respect to Culture and Context

The Christian gospel is not a Western gospel. In fact, the gospel first took root and experienced explosive growth in the Middle East, Asia Minor, and North Africa. Only after that did it travel to Europe and later to America. Sadly, however, many Western Christians have assumed that Western culture is superior and, therefore, that other cultures are inferior and even bad. In opposition to this flawed narrative of cultural superiority, the Bible gives us a gospel that is unique in its ability to be at home in any culture, while at the same time being an equal opportunity offender, exposing sin and idolatry in every culture.[20]

That is why the New Testament shows the apostles working hard to respect cultural contexts and minister in contextually effective manners, even while the gospel speaks prophetically against the sinful and idolatrous aspects of those cultures. Consider the way Paul shaped his speeches and sermons for each audience to whom he spoke. In Acts he communicates in a unique and culturally sensitive manner to the Jewish diaspora (Acts 13), a crowd of rural animists (ch. 14), the cultural power brokers of the Areopagus (ch. 17), a mob of Jewish nationalists (ch. 22), and the cultural elite of Syria-Palestine (ch. 26).[21] Similarly, the Gospel writers shaped their respective Gospels for specific audiences.

From the apostles, we learn significant lessons with respect to culture and context. We learn to minister faithfully, being careful that our words and deeds conform to the gospel rather than to Western forms. We learn to minister meaningfully, speaking and serving in ways that are meaningful for a particular context. And we learn to minister dialogically, learning from believers from other nations and eras as we work together to build a global witness to Christ.

A Witness Undeterred by Opposition

In a letter to his protégé, Timothy, the apostle Paul writes that "all who want to live a godly life in Christ Jesus will be persecuted" (2 Tim. 3:12). This is not a surprise to Jewish believers who have seen many of their prophets suffer and die at the hands of worldly leaders (Heb. 11:35–40). And it should not come as a surprise to twenty-first-century Christians. Missiologist Scott Moreau writes, "Far from being only a thing of the past, persecution today continues to be a reality faced by many Christians, particularly those in militant religious states. It is estimated that more Christians have lost their lives through persecution in this century than all other centuries combined, though generally there has been little publicity of this in the secular press of free countries."[22]

---

20. Among the many books exploring the universality of Christianity, three of the most significant are Lamin Sanneh, *Translating the Message* (Maryknoll, NY: Orbis, 2005); Andrew Walls, *The Missionary Movement in Christian History* (Maryknoll, NY: Orbis, 1996); and Kwame Bediako, *Christianity in Africa* (Maryknoll, NY: Orbis, 1995).

21. Eckhard Schnabel, *Paul the Missionary: Realities, Strategies, and Methods* (Downers Grove, IL: IVP Academic, 2008), 171.

22. A. Scott Moreau, "Persecution," in *Evangelical Dictionary of World Missions*, ed. A. Scott Moreau (Grand Rapids: Baker Books, 2000), 747.

Researcher David Barrett estimates that during the late twentieth century, some years saw upward of two hundred thousand Christians killed for the sake of their faith.[23] Most likely these trends will continue because so many of the world's unreached people groups live under oppressive religious or political ideologies.

The suffering and persecution of God's people is a constant theme throughout history and around the globe, and the twentieth century is no exception. One of the most striking images from my (Bruce's) childhood is a small newsletter, smuggled to the United States from the underground church in the Soviet Union, that carried two photographs side by side. The first photograph depicted an emaciated elderly man. The second portrayed an ox's yoke. Beneath the photos was a story detailing this elderly man's arrest at the hands of the secret police. He had been sent to a concentration camp in Siberia, where he was hooked to an ox's yolk and forced to grind wheat by treading in circles around an ancient gristmill. This man's crime? Worshiping Christ together with other believers in an underground church. During the last years before the fall of the Soviet Union, I read dozens more stories like his. I learned of believers who were dragged from their homes, thrown in concentration camps, tortured, and killed because of their determination to pledge allegiance to an authority higher than the Soviet state.

During college, I (Bruce) encountered the story of Richard Wurmbrand, a Romanian pastor who was persecuted under the regime of Nicolae Ceaușescu. Because the Romanian government considered Wurmbrand incorrigible in his efforts to preach outside officially approved avenues, he was imprisoned for fourteen years, with three of those years being served in solitary confinement. Wurmbrand tells the story of having atheist propaganda piped into his cell by loudspeaker for seventeen hours a day, for years on end, and of the intermittent torture he experienced at the same time.

> The tortures and brutality continued without interruption. When I lost consciousness or became too dazed to give the torturers any further hopes of confession, I would be returned to my cell. There I would lie, untended and half dead, to regain a little strength so they could work on me again. Many died at this stage, but somehow my strength always managed to return. In the ensuing years, they broke four vertebrae in my back, and many other bones. They carved me in a dozen places. They burned and cut eighteen holes in my body.[24]

23. David Barrett, "Annual Statistical Table on Global Mission: 2002," *IBMR* 26, no. 1 (January 2002): 23.
24. Richard Wurmbrand, *Tortured for Christ* (Bartlesville, OK: Living Sacrifice Publishers, 1967), 39.

In this and other accounts of his suffering, Wurmbrand is insistent that God worked in and through these evils to make him a conduit of the gospel. He believed that God sustained him through the persecution so that his witness to the other prisoners, to the Romanian regime, and to the Western church would be all the more powerful.

In the global South and East, Christians likewise often experience persecution. Consider the story of Joseph, a Masai warrior, who told his story to attendees at the International Conference for Itinerant Evangelists (Amsterdam) in the 1980s. One of the attendees, Michael Card, transcribed a portion of Joseph's testimony:

> One day Joseph, who was walking along one of these hot, dirty African roads, met someone who shared the gospel of Jesus Christ with him. Then and there he accepted Jesus as his Lord and Savior. The power of the Spirit began transforming his life; he was filled with such excitement and joy that the first thing he wanted to do was return to his own village and share that same Good News with the members of his local tribe.
>
> Joseph began going door-to-door, telling everyone he met about the Cross of Jesus and the salvation it offered, expecting to see their faces light up the way his had. To his amazement the villagers not only didn't care, they became violent. The men of the village seized him and held him to the ground while the women beat him with strands of barbed wire. He was dragged from the village and left to die alone in the bush.
>
> Joseph somehow managed to crawl to a waterhole, and there, after days of passing in and out of consciousness, found the strength to get up. He wondered about the hostile reception he had received from people he had known all his life. He decided he must have left something out or told the story of Jesus incorrectly. After rehearsing the message he had first heard, he decided to go back and share his faith once more.
>
> Joseph limped into the circle of huts and began to proclaim Jesus. "He died for you, so that you might find forgiveness and come to know the living God," he pleaded. Again he was grabbed by the men of the village and held while the women beat him, reopening wounds that had just begun to heal. Once more they dragged him unconscious from the village and left him to die.
>
> To have survived the first beating was truly remarkable. To live through the second was a miracle. Again, days later, Joseph awoke in the wilderness, bruised, scarred—and determined to go back.
>
> He returned to the small village and this time, they attacked him before he had a chance to open his mouth. As they flogged him for the third and probably the last time, he again spoke to them of Jesus Christ, the Lord. Before he passed out, the last thing he saw was that the women who were beating him began to weep.

This time he awoke in his own bed. The ones who had so severely beaten him were now trying to save his life and nurse him back to health. The entire village had come to Christ.[25]

Joseph's testimony weaves together a number of threads of Christian mission as revealed in the Bible. In this story, Joseph the Masai warrior understood that mission begins at home with one's own people. At risk to his life and in the midst of great pain and suffering, he proclaims to his people that Christ alone can save. His gospel words and deeds, combined with his willingness to suffer, were an act of public worship. His love for Christ overflowed into a love for his people. His trust and delight in Christ motivated him to invite members of his tribe to find their joy in Christ also. And his testimony to the International Conference drove the attendees to their knees, praying that God would act to bring salvation to the unreached people of the world.

The suffering of Aleksandr Solzhenitsyn, Richard Wurmbrand, Joseph, and countless others is unique in its ability to draw our attention to the unsurpassed worth and value of knowing and loving God. As persecuted Christians remain faithful in the midst of suffering, their witness makes clear that union with Christ is a greater treasure even than physical health and comfort. The suffering of these faithful Christians is also unique in drawing our attention to the significance and necessity of our international mission, our calling to be a light to the nations.

Conclusion

The most significant story at the turn of the century is not Fukuyama's triumph of liberal democracy. Nor is it Huntingdon's clash of civilizations or Friedman's hyperconnected "flat world." No, the most profound story at the beginning of the twenty-first century is the explosive growth of Christianity around the world. For Christians who have listened attentively to the biblical narrative, this comes as no surprise. As God promised throughout the Scriptures, he will make his people a light to the nations. And as he reveals in John's vision, his promise will find its fulfillment when Christ returns to receive the worship of vast multitudes from every tribe, tongue, people, and nation.

But that time has not yet come, and God's people remain in the middle of the script—a script in which we are called to immerse ourselves in the biblical

25. Michael Card, "Wounded in the House of Friends," *Virtue* (March/April 1991): 28–29, 69. I owe this citation to John Piper, *Let the Nations Be Glad! The Supremacy of God in Missions*, 2nd ed. (Grand Rapids: Baker Academic, 2003), 93–94.

narrative so that we can challenge the world's idols and ideologies with the axioms of the Bible and live faithfully in this time before Christ returns. Our mission is comprehensive, drawing on the totality of who we are as creatures made in God's image, radiating outward through word and deed into every sector of society and every sphere of culture, and extending to every nation and people even to the ends of the earth.

While our task is formidable, our company is more so: the supreme Lord of the universe goes with us and empowers us. He will be with us "always, to the end of the age" (Matt. 28:20). Even though the opposition seems daunting in our secular age and around the globe, the magnitude of our task is equaled and surpassed by the magnitude of our biblical convictions: that God is determined to win the nations to himself; that through Christ, he defeats the evil one and frees us from condemnation; that our task as the church in each generation is to bear witness to Christ through multiple dimensions of our lives and to the ends of the earth; and that God has given his Spirit to walk alongside us until Christ returns to set the world to rights.

SCRIPTURE INDEX

SUBJECT INDEX